Rethinking
the
Western
Tradition

Yale University Press

New Haven and London

Culture

and

Anarchy

by

Matthew Arnold

Edited by
Samuel Lipman

Commentary by
Maurice Cowling
Gerald Graff
Samuel Lipman
Steven Marcus

Published with assistance from the foundation established in memory of
James Wesley Cooper, Class of 1865, Yale College.

On p. 2: Facsimile of title page of first edition of *Culture and Anarchy,* courtesy
Beinecke Rare Book and Manuscript Library, Yale University.

Set in Times Roman type by The Composing Room of Michigan, Inc.,
Grand Rapids, Michigan. Printed in the United States of America
by Edwards Brothers, Inc., Ann Arbor, Michigan.

Library of Congress Cataloging-in-Publication Data
Arnold, Matthew, 1822–1888.
Culture and anarchy / by Matthew Arnold ; edited by Samuel Lipman ;
commentary by Maurice Cowling . . . [et al.].
p.   cm. — (Rethinking the Western tradition)
The text is that of the 1st ed., 1869.
Includes bibliographical references.
ISBN 0-300-05866-7 (cloth). — ISBN 0-300-05867-5 (pbk.)
1. Great Britain—Social conditions—19th century. 2. Culture. I. Lipman,
Samuel. II. Cowling, Maurice. III. Title. IV. Series.
HN389.A72   1993
306'.0941—dc20   93-2427 CIP

A catalogue record for this book is available from the British Library.

The paper in this book meets the guidelines for permanence and durability of
the Committee on Production Guidelines for Book Longevity of the Council
on Library Resources.

10 9 8 7 6 5 4 3 2

Contributors

Maurice Cowling is Fellow Emeritus of Peterhouse, Cambridge.

Gerald Graff is Professor of Humanities, English, and Education at the University of Chicago.

Samuel Lipman is publisher of *The New Criterion* and artistic director of the Waterloo Music Festival.

Steven Marcus is Delacorte Professor of the Humanities and Dean of Columbia College at Columbia University.

Contents

A Note on References

In the text of *Culture and Anarchy*, page references to the first edition (1869) are given in the margin. Arnold's own footnotes and the editor's comments on the text are marked by a dagger. Words and phrases that are defined in the glossary are marked by an asterisk; names and titles, routinely listed in the glossary, are not marked in the text.

Elsewhere, page references to the 1869 edition are given as [000]. References to volume and page in *The Complete Prose of Matthew Arnold*, ed. R. H. Super (Ann Arbor: University of Michigan Press, 1960–1977), are given as [Super 00:00].

Matthew Arnold:
A Brief Sketch

Matthew Arnold was born in 1822 and died in 1888. He lived his life fully, with a pleasant mien and a charm preferred to all (despite deep grief over the loss of three sons), a blissfully happy marriage, the honor of his countrymen, and the blessing of a quick death. He was one of the greatest poets of the middle third of the nineteenth century, the most important English literary critic of his time, a penetrating social observer, and a religious thinker whose reputation has suffered for his having been, much against his will, a prophet of our despair. He was a practical man as well: for more than three decades he served Her Majesty's Government as an Inspector of Schools, traveling widely, and fruitfully, in his own country and on the Continent. Intellectually there were several Matthew Arnolds, not just one, and each of them was suffused by a tragic view of life, the view that he expressed in the marvelous closing lines of his 1850s poem "Dover Beach":

> Ah, love, let us be true
> To one another! for the world, which seems
> To lie before us like a land of dreams,
> So various, so beautiful, so new,
> Hath really neither joy, nor love, nor light
> Nor certitude, nor peace, nor help for pain;
> And we are here as on a darkling plain
> Swept with confused alarms of struggle and flight,
> Where ignorant armies clash by night.

But whether by seriousness or by charm, he mastered his age, and his influence, whether we like it or not, is with us still.

He was fortunate in his parents. His father, the Reverend Thomas Arnold (1795–1842), was the most celebrated English schoolmaster of the century—the man who, it seemed single-handedly, established at Rugby School the model for the best in private secondary education the English-speaking world has yet known. His mother, Mary Penrose (1791–1873), with whom Arnold corresponded on intellectual as well as family matters to the end of her life, combined vivacity and a strong mind. For a short time the young Arnold attended Winchester, as had his father before him, but in 1837 he returned to Rugby to be under his father's firm but affectionate supervision.

At Rugby, the practice of modified self-government via a system of student monitors was already in place. What we know today of Rugby then, with its strong emphasis on moral conduct, we know best from that young person's classic of yesteryear, Thomas Hughes's enthralling *Tom Brown's Schooldays* (1857). Rugby was discipline itself disciplined by sympathy, and classical learning leavened by a strong appeal to its application to righteous conduct. Thomas Arnold, an orthodox Anglican churchman, intensely disliked the Tractarian movement of Hurrell Froude, John Keble, Edward Pusey, and, especially John Henry Newman; it is thus hardly surprising that his son, when he arrived at Oxford in 1840 as the winner of an Open Scholarship at Balliol College, seemed unaffected by the new conservative theology. But given his love and even adoration for the commanding moral presence of his father, it is also hardly surprising that in later years, long after Oxford had been left behind both by Arnold and by Newman (after 1845 a Roman Catholic), it was to Newman that Arnold looked for the spirit of the true Oxford, the home of beauty and what Arnold so movingly called "beaten causes" [035].

At Rugby Arnold had tried his hand at poetry, with some success. At Oxford, where his father had now added to his Rugby duties (sadly, only for a short time) the Regius Professorship of History, Arnold won the Newdigate Prize for his poem "Cromwell." Perhaps because he failed to apply himself to the necessary cramming, he only won a second class in the final examination in "Greats," but the disappointment was assuaged when he received a fellowship at Oriel College, where his father had been a fellow before him.

He continued to write poetry, and indeed within a few years of his leaving Oxford he was to complete the larger part of his life's work as a poet. Because his family was hardly wealthy and he had numerous brothers and sisters, he needed to earn a living. His path was chosen for him by an appointment as private secretary to the Whig Lord Lansdowne, president of the council in the government of Lord John Russell. Arnold

Matthew Arnold: A Brief Sketch

thoroughly enjoyed his brief sojourn in the great world, and may even have been sorry when it came to an end in 1851, when Lansdowne appointed him to an Inspectorship of Schools. Because Anglican schools were visited by Anglican clergymen, Arnold's beat (or so we would call it today) was the Dissenting or Nonconformist schools, establishments run, as were all schools, under private auspices but subject to state observation when state grants were involved. In truth, Arnold didn't like non-Establishment Protestants very much, but he did like children, and they him.

His work as an Inspector involved unceasing travel, under the primitive mid-century conditions of rail-travel and lodging then obtaining. But somehow he found time (and his job gave him the money) to marry, in 1851, Frances Lucy Wightman (d. 1901). They had six children, of whom only three survived into adulthood. By 1849 he had already published, to indifferent success, his first volume of poetry, *The Strayed Reveller, and Other Poems;* in 1852 he published yet another volume, *Empedocles on Etna, and Other Poems,* to an equally limp public response. The character of his work as a poet was now firmly established: a fondness for classical forms and a tendency to a profound melancholy surprising in a man of such charm and even, quite frequently, levity.

But his fortunes as a poet were to change with the publication in 1853 of a new volume, for the first time containing the author's full name on the title page; the earlier books had merely been signed "A." Now Arnold wrote a preface that gave his own theory of poetry, which he demonstrated by removing from the collection of his poems "Empedocles on Etna," the title work of the 1852 volume, precisely because he found in this poem of suicide no prospect of what he thought poetry must supply: relief, deliverance, and resistance. The modern mood was sour, and the words of the 1853 preface make the gloom clear: "What those who are familiar only with the great monuments of early Greek genius suppose to be its exclusive characteristics, have disappeared; the calm, the cheerfulness, the disinterested objectivity have disappeared; the dialogue of the mind with itself has commenced; modern problems have presented themselves; we hear already the doubts, we witness the discouragement, of Hamlet and of Faust." For a time Arnold fought this gloom and along with it a gathering premonition that his fate would be what he later described (as he had earlier in "Dover Beach") in "Stanzas from the Grande Chartreuse" (1855):

. . . as, on some far northern strand,
Thinking of his own Gods, a Greek
In pity and mournful awe might stand
Before some fallen Runic stone—
For both were faiths, and both are gone.

Wandering between two worlds, one dead,
The other powerless to be born,
With nowhere yet to rest my head . . .

The 1853 collection, followed by reprintings in 1854 and 1857 and a new selection in 1855, was a success. In 1857 Arnold was elected to the Professorship of Poetry at Oxford, and was the first to lecture in English rather than Latin. He occupied the chair, concurrently with his duties as a School Inspector, for ten years. His Inaugural Lecture, styled "On the Modern Element in Literature," found a similarity between Periclean Greece and his own England: both ages were modern in that they were "culminating" [Super 1:22] ages, seeking through literature a way of understanding their times. Among others of his Oxford Poetry lectures were three in 1860–1861 attacking Francis Newman (John Henry's brother) for what Arnold's biographer Park Honan calls a "feebly correct" translation of Homer [Honan 307]; still others included "The Study of Celtic Poetry," a subject about which Arnold actually knew quite little. His last lecture at Oxford, in 1867, was "Culture and Its Enemies," which the world now knows as the beginning of *Culture and Anarchy.*

During the period of his Oxford professorship Arnold had begun his brilliant career as a literary critic. *Essays in Criticism: First Series* was published in 1865 and subsequently (especially in the essay "Spinoza and the Bible") enlarged in later printings. But the most important work in the collection, and the work most significant for Arnold's critical reputation then as now, was the opening essay "The Function of Criticism at the Present Time." Here Arnold laid out a rationale and a plan for criticism, claiming for criticism a central role, not just in the preservation of literature, but also in its creation. He was bitterly aware of English insularism, its contented ignorance of developments in thought in France and Germany. His argument was simple but powerful: genius, though superior to mere criticism, could not create in a vacuum; it needed an "order of ideas" in which to "work freely" [Super 3:261]; such an order could only be provided by a criticism that had as its goal "in all branches of knowledge, theology, philosophy, history, art, science, to see the object as in itself it really is" [Super 3:261].[1] What that object was could only be found by "a disinterested endeavor to learn and propagate the best that is known and thought in the world" [Super 3:283] and thus (as he stated it in an earlier passage) to "create a current of true and fresh ideas" [Super 3:270]. For Arnold, criticism at its highest itself became literature, for, as he put it in another of the *Essays in Criticism*, "Joubert": "*a criticism of life* . . . The end and aim of all literature, if one considers it attentively, is, in truth, nothing but that" [Super 3:209].

It is clear that Arnold's duties as a School Inspector, which provided him with opportunities to see the state of education both in his own country and abroad, were directing his attentions precisely to that "criticism of life" which required detailed comment on English life as a whole. The immediate result of this new direction was the beginning in 1866 of *Friendship's Garland* (1871), a satirical exchange of letters between a cultured, if plain-spoken, Prussian and Arnold himself as a mock defender of the English status quo. It was, however, *Culture and Anarchy* wherein Arnold stated *sub specie aeternitatis* his diagnosis of England as Philistine and commercial, and his fears and hopes (the hopes to be achieved through culture) for his country's mind and society.

But Arnold's fears and hopes were hardly to be confined to England's mind and society. Arnold understood the massive loss of religious faith that underlay, as a malignancy can underlie the appearance of blossoming health, the expansive self-confidence of contemporary religious life and practice. He was not in the conventional sense a believer; he had no faith in a personal God. But he was a deeply religious man nonetheless. He recognized the existence, and the definition, of God in all that we know of ourselves and of life: "The Eternal *not ourselves* which makes for righteousness" [Super 6:311] and "the stream of tendency by which all things seek to fulfill the law of their being" [Super 6:189].

Almost the last two decades of Arnold's life were devoted to his thoughts on a religion that might bring, in the words of his poem "Obermann Once More" (c. 1866), "joy whose grounds are true." The three great religious collections of his maturity, *St. Paul and Protestantism* (1870), *Literature and Dogma* (1873), and *God and the Bible* (1875), are devoted to saving the basis of religion from its dependence on the literal

---

1. Here in this formulation was the clearest possible link between Arnold the critic and Arnold the Rugby classicist son of his father: in the early sonnet "To a Friend" (c. 1848) Arnold had written of Sophocles as a man "Who saw life steadily, and saw it whole." In this notion of the artist as judge Arnold integrated his own work as poet and critic.

reading of the Bible and a belief in miracles. For Arnold, conduct at its most transcendent—what he calls in *Last Essays on Church and Religion* (1877) "kindness and pureness, charity and chastity" [Super 8:156]—was three-quarters of life [Super 6:180]; it is not too much to think that as he came to the end of his life, conduct became all.

He lectured a lot in his last years, coming twice to America. His *Discourses in America* (1885), perhaps unsuccessful as talks (because his style of delivery was so weak), remain remarkable for their courage in speaking to the former colonists on the problems of democracy and of building a democratic culture; in so doing, he only extended the message of the need for a true high culture he had begun in *Essays in Criticism* and *Culture and Anarchy*. It required a remarkable man indeed to begin a scarcely enthusiastic lecture on Emerson in hardly papist Boston—Emerson had been dead less than two years—with what amounted to an ode to Newman, only several years before made a Cardinal. It took courage to be Arnold; it takes some courage even today, in these unctuously correct times, to read him, and perhaps even more courage to take him seriously.

Culture and Anarchy:
A Publishing History

What we now know as *Culture and Anarchy* originated in six articles published by Arnold in the *Cornhill Magazine* in 1867 and 1868. The mission of the *Cornhill*, founded in 1860 with William Makepeace Thackeray as its first editor, was to provide in each issue, at the cost of a shilling, a serial installment of a novel, short stories, poetry, and diverse articles. Early issues included serialized excerpts of novels by both Thackeray and Anthony Trollope. Other contributors included John Ruskin and the antidemocrat James Fitzjames Stephen (1829–94), an old antagonist of Arnold whose attack on him in the *Saturday Review* eventually inspired Arnold in 1867 to devote the last of his lectures as Oxford Professor of Poetry to the subject "Culture and Its Enemies."

"Culture and Its Enemies" was published in the *Cornhill* in July 1867, followed at short intervals by five more articles, all under the title "Anarchy and Authority." As they appeared, they attracted great interest in the then-flourishing periodical press. In completing the series of articles, Arnold often took careful account of his critics' positions. The first publication of this material in book form, under the memorable title *Culture and Anarchy,* a brilliant conflation of the two titles under which the articles had first appeared, was in 1869 under the imprint of Smith, Elder & Co.

Two further editions followed during Arnold's lifetime, the second in 1875 and the third in 1882. Arnold made many changes as the text progressed from its original appearance in the *Cornhill* through the three book editions; all of these changes are brilliantly documented in R. W. Super's remarkable edition of *Culture and Anarchy* in volume 5 of *The Complete Prose Works of Matthew Arnold* (1960–1977). To make up the first edition, Arnold added to the *Cornhill* articles an extensive preface, a brief introduction, and a shorter conclusion. Elsewhere, apart from correcting what Arnold must have felt were mere stylistic infelicities, the changes he made as the work was published and republished were to remove the names of many people he had attacked, often quite stringently. In addition, he added chapter headings to the sections that in the first edition had only been identified by Roman numerals:

Sweetness and Light [I]
Doing as One Likes [II]
Barbarians, Philistines, Populace [III]
Hebraism and Hellenism [IV]
Porro Unum Est Necessarium [V]
Our Liberal Practitioners [VI]

Arnold did make one major alteration, however, after the publication of the first edition. In the original publication of the conclusion, in discussing the need for order as a prerequisite for society and for human perfection, Arnold continued with a clear allusion to the 1866 Hyde Park riots in support of the expansion of the franchise:

> With me, indeed, this rule of conduct is hereditary. I remember my father, in one of his unpublished letters written more than forty years ago, when the political and social state of the country was gloomy and troubled, and there were riots in many places, goes on, after strongly insisting on the badness and foolishness of the government, and on the harm and dangerousness of our feudal and aristocratical constitution of society, and ends thus: "As for rioting, the old Roman way of dealing with *that* is always the right one; flog the rank and file, and fling the ringleaders from the Tarpeian Rock! [258][1]

This passage was excised in toto from the second and third editions, and it has seemed to me that in justice to the historical document that *Culture and Anarchy* undoubtedly is, these words must be printed in full, in their original context.[2]

Beyond this single passage of such singular importance, there has also seemed every reason to publish a text that retains all of the names and the

---

1. A rock on the Capitoline Hill in Rome from which aristocratic traitors were thrown.
2. Dover Wilson's 1932 edition of *Culture and Anarchy* (reprinted, with corrections, in 1935), though it is based on the first edition of 1869 and does include the passage, unaltered, about flinging the rioters from the Tarpeian Rock as well as the names omitted from later editions, also incorporates Arnold's later stylistic changes. Ian Gregor's 1971 edition is based on Arnold's third edition of 1882.

A Publishing History

descriptions that made *Culture and Anarchy* so deeply topical. Arnold, after all, talked of literature as a criticism of life; criticism requires not simply the statement of general principles but also the vivid personal examples that only life itself can give to illustrate these principles. The first edition of *Culture and Anarchy,* in the pointed references to those people whom Arnold particularly scorned, still smacks of the heat with which it was written; later considerations, no matter how gentlemanly and in what good taste, can only serve to render abstract that which Arnold had originally seen as concrete. Arnold's topical examples are important to us today, not in themselves, but for the necessary burden they place on us of finding our own examples of the contemporary reality about which *Culture and Anarchy* has so much to say.

Chronology of Arnold's Life

1822   Born at Laleham, Surrey, the eldest son of the Reverend Thomas Arnold and Mary Penrose.

1836   Enters Winchester.

1837   Enters Rugby, where his father had become the reforming headmaster in 1828.

1840   Enters Oxford, winning a classical scholarship at Balliol.

1841   Begins friendship with the poet Arthur Hugh Clough.

1842   Death of his father (b. 1795).

1843   Wins the Newdigate Prize for the poem "Cromwell."

1844   Receives a second in "Greats."

1845   Elected to a fellowship at Oriel College, Oxford.

1846   Travels in France, visits George Sand, and sees the great actress Rachel.

1847   Becomes private secretary to the marquis of Lansdowne, a prominent Whig politician.

1848   Visits Switzerland, meeting his first love, Mary Claude.

1849   Publishes *The Strayed Reveller, and Other Poems.*

1850   Publishes "Memorial Verses" on Wordsworth.

1851   Appointed Inspector of Schools by Lord Lansdowne; marries Frances Lucy Wightman. At about this time, works on (but does not publish) his most famous poem, "Dover Beach."

1852   Publishes *Empedocles on Etna, and Other Poems.*

1853   Publishes *Poems, a New Edition*

1854   Publishes *Poems. Second Series.*

1855   Publishes "Stanzas from the Grande Chartreuse."

1857   Elected Professor of Poetry at Oxford; inaugural lecture "On the Modern Element in Literature."

1859   Travels in France, Holland, and Switzerland as an officer of the Newcastle Commission on Elementary Education.

1861   Publishes *On Translating Homer* and *The Popular Education of France.* Death of Clough.

1862   Attacks official government position on awarding education grants by results rather than curriculum.

1864   Publishes *A French Eton.*

1865   Publishes *Essays in Criticism: First Series;* travels in France, Italy, Germany, and Switzerland as an official of the Taunton Commission studying foreign education.

1866   Publishes "Thyrsis," his elegy on Clough.

1868   Deaths of infant son Basil Francis (b. 1866) and eldest son Thomas (b. 1852).

1869   Publishes *Culture and Anarchy;* also publishes first collected edition (including the previously unpublished "Dover Beach") of his *Poems.*

1870   Publishes *St. Paul and Protestantism.*

1871   Publishes *Friendship's Garland.*

1872   Death of son Trevenen William (b. 1853).

1873   Publishes *Literature and Dogma;* death of mother (b. 1791).

1875   Publishes *God and the Bible,* answering objections to *Literature and Dogma.*

1877   Publishes *Last Essays on Church and Religion;* satirically portrayed as "Mr. Luke" in W. H. Mallock's *The New Republic.*

1879   Publishes *Mixed Essays.*

1882   Publishes *Irish Essays.*

1883   Accepts a Civil List pension of £250; begins lecture tour in America, lasting into 1884.

1884   Becomes Chief Inspector of Schools.

1885   Publishes *Discourses in America;* travels in Germany for the Education Department.

1886   Travels in France, Switzerland, and Germany for Royal Commission. Second visit to America.

1888   Dies in Liverpool while awaiting return of his daughter Lucy from America. Posthumous publication of *Essays in Criticism: Second Series.*

1901   Death of wife, Frances Lucy (b. 1825).

1908   Death of son Richard Penrose (b. 1855).

1934   Death of daughter Lucy Charlotte (b. 1858).

1936   Death of last surviving child, daughter Eleanor Mary Caroline (b. 1861).

Culture
and
Anarchy

a. Macmillan.
with sincere regard
from the author —

CULTURE AND ANARCHY:

AN ESSAY

IN

POLITICAL AND SOCIAL CRITICISM.

BY

MATTHEW ARNOLD.

LONDON:
SMITH, ELDER AND CO., 15, *WATERLOO PLACE.*
1869.

Preface

My foremost design in writing this Preface is to address a word of exhortation to the Society for Promoting Christian Knowledge. In the essay which follows, the reader will often find Bishop Wilson quoted. To me and to the members of the Society for Promoting Christian Knowledge his name and writings are still, no doubt, familiar; but the world is fast going away from old-fashioned people of his sort, and I learnt with consternation lately from a brilliant and distinguished votary of the natural sciences, that he had never so much as heard of Bishop Wilson, and that he imagined me to have invented him. At a moment when the Courts of Law have just taken off the embargo from the *recreative religion† furnished on Sundays by my gifted acquaintance and others, and when St. Martin's Hall and the Alhambra will soon be beginning again to resound with their pulpit-eloquence, it distresses one to think that the new lights should not only have, in general, a very low opinion of the preachers of the old religion, but that they should have it without knowing the best that these preachers can do. And that they are in this case is owing in part, certainly, to the negligence of the Christian Knowledge Society. In old times they used to print and spread abroad Bishop Wilson's *Maxims of Piety and Christianity;* the copy of this work which I use is one of their publications, bearing their imprint, and bound in the well-known brown calf which they made familiar to our childhood; but the date of my copy is 1812. I know of no copy besides, and I believe the work is no longer one of those printed and circulated by the Society. Hence the error, flattering, I own, to me personally, yet in itself to be regretted, of the distinguished physicist already mentioned.

But Bishop Wilson's *Maxims* deserve to be circulated as a religious book, not only by comparison with the cartloads of rubbish circulated at present under this designation, but for their own sake, and even by com-

iv

---

† An asterisk marks the first word of a phrase that is explained in the Glossary—ED.

v   parison with the other works of the same author. Over the far better known *Sacra Privata* they have this advantage, that they were prepared by him for his own private use, while the *Sacra Privata* were prepared by him for the use of the public. The *Maxims* were never meant to be printed, and have on that account, like a work of, doubtless, far deeper emotion and power, the *Meditations* of Marcus Aurelius, something peculiarly sincere and first-hand about them. Some of the best things from the *Maxims* have passed into the *Sacra Privata;* still, in the *Maxims,* we have them as they first arose; and whereas, too, in the *Sacra Privata* the writer speaks very often as one of the clergy, and as addressing the clergy, in the *Maxims* he almost always speaks solely as a man. I am not saying a word against the *Sacra Privata,* for which I have the highest respect; only the *Maxims* seem to me a better and a more edifying book still. They should be read, as Joubert says Nicole should be read, with a direct aim at practice. The reader will leave on one side things which, from the change of time and from the changed point of view which the change of time inevitably brings with it,

vi   no longer suit him; enough will remain to serve as a sample of the very best, perhaps, which our nation and race can do in the way of religious writing. Monsieur Michelet makes it a reproach to us that, in all the doubt as to the real author of the *Imitation,* no one has ever dreamed of ascribing that work to an Englishman. It is true, the *Imitation* could not well have been written by an Englishman; the religious delicacy and the profound asceticism of that admirable book are hardly in our nature. This would be more of a reproach to us if in poetry, which requires, no less than religion, a true delicacy of spiritual perception, our race had not done such great things; and if the *Imitation,* exquisite as it is, did not, as I have elsewhere remarked, belong to a class of works in which the perfect balance of human nature is lost, and which have therefore, as spiritual productions, in their contents something excessive and morbid, in their form something not thoroughly sound. On a lower range than the *Imitation,* and awakening in our nature chords less poetical and delicate, the *Maxims* of Bishop Wilson are, as a religious work, far more solid. To the most sincere ardour and unction, Bishop Wilson unites, in these *Maxims,* that downright

vii   honesty and plain good sense which our English race has so powerfully applied to the divine impossibilities of religion; by which it has brought religion so much into practical life, and has done its allotted part in promoting upon earth the kingdom of God. But with ardour and unction religion, as we all know, may still be fanatical; with honesty and good sense, it may still be prosaic; and the fruit of honesty and good sense united with ardour and unction is often only a prosaic religion held fanatically. Bishop Wilson's excellence lies in a balance of the four qualities, and in a fulness and perfection of them, which makes this untoward result impossible; his unction is so perfect, and in such happy alliance with his good sense, that it becomes tenderness and fervent charity; his good sense is so perfect and in such happy alliance with his unction, that it becomes moderation and insight. While, therefore, the type of religion exhibited in his *Maxims* is English, it is yet a type of a far higher kind than is in general reached by Bishop Wilson's countrymen; and yet, being English, it is possible and attainable for them. And so I conclude as I began, by saying that a work of this sort is one which the Society for Promoting Christian Knowledge should not suffer to remain out of print or out of currency.

To pass now to the matters canvassed in the following essay. The whole scope of the essay is to recommend culture as the great help out of our present difficulties; culture being a pursuit of our total perfection by means of getting to know, on all the matters which most concern us, the best which has been thought and said in the world, and, through this knowledge, turning a stream of fresh and free thought upon our stock notions and habits, which we now follow staunchly but mechanically, vainly imagining that there is a virtue in following them staunchly which makes up for the mischief of following them mechanically. This, and this alone, is the scope of the following essay. I say again here, what I have said in the pages which follow, that from the faults and weaknesses of bookmen a notion of something bookish, pedantic, and futile has got itself more or less connected with the word culture, and that it is a pity we cannot use a word more perfectly free from all shadow of reproach. And yet, futile as are many bookmen, and helpless as books and reading often prove for bringing nearer to perfection those who use them, one must, I think, be struck more and more, the longer one lives, to find how much, in our present society, a man's life of each day depends for its solidity and value on whether he reads during that day, and, far more still, on what he reads during it. More and more he who examines himself will find the difference it makes to him, at the end of any given day, whether or no he has pursued his avocations throughout it without reading at all; and whether or no, having read something, he has read the newspapers only. This, however, is a matter for each man's private conscience and experience. If a man without books or reading, or reading nothing but his letters and the newspapers, gets nevertheless a fresh and free play of the best thoughts upon his stock notions and habits, he has got culture. He has got that for which we prize and recommend culture; he has got that which at the present moment we seek culture that it may give us. This inward operation is the very life and essence of culture, as we conceive it.

Nevertheless, it is not easy so to frame one's discourse concerning the operation of culture, as to avoid giving frequent occasion to a misunderstanding whereby the essential inwardness of the operation is lost sight of. We are supposed, when we criticise by the help of culture some imperfect doing or other, to have in our eye some well-known rival plan of doing, which we want to serve and recommend. Thus, for instance, because I have freely pointed out the dangers and inconveniences to which our literature is exposed in the absence of any centre of taste and authority like the French Academy, it is constantly said that I want to introduce here in England an institution like the French Academy. I have indeed expressly declared that I wanted no such thing; but let us notice how it is just our worship of machinery, and of external doing, which leads to this charge being brought; and how the inwardness of culture makes us seize, for watching and cure, the faults to which our want of an Academy inclines us, and yet prevents us from trusting to an arm of flesh, as the Puritans say,—from blindly flying to this outward machinery of an Academy, in order to help ourselves. For the very same culture and free inward play of thought which shows us how the Corinthian style, or the whimsies about the *One Primeval Language are generated and strengthened in the absence of an Academy, shows us, too, how little any Academy, such as we should be likely to get, would cure them. Every one who knows the characteristics of our national life, and the tendencies so fully discussed in the following pages, knows exactly what an English Academy would be like. One can see the happy family in one's mind's eye as distinctly as if it was already constituted. Lord Stanhope, the Bishop of Oxford, Mr. Gladstone, the Dean of Westminster, Mr. Froude, Mr. Henry Reeve,—everything which is influential, accomplished, and distinguished; and then, some fine morning, a dissatisfaction of the public mind with this brilliant and select coterie, a flight of Corinthian leading articles, and an irruption of Mr. G. A. Sala. Clearly, this is not what will do us good. The very same faults,—the want of sensitiveness of intellectual conscience, the disbelief in right reason, the dislike of authority,—which have hindered our having an Academy and have worked injuriously in our literature, would also hinder us from making our Academy, if we established it, one which would really correct them. And culture, which shows us truly the faults, shows us this also just as truly.

It is by a like sort of misunderstanding, again, that Mr. Oscar Browning, one of the assistant-masters at Eton, takes up in the *Quarterly Review* the cudgels for Eton, as if I had attacked Eton, because I have said, in a book about foreign schools, that a man may well prefer to teach his three or four hours a day without keeping a boarding-house; and that there are great dangers in cramming little boys of eight or ten and making them compete for an object of great value to their parents; and, again, that the manufacture and supply of school-books, in England, much needs regulation by some competent authority. Mr. Oscar Browning gives us to understand that at Eton he and others, with perfect satisfaction to themselves and the public, combine the functions of teaching and of keeping a boarding-house; that he knows excellent men (and, indeed, well he may, for a brother of his own, I am told, is one of the best of them,) engaged in preparing little boys for competitive examinations, and that the result, as tested at Eton, gives perfect satisfaction. And as to school-books he adds, finally, that Dr. William Smith, the learned and distinguished editor of the *Quarterly Review*, is, as we all know, the compiler of school-books meritorious and many. This is what Mr. Oscar Browning gives us to understand in the *Quarterly Review*, and it is impossible not to read with pleasure what he says. For what can give a finer example of that frankness and manly self-confidence which our great public schools, and none of them so much as Eton, are supposed to inspire, of that buoyant ease in holding up one's head, speaking out what is in one's mind, and flinging off all sheepishness and awkwardness, than to see an Eton assistant-master offering in fact himself as evidence that to combine boarding-house-keeping with teaching is a good thing, and his brother as evidence that to train and race little boys for competitive examinations is a good thing? Nay, and one sees that this frank-hearted Eton self-confidence is contagious; for has not Mr. Oscar Browning managed to fire Dr. William Smith (himself, no doubt, the modestest man alive, and never trained at Eton) with the same spirit, and made him insert in his own *Review* a puff, so to speak, of his own school-books, declaring that they are (as they are) meritorious and many? Nevertheless, Mr. Oscar Browning is wrong in thinking that I wished to run down Eton; and his repetition on behalf of Eton, with this idea in his head, of the strains of his heroic ancestor, *Malvina's Oscar, as they are recorded by the family poet, Ossian, is unnecessary. "The wild boar rushes over their tombs, but he does not disturb their repose. They still love the sport of their youth, and mount the wind with joy." All I meant to say was, that there were unpleasantnesses in uniting the keeping a boarding-house with teaching, and dangers in cramming and racing little boys for competitive examinations, and charlatanism and extravagance in the manufacture and supply of our school-books. But when Mr. Oscar

xiii

xiv

Browning tells us that all these have been happily got rid of in his case, and his brother's case, and Dr. William Smith's case, then I say that this is just what I wish, and I hope other people will follow their good example. All I seek is that such blemishes should not through any negligence, self-love, or want of due self-examination, be suffered to continue.

Natural, as we have said, the sort of misunderstanding just noticed is; yet our usefulness depends upon our being able to clear it away, and to convince those who mechanically serve some stock notion or operation, and thereby go astray, that it is not culture's work or aim to give the victory to some rival fetish, but simply to turn a free and fresh stream of thought upon the whole matter in question. In a thing of more immediate interest, just now, than either of the two we have mentioned, the like misunderstanding prevails; and until it is dissipated, culture can do no good work in the matter. When we criticise the present operation of disestablishing the Irish Church, not by the power of reason and justice, but by the power of the antipathy of the Protestant Nonconformists, English and Scotch, to establishments, we are charged with being dreamers of dreams, which the national will has rudely shattered, for endowing the religious sects all round; or we are called enemies of the Nonconformists, blind partisans of the Anglican Establishment. More than a few words we must give to showing how erroneous are these charges; because if they were true, we should be actually subverting our own design, and playing false to that culture which it is our very purpose to recommend.

Certainly we are no enemies of the Nonconformists; for, on the contrary, what we aim at is their perfection. Culture, which is the study of perfection, leads us, as we in the following pages have shown, to conceive of true human perfection as a *harmonious* perfection, developing all sides of our humanity; and as a *general* perfection, developing all parts of our society. For if one member suffer, the other members must suffer with it; and the fewer there are that follow the true way of salvation the harder that way is to find. And while the Nonconformists, the successors and representatives of the Puritans, and like them staunchly walking by the best light they have, make a large part of what is strongest and most serious in this nation and therefore attract our respect and interest, yet all that, in what follows, is said about Hebraism and Hellenism, has for its main result to show how our Puritans, ancient and modern, have not enough added to their care for walking staunchly by the best light they have, a care that that light be not darkness; how they have developed one side of their humanity at the expense of all others, and have become incomplete and mutilated men in consequence. Thus falling short of harmonious perfection, they fail to follow the true way of salvation. Therefore that way is made the harder for others to find, general perfection is put further off out of our reach, and the confusion and perplexity in which our society now labours is increased by the Nonconformists rather than diminished by them. So while we praise and esteem the zeal of the Nonconformists in walking staunchly by the best light they have, and desire to take no whit from it, we seek to add to this what we call sweetness and light, and develope their full humanity more perfectly; and to seek this is certainly not to be the enemy of the Nonconformists.

But now, with these ideas in our head, we come across the present operation for disestablishing the Irish Church by the power of the Nonconformists' antipathy to religious establishments and endowments. And we see Liberal statesmen, for whose purpose this antipathy happens to be convenient, flattering it all they can; saying that though they have no intention of laying hands on an Establishment which is efficient and popular, like the Anglican Establishment here in England, yet it is in the abstract a fine and good thing that religion should be left to the voluntary xviii support of its promoters, and should thus gain in energy and independence; and Mr. Gladstone has no words strong enough to express his admiration of the refusal of State-aid by the Irish Roman Catholics, who have never yet been seriously asked to accept it, but who would a good deal embarrass him if they demanded it. And we see philosophical politicians, with a turn for swimming with the stream, like Mr. Baxter or Mr. Charles Buxton, and philosophical divines with the same turn, like the Dean of Canterbury, seeking to give a sort of grand stamp of generality and solemnity to this antipathy of the Nonconformists, and to dress it out as a law of human progress in the future. Now, nothing can be pleasanter than swimming with the stream; and we might gladly, if we could, try in our unsystematic way to help Mr. Baxter, and Mr. Charles Buxton, and the Dean of Canterbury, in their labours at once philosophical and popular. But we have got fixed in our minds that a more full and harmonious development of their humanity is what the Nonconformists most want, that narrowness, one-sidedness, and incompleteness is what they most suffer from; in a word, that in what we call *provinciality* they abound, but xix in what we may call *totality* they fall short.

And they fall short more than the members of Establishments. The great works by which, not only in literature, art, and science generally, but in religion itself, the human spirit has manifested its approaches to totality, and a full, harmonious perfection, and by which it stimulates and helps forward the world's general perfection, come, not from Nonconformists, but from men who either belong to Establishments or have been trained in them. A Nonconformist minister, the Rev. Edward White, who has lately written a temperate and well-reasoned pamphlet against Church Establishments, says that "the unendowed and unestablished communities of England exert full as much moral and ennobling influence upon the conduct of statesmen as that Church which is both established and endowed." That depends upon what one means by moral and ennobling influence. The believer in machinery may think that to get a Government to abolish *Church-rates or to legalise *marriage with a deceased wife's sister is to exert a moral and ennobling influence upon Government. But a lover of perfection, who looks to inward ripeness for the true springs of conduct, will surely think that as Shakespeare has done more for the inward ripeness of our statesmen than Dr. Watts, and has, therefore, done more to moralise and ennoble them, so an Establishment which has produced Hooker, Barrow, Butler, has done more to moralise and ennoble English statesmen and their conduct than communities which have produced the Nonconformist divines. The fruitful men of English Puritanism and Nonconformity are men who were trained within the pale of the Establishment, —Milton, Baxter, Wesley. A generation or two outside the Establishment, and Puritanism produces men of national mark no more. With the same doctrine and discipline, men of national mark are produced in Scotland; but in an Establishment. With the same doctrine and discipline, men of national and even European mark are produced in Germany, Switzerland, France; but in Establishments. Only two religious disciplines seem exempted, or comparatively exempted, from the operation of the law which seems to forbid the rearing, outside of national establishments, of men of the highest spiritual significance. These two are the Roman Catholic and the Jewish. And these, both of them, rest on Establishments, which, though not indeed national, are cosmopolitan; and perhaps here, what the individual man does not lose by these conditions of his rearing, the citizen, and the State of which he is a citizen, loses.

What, now, can be the reason of this undeniable provincialism of the English Puritans and Protestant Nonconformists, a provincialism which has two main types,—a bitter type and a smug type,—but which in both its types is vulgarising, and thwarts the full perfection of our humanity? Men of genius and character are born and reared in this medium as in any other. From the faults of the mass such men will always be comparatively free, and they will always excite our interest; yet in this medium they seem to have a special difficulty in breaking through what bounds them, and in developing their totality. Surely the reason is, that the Nonconformist is not in contact with the main current of national life, like the member of an Establishment. In a matter of such deep and vital concern as religion, this separation from the main current of the national life has peculiar impor- tance. In the following essay we have discussed at length the tendency in us to *Hebraise,* as we call it; that is, to sacrifice all other sides of our being to the religious side. This tendency has its cause in the divine beauty and grandeur of religion, and bears affecting testimony to them; but we have seen that it has dangers for us, we have seen that it leads to a narrow and twisted growth of our religious side itself, and to a failure in perfection. But if we tend to Hebraise even in an Establishment, with the main current of national life flowing round us, and reminding us in all ways of the variety and fulness of human existence,—by a Church which is historical as the State itself is historical, and whose order, ceremonies, and monuments reach, like those of the State, far beyond any fancies and devisings of ours, and by institutions such as the Universities, formed to defend and advance that very culture and many-sided development which it is the danger of Hebraising to make us neglect,—how much more must we tend to Hebraise when we lack these preventives. One may say that to be reared a member of an Establishment is in itself a lesson of religious moderation, and a help towards culture and harmonious perfection. Instead of battling for his own private forms for expressing the inexpressible and defining the undefinable, a man takes those which have commended themselves most to the religious life of his nation; and while he may be sure that within those forms the religious side of his own nature may find its satisfaction, he has leisure and composure to satisfy other sides of his nature as well.

But with the member of a Nonconforming or self-made religious community how different! The sectary's *eigene grosse Erfindungen,* as Goethe calls them,—the precious discoveries of himself and his friends for expressing the inexpressible and defining the undefinable in peculiar forms of their own, cannot but, as he has voluntarily chosen them, and is personally responsible for them, fill his whole mind. He is zealous to do battle for them and affirm them, for in affirming them he affirms himself, and that is what we all like. Other sides of his being are thus neglected, because the religious side, always tending in every serious man to predominance over our other spiritual sides, is in him made quite absorbing and tyrannous by the condition of self-assertion and challenge which he has chosen for himself. And just what is not essential in religion he comes to mistake for essential, and a thousand times the more readily because he has chosen it of himself; and religious activity he fancies to consist in battling for it. All this leaves him little leisure or inclination for culture; to which, besides, he has no great institutions not of his own making, like the Universities connected with the national Establishment, to invite him; but only such institutions as, like the order and discipline of his religion, he may have invented for himself, and invented under the sway of the narrow and tyrannous notions of religion fostered in him as we have seen. Thus, while a national Establishment of religion favours totality, *hole-and-corner* forms of religion (to use an expressive popular word) inevitably favour provincialism.

But the Nonconformists, and many of our Liberal friends along with them, have a plausible plan for getting rid of this provincialism, if, as they can hardly quite deny, it exists. "Let us all be in the same boat," they cry; "open the Universities to everybody, and let there be no establishment of religion at all!" Open the Universities by all means; but, as to the second point about establishment, let us sift the proposal a little. It does seem at first a little like that proposal of the fox, who had lost his own tail, to put all the other foxes in the same boat by a general cutting off of tails; and we know that moralists have decided that the right course here was, not to adopt this plausible suggestion, and cut off tails all round, but rather that the other foxes should keep their tails, and that the fox without a tail should get one. And so we might be inclined to urge that, to cure the evil of the Nonconformists' provincialism, the right way can hardly be to provincialise us all round.

However, perhaps we shall not be provincialised. For the Rev. Edward White says that probably, "when all good men alike are placed in a condition of religious equality, and the whole complicated iniquity of Government Church patronage is swept away, more of moral and ennobling influence than ever will be brought to bear upon the action of statesmen." We already have an example of religious equality in our colonies. "In the colonies," says *The Times,* "we see religious communities unfettered by State-control, and the State relieved from one of the most troublesome and irritating of responsibilities." But America is the great example alleged by those who are against establishments for religion. Our topic at this moment is the influence of religious establishments on culture; and it is remarkable that Mr. Bright, who has taken lately to representing himself as, above all, a promoter of reason and of the simple natural truth of things, and his policy as a fostering of the growth of intelligence,—just the aims, as is well known, of culture also,—Mr. Bright, in a speech at Birmingham about education, seized on the very point which seems to concern our topic, when he said: "I believe the people of the United States have offered to the world more valuable information during the last forty

years than all Europe put together." So America, without religious establishments, seems to get ahead of us all in culture and totality; and these are
the cure for provincialism.

On the other hand, another friend of reason and the simple natural truth
of things, Monsieur Renan, says of America, in a book he has recently
published, what seems to conflict violently with what Mr. Bright says.
Mr. Bright affirms that, not only have the United States thus informed
Europe, but they have done it without a great apparatus of higher and
scientific instruction, and by dint of all classes in America being "sufficiently educated to be able to read, and to comprehend, and to think; and
that, I maintain, is the foundation of all subsequent progress." And then
comes Monsieur Renan, and says: "The sound instruction of the people is
an effect of the high culture of certain classes. The countries which, like
the United States, have created a considerable popular instruction without
any serious higher instruction, will long have to expiate this fault by their
intellectual mediocrity, their vulgarity of manners, their superficial spirit,
their lack of general intelligence."†

Now, which of these two friends of culture are we to believe? Monsieur
Renan seems more to have in his eye what we ourselves mean by culture;
because Mr. Bright always has in his eye what he calls "a commendable
interest" in politics and political agitations. As he said only the other day at
Birmingham: "At this moment,—in fact, I may say at every moment in
the history of a free country,—there is nothing that is so much worth
discussing as politics." And he keeps repeating, with all the powers of his
noble oratory, the old story, how to the thoughtfulness and intelligence of
the people of great towns we owe all our improvements in the last thirty
years, and how these improvements have hitherto consisted in Parliamentary reform, and free trade, and abolition of Church rates, and so on; and
how they are now about to consist in getting rid of minority-members, and
in introducing a free breakfast-table, and in abolishing the Irish Church by
the power of the Nonconformists' antipathy to establishments, and much
more of the same kind. And though our pauperism and ignorance, and all
the questions which are called social, seem now to be forcing themselves
upon his mind, yet he still goes on with his glorifying of the great towns,
and the *Liberals, and their operations for the last thirty years. It never

† "Les pays qui comme les États-Unis ont créé un enseignement populaire considérable
sans instruction supérieure sérieuse, expieront longtemps encore leur faute par leur
médiocrité intellectuelle, leur grossièreté de mœurs, leur esprit superficiel, leur manque
d'intelligence générale."

Preface

seems to occur to him that the present troubled state of our social life has anything to do with the thirty years' blind worship of their nostrums by himself and our Liberal friends, or that it throws any doubts upon the sufficiency of this worship. But he thinks what is still amiss is due to the stupidity of the Tories, and will be cured by the thoughtfulness and intelligence of the great towns, and by the Liberals going on gloriously with their political operations as before; or that it will cure itself. So we see what Mr. Bright means by thoughtfulness and intelligence, and in what manner, according to him, we are to grow in them. And, no doubt, in America all classes read their newspaper and take a commendable interest in politics more than here or anywhere else in Europe.

But, in the following essay, we have been led to doubt the sufficiency of all this political operating of ours, pursued mechanically as we pursue it; and we found that *general intelligence,* as Monsieur Renan calls it, or, in our own words, a reference of all our operating to a firm intelligible law of things, was just what we were without, and that we were without it

because we worshipped our machinery so devoutly. Therefore, we conclude that Monsieur Renan, more than Mr. Bright, means by reason and intelligence the same thing as we do; and when he says that America, that chosen home of newspapers and politics, is without general intelligence, we think it likely, from the circumstances of the case, that this is so; and that, in culture and totality, America, instead of surpassing us all, falls short.

And,—to keep to our point of the influence of religious establishments upon culture and a high development of our humanity,—we can surely see reasons why, with all her energy and fine gifts, America does not show more of this development, or more promise of this. In the following essay it will be seen how our society distributes itself into Barbarians, Philistines, and Populace; and America is just ourselves, with the Barbarians quite left out, and the Populace nearly. This leaves the Philistines for the great bulk of the nation;—a livelier sort of Philistine than ours, and with the pressure and false ideal of our Barbarians taken away, but left all the more to himself and to have his full swing. And as we have found that the

strongest and most vital part of English Philistinism was the Puritan and Hebraising middle-class, and that its Hebraising keeps it from culture and totality, so it is notorious that the people of the United States issues from this class, and reproduces its tendencies,—its narrow conception of man's spiritual range and of his one thing needful. From Maine to Florida, and back again, all America Hebraises. Difficult as it is to speak of a people merely from what one reads, yet that, I think, one may, without much fear of contradiction say. I mean, when, in the United States, any spiritual side in a man is wakened to activity, it is generally the religious side, and the religious side in a narrow way. Social reformers go to Moses or St. Paul for their doctrines, and have no notion there is anywhere else to go to; earnest young men at schools and universities, instead of conceiving salvation as a harmonious perfection only to be won by unreservedly cultivating many sides in us, conceive of it in the old Puritan fashion, and fling themselves ardently upon it in the old, false ways of this fashion, which we know so well, and such as Mr. Hammond, the American revivalist, has lately, at Mr. Spurgeon's Tabernacle, been refreshing our memory with. Now, if America thus Hebraises more than either England or xxxii Germany, will any one deny that the absence of religious establishments has much to do with it? We have seen how establishments tend to give us a sense of a historical life of the human spirit, outside and beyond our own fancies and feelings; how they thus tend to suggest new sides and sympathies in us to cultivate; how, further, by saving us from having to invent and fight for our own forms of religion, they give us leisure and calm to steady our view of religion itself,—the most overpowering of objects, as it is the grandest,—and to enlarge our first crude notions of the one thing needful. But, in a serious people, where every one has to choose and strive for his own order and discipline of religion, the contention about these non-essentials occupies his mind, his first crude notions about the one thing needful do not get purged, and they invade the whole spiritual man in him, and then, making a solitude, they call it heavenly peace.

I remember a Nonconformist manufacturer, in a town of the Midland counties, telling me that when he first came there, some years ago, the place had no Dissenters; but he had opened an Independent chapel in it, xxxiii and now Church and Dissent were pretty equally divided, with sharp contests between them. I said, that seemed a pity. "A pity?" cried he; "not at all! Only think of all the zeal and activity which the collision calls forth!" "Ah, but, my dear friend," I answered, "only think of all the nonsense which you now hold quite firmly, which you would never have held if you had not been contradicting your adversary in it all these years!" The more serious the people, and the more prominent the religious side in it, the greater is the danger of this side, if set to choose out forms for itself and fight for existence, swelling and spreading till it swallows all other spiritual sides up, intercepts and absorbs all nutriment which should have gone to them, and leaves Hebraism rampant in us and Hellenism stamped out.

Culture, and the harmonious perfection of our whole being, and what we call totality, then become secondary matters; and the institutions, which should develope these, take the same narrow and partial view of humanity and its wants as the free religious communities take. Just as the free churches of Mr. Beecher or Brother Noyes, with their provincialism and want of centrality, make mere Hebraisers in religion, and not perfect men, so the university of Mr. Ezra Cornell, a really noble monument of his munificence, yet seems to rest on a provincial misconception of what culture truly is, and to be calculated to produce miners, or engineers, or architects, not sweetness and light.

And, therefore, when the Rev. Edward White asks the same kind of question about America that he has asked about England, and wants to know whether, without religious establishments, as much is not done in America for the higher national life as is done for that life here, we answer in the same way as we did before, that as much is not done. Because to enable and stir up people to read their Bible and the newspapers, and to get a practical knowledge of their business, does not serve to the higher spiritual life of a nation so much as culture, truly conceived, serves; and a true conception of culture is, as Monsieur Renan's words show, just what America fails in.

To the many who think that culture, and sweetness, and light, are all moonshine, this will not appear to matter much; but with us, who value them, and who think that we have traced much of our present discomfort to the want of them, it weighs a great deal. So not only do we say that the Nonconformists have got provincialism and lost totality by the want of a religious establishment, but we say that the very example which they bring forward to help their case makes against them; and that when they triumphantly show us America without religious establishments, they only show us a whole nation touched, amidst all its greatness and promise, with that provincialism which it is our aim to extirpate in the English Nonconformists.

But now to evince the disinterestedness which culture, as I have said, teaches us. We have seen the narrowness generated in Puritanism by its hole-and-corner organisation, and we propose to cure it by bringing Puritanism more into contact with the main current of national life. Here we are fully at one with the Dean of Westminster; and, indeed, he and we were trained in the same school to mark the narrowness of Puritanism, and to wish to cure it. But he and others would give to the present Anglican Establishment a character the most latitudinarian, as it is called, possible; availing themselves for this purpose of the diversity of tendencies and doctrines which does undoubtedly exist already in the Anglican formularies; and they would say to the Puritans: "Come all of you into this liberally conceived Anglican Establishment." But to say this is hardly, perhaps, to take sufficient account of the course of history, or of the strength of men's feelings in what concerns religion, or of the gravity which may have come to attach itself to points of religious order and discipline merely. When the Rev. Edward White talks of "sweeping away the whole complicated iniquity of Government Church patronage," he uses language which has been forced upon him by his position, but which is, as we have seen, devoid of any real solidity. But when he talks of the religious communities "which have for three hundred years contended for the power of the congregation in the management of their own affairs," then he talks history; and his language has behind it, in my opinion, facts which make the latitudinarianism of our Broad Churchmen quite illusory. Certainly, culture will never make us think it an essential of religion whether we have in our Church discipline "a popular authority of elders," as Hooker calls it, or whether we have Episcopal jurisdiction. Certainly, xxxvii Hooker himself did not think it an essential; for in the dedication of his *Ecclesiastical Polity,* speaking of these questions of Church discipline which gave occasion to his great work, he says they are "in truth, for the greatest part, such silly things, that very easiness doth make them hard to be disputed of in serious manner." Hooker's great work against the impugners of the order and discipline of the Church of England was written (and this is too indistinctly seized by many who read it), not because Episcopalianism is essential, but because its impugners maintained that Presbyterianism is essential, and that Episcopalianism is sinful. Neither the one nor the other is either essential or sinful, and much may be said on behalf of both. But what is important to be remarked is that *both were in the Church of England at the Reformation,* and that Presbyterianism was only extruded gradually. We have mentioned Hooker, and nothing better illustrates what has just been asserted than the following incident in Hooker's own career, which every one has read, for it is related in Isaac Walton's *Life of Hooker,* but of which, probably, the significance has been xxxviii fully grasped by not one-half of those who have read it.

Hooker was through the influence of Archbishop Whitgift appointed, in 1585, Master of the *Temple; but a great effort had just been made to obtain the place for a Mr. Walter Travers, well known in that day, though now it is Hooker's name which alone preserves his. This Travers was then afternoon-lecturer at the Temple. The Master whose death made the vacancy, Alvey, recommended on his deathbed Travers for his successor, the society was favourable to him, and he had the support of the Lord Treasurer Burghley. After Hooker's appointment to the Mastership, Travers remained afternoon-lecturer, and combated in the afternoons the doctrine which Hooker preached in the mornings. Now, this Travers, originally a Fellow of Trinity College, Cambridge, afterwards afternoon-lecturer at the Temple, recommended for the Mastership by the foregoing Master, whose opinions, it is said, agreed with his, favoured by the society of the Temple, and supported by the Prime Minister,—this Travers was not an Episcopally ordained clergyman at all; he was a Presbyterian, a partisan of the *Geneva church-discipline, as it was then called, and "had taken orders," says Walton, "by the Presbyters in Antwerp." In another place Walton speaks of his orders yet more fully:—"He had disowned," he says, "the English Established Church and Episcopacy, and went to Geneva, and afterwards to Antwerp, to be ordained minister, as he was by Villers and Cartwright and others the heads of a congregation there; and so came back again more confirmed for the discipline." Villers and Cartwright are in like manner examples of Presbyterianism within the Church of England, which was common enough at that time; but perhaps nothing can better give us a lively sense of its presence there than this history of Travers, which is as if Mr. Binney were now afternoon-reader at Lincoln's Inn or the Temple, were to be a candidate, favoured by the benchers and by the Prime Minister, for the Mastership, and were only kept out of the post by the accident of the Archbishop of Canterbury's influence with the Queen carrying a rival candidate.

Presbyterianism, with its popular principle of the power of the congregation in the management of their own affairs, was extruded from the Church of England, and men like Travers can no longer appear in her pulpits. Perhaps if a government like that of Elizabeth, with secular statesmen like the Cecils, and ecclesiastical statesmen like Whitgift, could have been prolonged, Presbyterianism might, by a wise mixture of concession and firmness, have been absorbed in the Establishment. Lord Bolingbroke, on a matter of this kind a very clear-judging and impartial witness, says, in a work far too little read, his *Remarks on English History:*—"The measures pursued and the temper observed in Queen Elizabeth's time tended to diminish the religious opposition by a slow, a gentle, and for that very reason an effectual progression. There was even room to hope that when the first fire of the Dissenters' zeal was passed, reasonable terms of union with the Established Church might be accepted by such of them as were not intoxicated with fanaticism. These were friends to order, though they disputed about it. If these friends of Calvin's discipline had been once incorporated with the Established Church, the remaining sectaries would

xxxix

xl

have been of little moment, either for numbers or reputation; and the very means which were proper to gain these friends, were likewise the most effectual to hinder the increase of them, and of the other sectaries in the meantime." The temper and ill judgment of the Stuarts made shipwreck of all policy of this kind. Yet speaking even of the time of the Stuarts, but their early time, Clarendon says that if Bishop Andrewes had succeeded Bancroft at Canterbury, the disaffection of separatists might have been stayed and healed. This, however, was not to be; and Presbyterianism, after exercising for some years the law of the strongest, itself in Charles the Second's reign suffered under this law, and was finally cast out from the Church of England.

Now the points of church discipline at issue between Presbyterianism and Episcopalianism are, as has been said, not essential. They might probably once have been settled in a sense altogether favourable to Episcopalianism. Hooker may have been right in thinking that there were in his time circumstances which made it essential that they should be settled in this sense, though the points in themselves were not essential. But by the very fact of the settlement not having then been effected, of the breach having gone on and widened, of the Nonconformists not having been amicably incorporated with the Establishment but violently cast out from it, the circumstances are now altogether altered. Isaac Walton, a fervent Churchman, complains that "the principles of the Nonconformists grew at last to such a height and were vented so daringly, that, beside the loss of life and limbs, the Church and State were both forced to use such other severities as will not admit of an excuse, if it had not been to prevent confusion and the perilous consequences of it." But those very severities have of themselves made union on an Episcopalian footing impossible. Besides, Presbyterianism, the popular authority of elders, the power of the congregation in the management of their own affairs, has that warrant given to it by Scripture and by the proceedings of the early Christian Churches, it is so consonant with the spirit of Protestantism which made the Reformation and which has such strength in this country, it is so predominant in the practice of other reformed churches, it was so strong in the original reformed Church of England, that one cannot help doubting whether any settlement which suppressed it could have been really permanent, and whether it would not have kept appearing again and again, and causing dissension.

Well, then, if culture is the disinterested endeavour after man's perfection, will it not make us wish to cure the provincialism of the Nonconformists, not by making Churchmen provincial along with them, but by letting their popular church discipline, formerly found in the National Church, and still found in the affections and practice of a good part of the nation, appear in the National Church once more; and thus to bring Nonconformists into contact again, as their greater fathers were, with the main stream of national life? Why should not a Presbyterian or Congregational Church, based on this considerable and important, though not essential principle, of the congregation's power in the church management, be established,—with equal rank for its chiefs with the chiefs of Episcopacy, and with admissibility of its ministers, under a revised system of patronage and preferment, to benefices,—side by side with the Episcopal Church, as the Calvinist and Lutheran Churches are established side by side in France and Germany? Such a Congregational Church would unite

xliv the main bodies of Protestants who are now separatists; and separation would cease to be the law of their religious order. Then,—through this concession on a really considerable point of difference,—that endless splitting into hole-and-corner churches on quite inconsiderable points of difference, which must prevail so long as separatism is the first law of a Nonconformist's religious existence, would be checked. Culture would then find a place among English followers of the popular authority of elders, as it has long found it among the followers of Episcopal jurisdiction; and this we should gain by merely recognising, regularising, and restoring an element which appeared once in the reformed National Church, and which is considerable and national enough to have a sound claim to appear there still.

So far, then, is culture from making us unjust to the Nonconformists because it forbids us to worship their fetishes, that it even leads us to propose to do more for them than they themselves venture to claim. It leads us, also, to respect what is solid and respectable in their convictions, while their latitudinarian friends make light of it. Not that the forms in which the human spirit tries to express the inexpressible, or the forms by

xlv which man tries to worship, have or can have, as has been said, for the follower of perfection, anything necessary or eternal. If the New Testament and the practice of the primitive Christians sanctioned the popular form of church government a thousand times more expressly than they do, if the Church since Constantine were a thousand times more of a departure from the scheme of primitive Christianity than it can be shown to be, that does not at all make, as is supposed by men in bondage to the letter, the popular form of church government alone and always sacred and binding, or the work of Constantine a thing to be regretted. What is alone and always sacred and binding for man is the climbing towards his total perfection, and the machinery by which he does this varies in value according as it helps him to do it. The planters of Christianity had their roots in deep and rich grounds of human life and achievement, both Jewish and also Greek; and had thus a comparatively firm and wide basis amidst all the vehement inspiration of their mighty movement and change. By their strong inspiration they carried men off the old basis of life and culture, whether Jewish or Greek, and generations arose who had their roots in neither world, and were in contact therefore with no full and great stream of human life. Christianity might have lost herself, if it had not been for some such change as that of the fourth century, in a multitude of *hole-and-corner churches like the churches of English Nonconformity after its founders departed; churches without great men, and without furtherance for the higher life of humanity. At a critical moment came Constantine, and placed Christianity,—or let us rather say, placed the human spirit, whose totality was endangered,—in contact with the main current of human life. And his work was justified by its fruits, in men like Augustine and Dante, and indeed in all the great men of Christianity, Catholics or Protestants, ever since. And one may go beyond this. Monsieur Albert Réville, whose religious writings are always interesting, says that the conception which cultivated and philosophical Jews now entertain of Christianity and its founder, is probably destined to become the conception which Christians themselves will entertain. Socinians are fond of saying the same thing about the Socinian conception of Christianity. Even if this were true, it would still have been better for a man, through the last eighteen hundred years, to have been a Christian, and a member of one of the great Christian communions, than to have been a Jew or a Socinian; because the being in contact with the main stream of human life is of more moment for a man's total spiritual growth, and for his bringing to perfection the gifts committed to him, which is his business on earth, than any speculative opinion which he may hold or think he holds. Luther,—whom we have called a Philistine of genius, and who, because he was a Philistine, had a coarseness and lack of spiritual delicacy which have harmed his disciples, but who, because he was a genius, had splendid flashes of spiritual insight,—Luther says admirably in his Commentary on the Book of Daniel: "A God is simply *that* whereon the human heart rests with trust, faith, hope and love. If the resting is right, then the God too is right; if the resting is wrong, then the God too is illusory." In other words, the worth of what a man thinks about God and the objects of religion depends on what the man *is;* and what the man *is,* depends upon his having more or less reached the measure of a perfect and total man.

xlviii   All this is true; and yet culture, as we have seen, has more tenderness
for scruples of the Nonconformists than have their Broad Church friends.
That is because culture, disinterestedly trying, in its aim at perfection, to
see things as they really are, sees how worthy and divine a thing is the
religious side in man, though it is not the whole of man. And when Mr.
Greg, who differs from us about edification, (and certainly we do not seem
likely to agree with him as to what edifies), finding himself moved by
some extraneous considerations or other to take a Church's part against its
enemies, calls taking a Church's part *returning to base uses,* culture
teaches us how out of place is this language, and that to use it shows an
inadequate conception of human nature, and that no Church will thank a
man for taking its part in this fashion, but will leave him with indifference
to the tender mercies of his Benthamite friends. But avoiding Bentham-
ism, or an inadequate conception of the religious side in man, culture
makes us also avoid Mialism, or an inadequate conception of man's totality. Therefore to the worth and grandeur of the religious side in man,
xlix   culture is rejoiced and willing to pay any tribute, except the tribute of
man's totality. True, the order and liturgy of the Church of England one
may be well contented to live and to die with, and they are such as to
inspire an affectionate and revering attachment. True, the reproaches of
Nonconformists against this order for "retaining badges of Antichristian
recognisance;" and for "corrupting the right form of Church polity with
manifold Popish rites and ceremonies;" true, their assertion of the essentialness of their own supposed Scriptural order, and their belief in its
eternal fitness, are founded on illusion. True, the whole attitude of horror
and holy superiority assumed by Puritanism towards the Church of Rome,
is wrong and false, and well merits Sir Henry Wotton's rebuke:—"Take
heed of thinking that the farther you go from the Church of Rome, the
nearer you are to God." True, one of the best wishes one could form for
Mr. Spurgeon or Father Jackson is, that they might be permitted to learn on
this side the grave (for if they do not, a considerable surprise is certainly
reserved for them on the other) that Whitfield and Wesley were not at all
better than St. Francis, and that they themselves are not at all better than
l   Lacordaire. Yet, in spite of all this, so noble and divine a thing is religion,
so respectable is that earnestness which desires a prayer-book with one
strain of doctrine, so attaching is the order and discipline by which we are
used to have our religion conveyed, so many claims on our regard has that
popular form of church government for which Nonconformists contend,
so perfectly compatible is it with all progress towards perfection, that
culture would make us shy even to propose to Nonconformists the accep-

tance of the Anglican prayer-book and the episcopal order; and would be forward to wish them a prayer-book of their own approving, and the church discipline to which they are attached and accustomed.

Only not at the price of Mialism; that is, of a doctrine which leaves the Nonconformists in holes and corners, out of contact with the main current of national life. One can lay one's finger, indeed, on the line by which this doctrine has grown up, and see how the essential part of Nonconformity is a popular church-discipline analogous to that of the other reformed churches, and how its voluntaryism is an accident. It contended for the establishment of its own church-discipline as the only true one; and beaten in this contention, and seeing its rival established, it came down to the more plausible proposal "to place all good men alike in a condition of religious equality;" and this plan of proceeding, originally taken as a mere second-best, became, by long sticking to it and preaching it up, first fair, then righteous, then the only righteous, then at last necessary to salvation. This is the plan for remedying the Nonconformists' divorce from contact with the national life by divorcing churchmen too from contact with it; that is, as we have familiarly before put it, the tailless foxes are for cutting off tails all round. But this the other foxes could not wisely grant, unless it were proved that tails are of no value. And so, too, unless it is proved that contact with the main current of national life is of no value (and we have shown that it is of the greatest value), we cannot safely, even to please the Nonconformists in a matter where we would please them as much as possible, admit Mialism.

But now, as we have shown the disinterestedness which culture enjoins, and its obedience not to likings or dislikings, but to the aim of perfection, let us show its flexibility,—its independence of *machinery. That other and greater prophet of intelligence, and reason, and the simple natural truth of things,—Mr. Bright,—means by these, as we have seen, a certain set of measures which suit the special ends of Liberal and Nonconformist partisans. For instance, reason and justice towards Ireland mean the abolishment of the iniquitous Protestant ascendency in such a particular way as to suit the Nonconformists' antipathy to establishments. Reason and justice pursued in a different way, by distributing among the three main Churches of Ireland,—the Roman Catholic, the Anglican, and the Presbyterian,—the church property of Ireland, would immediately cease, for Mr. Bright and the Nonconformists, to be reason and justice at all, and would become, as Mr. Spurgeon says, "a setting up of the Roman image." Thus we see that the sort of intelligence reached by culture is more disinterested than the sort of intelligence reached by belonging to the Liberal party in the great towns, and taking a commendable interest in politics. But still more striking is the difference between the two views of intelligence, when we see that culture not only makes a quite disinterested choice of the machinery proper to carry us towards sweetness and light, and to make reason and the will of God prevail, but by even this machinery does not hold stiffly and blindly, and easily passes on beyond it to that for the sake of which it chose it.

liii

For instance: culture leads us to think that the ends of human perfection might be best served by establishing,—that is, by bringing into contact with the main current of the national life,—in Ireland the Roman Catholic and the Presbyterian Churches along with the Anglican Church; and, in England, a Presbyterian or Congregational Church of like rank and *status* with our Episcopalian one. It leads us to think that we should really, in this way, be working to make reason and the will of God prevail; because we should be making Roman Catholics better citizens, and Nonconformists,—nay, and Churchmen along with them,—larger-minded and more complete men. But undoubtedly there are great difficulties in such a plan as this; and the plan is not one which looks very likely to be adopted. It is a plan more for a time of creative statesmen, like the time of Elizabeth, than for a time of instrumental statesmen like the present. The Churchman must rise above his ordinary self in order to favour it; and the Nonconformist has worshipped his fetish of separatism so long that he is likely to wish still to remain, like Ephraim, "a wild ass alone by himself." The centre of power being where it is, our instrumental statesmen have every temptation, as is shown more at large in the following essay, in the first place, to "relieve themselves," as *The Times* says, "of troublesome and irritating responsibilities;" in the second place, when they must act, to go along, as they do, with the ordinary self of those on whose favour they depend, to adopt as their own its desires, and to serve them with fidelity, and even, if possible, with impulsiveness. This is the more easy for them, because there are not wanting,—and there never will be wanting,—thinkers like Mr. Baxter, Mr. Charles Buxton, and the Dean of Canterbury, to swim with the stream, but to swim with it philosophically; to call the desires of the ordinary self of any great section of the community edicts of the national mind and laws of human progress, and to give them a general, a philosophic, and an imposing expression. A generous statesman may honestly, therefore, soon unlearn any disposition to put his tongue in his cheek in advocating these desires, and may advocate them with fervour and impulsiveness. Therefore a plan such as that which we have indicated does not seem a plan so likely to find favour as a plan for abolishing the

liv

lv

Irish Church by the power of the Nonconformists' antipathy to establishments.

But to tell us that our fond dreams are on that account shattered is inexact, and is the sort of language which ought to be addressed to the promoters of intelligence through public meetings and a commendable interest in politics, when they fail in their designs, and not to us. For we are fond stickers to no machinery, not even our own; and we have no doubt that perfection can be reached without it,—with free churches as with established churches, and with instrumental statesmen as with creative statesmen. But it can never be reached without seeing things as they really are; and it is to this, therefore, and to no machinery in the world, that culture sticks fondly. It insists that men should not mistake, as they are prone to mistake, their natural taste for the bathos for a relish for the sublime; and if statesmen, either with their tongue in their cheek or   lvi through a generous impulsiveness, tell them their natural taste for the bathos is a relish for the sublime, there is the more need for culture to tell them the contrary. It is delusion on this point which is fatal, and against delusion on this point culture works. It is not fatal to our Liberal friends to labour for free trade, extension of the suffrage, and abolition of church-rates, instead of graver social ends; but it is fatal to them to be told by their flatterers, and to believe, with our pauperism increasing more rapidly than our population, that they have performed a great, an heroic work, by occupying themselves exclusively, for the last thirty years, with these Liberal nostrums, and that the right and good course for them now is to go on occupying themselves with the like for the future. It is not fatal to Americans to have no religious establishments and no effective centres of high culture; but it is fatal to them to be told by their flatterers, and to believe, that they are the most intelligent people in the whole world, when of intelligence, in the true and fruitful sense of the word, they even singularly, as we have seen, come short. It is not fatal to the Nonconform-   lvii ists to remain with their separated churches; but it is fatal to them to be told by their flatterers, and to believe, that theirs is the one pure and Christ-ordained way of worshipping God, that provincialism and loss of totality have not come to them from following it, or that provincialism and loss of totality are not evils. It is not fatal to the English nation to abolish the Irish Church by the power of the Nonconformists' antipathy to establishments; but it is fatal to it to be told by its flatterers, and to believe, that it is abolishing it through reason and justice, when it is really abolishing it through this power; or to expect the fruits of reason and justice from anything but the spirit of reason and justice themselves.

Now culture, because of its keen sense of what is really fatal, is all the more disposed to be pliant and easy about what is not fatal. And because machinery is the bane of politics, and an inward working, and not machinery, is what we most want, we keep advising our ardent young Liberal friends to think less of machinery, to stand more aloof from the arena of politics at present, and rather to try and promote, with us, an inward working. They do not listen to us, and they rush into the arena of politics, where their merits, indeed, seem to be little appreciated as yet; and then they complain of the reformed constituencies, and call the new Parliament a Philistine Parliament. As if a nation, nourished and reared in Hebraising, could give us, just yet, anything better than a Philistine Parliament!— for would a Barbarian Parliament be even so good, or a Populace Parliament? For our part, we rejoice to see our dear old friends, the Hebraising Philistines, gathered in force in the Valley of Jehoshaphat before their final conversion, which will certainly come; but for this conversion we must not try to oust them from their places, and to contend for machinery with them, but we must work on them inwardly and cure them of Hebraising.

Yet *the days of Israel are innumerable;* and in its blame of Hebraising too, and in its praise of Hellenising, culture must not fail to keep its flexibility, and to give to its judgments that passing and provisional character which we have seen it impose on its preferences and rejections of machinery. Now, and for us, it is a time to Hellenise, and to praise knowing; for we have Hebraised too much, and have over-valued doing. But the habits and discipline received from Hebraism remain for our race an eternal possession; and, as humanity is constituted, one must never assign them the second rank to-day, without being ready to restore them to the first rank to-morrow. To walk staunchly by the best light one has, to be strict and sincere with oneself, not to be of the number of those who say and do not, to be in earnest,—this is the discipline by which alone man is enabled to rescue his life from thraldom to the passing moment and to his bodily senses, to ennoble it, and to make it eternal. And this discipline has been nowhere so effectively taught as in the school of Hebraism. Sophocles and Plato knew as well as the author of the Epistle to the Hebrews that "without holiness no man shall see God," and their notion of what goes to make up holiness was larger than his. But the intense and convinced energy with which the Hebrew, both of the Old and of the New Testament, threw himself upon his ideal, and which inspired the incomparable definition of the great Christian virtue, Faith,—*the substance of things hoped for, the evidence of things not seen,*—this energy of faith in its ideal has belonged to Hebraism alone. As our idea of holiness enlarges, and our scope of perfection widens beyond the narrow limits to which the over-rigour of Hebraising has tended to confine it, we shall come again to Hebraism for that devout energy in embracing our ideal, which alone can give to man the happiness of doing what he knows. "If ye know these things, happy are ye if ye do them!"—the last word for infirm humanity will always be that. For this word, reiterated with a power now sublime, now affecting, but always admirable, our race will, as long as the world lasts, return to Hebraism; and the Bible, which preaches this word, will forever remain, as Goethe called it, not only a national book, but the Book of the Nations. Again and again, after what seemed breaches and separations, the prophetic promise to Jerusalem will still be true:—*Lo, thy sons come, whom thou sentest away; they come gathered from the west unto the east by the word of the Holy One, rejoicing in the remembrance of God.*

Culture and Anarchy

[Introduction]

In one of his speeches a year or two ago, that fine speaker and famous Liberal, Mr. Bright, took occasion to have a fling at the friends and preachers of culture. "People who talk about what they call *culture!*" said he contemptuously; "by which they mean a smattering of the two dead languages of Greek and Latin." And he went on to remark, in a strain with which modern speakers and writers have made us very familiar, how poor a thing this culture is, how little good it can do to the world, and how
2   absurd it is for its possessors to set much store by it. And the other day a younger Liberal than Mr. Bright, one of a school whose mission it is to bring into order and system that body of truth of which the earlier Liberals merely touched the outside, a member of the University of Oxford, and a very clever writer, Mr. Frederic Harrison, developed, in the systematic and stringent manner of his school, the thesis which Mr. Bright had propounded in only general terms. "Perhaps the very silliest cant of the day," said Mr. Frederic Harrison, "is the cant about culture. Culture is a desirable quality in a critic of new books, and sits well on a possessor of *belles lettres;* but as applied to politics, it means simply a turn for small faultfinding, love of selfish ease, and indecision in action. The man of culture is in politics one of the poorest mortals alive. For simple pedantry and want of good sense no man is his equal. No assumption is too unreal, no end is too unpractical for him. But the active exercise of politics requires common sense, sympathy, trust, resolution and enthusiasm, qualities which your man of culture has carefully rooted up, lest they damage the delicacy of his critical olfactories. Perhaps they are the only
3   class of responsible beings in the community who cannot with safety be entrusted with power."

Now for my part I do not wish to see men of culture asking to be entrusted with power; and, indeed, I have freely said, that in my opinion the speech most proper, at present, for a man of culture to make to a body

of his fellow-countrymen who get him into a committee-room, is Socrates's: *Know thyself!* and this is not a speech to be made by men wanting to be entrusted with power. For this very indifference to direct political action I have been taken to task by the *Daily Telegraph,* coupled, by a strange perversity of fate, with just that very one of the Hebrew prophets whose style I admire the least, and called "an elegant Jeremiah." It is because I say (to use the words which the *Daily Telegraph* puts in my mouth):—"You mustn't make a fuss because you have no vote,—that is vulgarity; you mustn't hold big meetings to agitate for reform bills and to repeal corn laws,—that is the very height of vulgarity,"—it is for this reason that I am called, sometimes an elegant Jeremiah, sometimes a spurious Jeremiah, a Jeremiah about the reality of whose mission the writer in the *Daily Telegraph* has his doubts. It is evident, therefore, that I   4
have so taken my line as not to be exposed to the whole brunt of Mr. Frederic Harrison's censure. Still, I have often spoken in praise of culture; I have striven to make all my works and ways serve the interests of culture; I take culture to be something a great deal more than what Mr. Frederic Harrison and others call it: "a desirable quality in a critic of new books." Nay, even though to a certain extent I am disposed to agree with Mr. Frederic Harrison, that men of culture are just the class of responsible beings in this community of ours who cannot properly, at present, be entrusted with power, I am not sure that I do not think this the fault of our community rather than of the men of culture. In short, although, like Mr. Bright and Mr. Frederic Harrison, and the editor of the *Daily Telegraph,* and a large body of valued friends of mine, I am a liberal, yet I am a liberal tempered by experience, reflection, and renouncement, and I am, above all, a believer in culture. Therefore I propose now to try and enquire, in the simple unsystematic way which best suits both my taste and my powers, what culture really is, what good it can do, what is our own special need of   5
it; and I shall seek to find some plain grounds on which a faith in culture— both my own faith in it and the faith of others,—may rest securely.

I. [Sweetness and Light]

The disparagers of culture make its motive curiosity; sometimes, indeed, they make its motive mere exclusiveness and vanity. The culture which is supposed to plume itself on a smattering of Greek and Latin is a culture which is begotten by nothing so intellectual as curiosity; it is valued either out of sheer vanity and ignorance, or else as an engine of social and class distinction, separating its holder, like a badge or title, from other people

who have not got it. No serious man would call this *culture,* or attach any value to it, as culture, at all. To find the real ground for the very differing estimate which serious people will set upon culture, we must find some
6   motive for culture in the terms of which may lie a real ambiguity; and such a motive the word *curiosity* gives us. I have before now pointed out that in English we do not, like the foreigners, use this word in a good sense as well as in a bad sense; with us the word is always used in a somewhat disapproving sense; a liberal and intelligent eagerness about the things of the mind may be meant by a foreigner when he speaks of curiosity, but with us the word always conveys a certain notion of frivolous and unedifying activity. In the *Quarterly Review,* some little time ago, was an estimate of the celebrated French critic, Monsieur Sainte-Beuve, and a very inadequate estimate it, in my judgment, was. And its inadequacy consisted chiefly in this: that in our English way it left out of sight the double sense really involved in the word *curiosity,* thinking enough was said to stamp Monsieur Sainte-Beuve with blame if it was said that he was impelled in his operations as a critic by curiosity, and omitting either to perceive that Monsieur Sainte-Beuve himself, and many other people with him, would consider that this was praiseworthy and not blameworthy, or to point out
7   why it ought really to be accounted worthy of blame and not of praise. For as there is a curiosity about intellectual matters which is futile, and merely a disease, so there is certainly a curiosity,—a desire after the things of the mind simply for their own sakes and for the pleasure of seeing them as they are,—which is, in an intelligent being, natural and laudable. Nay, and the very desire to see things as they are implies a balance and regulation of mind which is not often attained without fruitful effort, and which is the very opposite of the blind and diseased impulse of mind which is what we mean to blame when we blame curiosity. Montesquieu says:—"The first motive which ought to impel us to study is the desire to augment the excellence of our nature, and to render an intelligent being yet more intelligent." This is the true ground to assign for the genuine scientific passion, however manifested, and for culture, viewed simply as a fruit of this passion; and it is a worthy ground, even though we let the term *curiosity* stand to describe it.

But there is of culture another view, in which not solely the scientific passion, the sheer desire to see things as they are, natural and proper in an
8   intelligent being, appears as the ground of it. There is a view in which all the love of our neighbour, the impulses towards action, help, and beneficence, the desire for stopping human error, clearing human confusion, and diminishing the sum of human misery, the noble aspiration to leave the

world better and happier than we found it,—motives eminently such as are called social,— come in as part of the grounds of culture, and the main and pre-eminent part. Culture is then properly described not as having its origin in curiosity, but as having its origin in the love of perfection; it is *a study of perfection.* It moves by the force, not merely or primarily of the scientific passion for pure knowledge, but also of the moral and social passion for doing good. As, in the first view of it, we took for its worthy motto Montesquieu's words: "To render an intelligent being yet more intelligent!" so, in the second view of it, there is no better motto which it can have than these words of Bishop Wilson: "To make reason and the will of God prevail!" Only, whereas the passion for doing good is apt to be overhasty in determining what reason and the will of God say, because its turn is for acting rather than thinking, and it wants to be beginning to act; 9 and whereas it is apt to take its own conceptions, which proceed from its own state of development and share in all the imperfections and imma- turities of this, for a basis of action; what distinguishes culture is, that it is possessed by the scientific passion, as well as by the passion of doing good; that it has worthy notions of reason and the will of God, and does not readily suffer its own crude conceptions to substitute themselves for them; and that, knowing that no action or institution can be salutary and stable which are not based on reason and the will of God, it is not so bent on acting and instituting, even with the great aim of diminishing human error and misery ever before its thoughts, but that it can remember that acting and instituting are of little use, unless we know how and what we ought to act and to institute.

This culture is more interesting and more far-reaching than that other, which is founded solely on the scientific passion for knowing. But it needs times of faith and ardour, times when the intellectual horizon is opening and widening all round us, to flourish in. And is not the close and bounded intellectual horizon within which we have long lived and moved now 10 lifting up, and are not new lights finding free passage to shine in upon us? For a long time there was no passage for them to make their way in upon us, and then it was of no use to think of adapting the world's action to them. Where was the hope of making reason and the will of God prevail among people who had a routine which they had christened reason and the will of God, in which they were inextricably bound, and beyond which they had no power of looking? But now the iron force of adhesion to the old routine,—social, political, religious,—has wonderfully yielded; the iron force of exclusion of all which is new has wonderfully yielded; the danger now is, not that people should obstinately refuse to allow anything but their old routine to pass for reason and the will of God, but either that they should allow some novelty or other to pass for these too easily, or else that they should underrate the importance of them altogether, and think it enough to follow action for its own sake, without troubling themselves to make reason and the will of God prevail therein.

11   Now, then, is the moment for culture to be of service, culture which believes in making reason and the will of God prevail, believes in perfection, is the study and pursuit of perfection, and is no longer debarred, by a rigid invincible exclusion of whatever is new, from getting acceptance for its ideas, simply because they are new.

The moment this view of culture is seized, the moment it is regarded not solely as the endeavour to see things as they are, to draw towards a knowledge of the universal order which seems to be intended and aimed at in the world, and which it is a man's happiness to go along with or his misery to go counter to,—to learn, in short, the will of God,—the moment, I say, culture is considered not merely as the endeavour to *see* and *learn* this, but as the endeavour, also, to make it *prevail*, the moral, social, and beneficent character of culture becomes manifest. The mere endeavour to see and learn it for our own personal satisfaction is indeed a commencement for making it prevail, a preparing the way for this, which always serves this, and is wrongly, therefore, stamped with blame absolutely in itself, and not only in its caricature and degeneration. But perhaps it has got stamped with blame, and disparaged with the dubious title of

12   curiosity, because in comparison with this wider endeavour of such great and plain utility it looks selfish, petty, and unprofitable.

And religion, the greatest and most important of the efforts by which the human race has manifested its impulse to perfect itself,—religion, that voice of the deepest human experience,—does not only enjoin and sanction the aim which is the great aim of culture, the aim of setting ourselves to ascertain what perfection is and to make it prevail; but also, in determining generally in what human perfection consists, religion comes to a conclusion identical with that which culture,—seeking the determination of this question through all the voices of human experience which have been heard upon it, art, science, poetry, philosophy, history, as well as religion, in order to give a greater fulness and certainty to its solution,— likewise reaches. Religion says: *The kingdom of God is within you;* and culture, in like manner, places human perfection in an *internal* condition, in the growth and predominance of our humanity proper, as distinguished from our animality, in the ever-increasing efficaciousness and in the gen-

13   eral harmonious expansion of those gifts of thought and feeling which

make the peculiar dignity, wealth, and happiness of human nature. As I have said on a former occasion: "It is in making endless additions to itself, in the endless expansion of its powers, in endless growth in wisdom and beauty, that the spirit of the human race finds its ideal. To reach this ideal, culture is an indispensable aid, and that is the true value of culture." Not a having and a resting, but a growing and a becoming, is the character of perfection as culture conceives it; and here, too, it coincides with religion. And because men are all members of one great whole, and the sympathy which is in human nature will not allow one member to be indifferent to the rest, or to have a perfect welfare independent of the rest, the expansion of our humanity, to suit the idea of perfection which culture forms, must be a *general* expansion. Perfection, as culture conceives it, is not possible while the individual remains isolated: the individual is obliged, under pain of being stunted and enfeebled in his own development if he disobeys, to carry others along with him in his march towards perfection, to be continu- 14 ally doing all he can to enlarge and increase the volume of the human stream sweeping thitherward; and here, once more, it lays on us the same obligation as religion, which says, as Bishop Wilson has admirably put it, that "to promote the kingdom of God is to increase and hasten one's own happiness." Finally, perfection,—as culture, from a thorough disin- terested study of human nature and human experience, learns to conceive it,—is an harmonious expansion of *all* the powers which make the beauty and worth of human nature, and is not consistent with the over- development of any one power at the expense of the rest. Here it goes beyond religion, as religion is generally conceived by us.

If culture, then, is a study of perfection, and of harmonious perfection, general perfection, and perfection which consists in becoming something rather than in having something, in an inward condition of the mind and spirit, not in an outward set of circumstances,—it is clear that culture, instead of being the frivolous and useless thing which Mr. Bright, and Mr. Frederic Harrison, and many other liberals are apt to call it, has a very important function to fulfil for mankind. And this function is particularly important in our modern world, of which the whole civilisation is, to a 15 much greater degree than the civilisation of Greece and Rome, mechani- cal and external, and tends constantly to become more so. But above all in our own country has culture a weighty part to perform, because here that mechanical character, which civilisation tends to take everywhere, is shown in the most eminent degree. Indeed nearly all the characters of perfection, as culture teaches us to fix them, meet in this country with some powerful tendency which thwarts them and sets them at defiance.

The idea of perfection as an *inward* condition of the mind and spirit is at variance with the mechanical and material civilisation in esteem with us, and nowhere, as I have said, so much in esteem as with us. The idea of perfection as a *general* expansion of the human family is at variance with our strong individualism, our hatred of all limits to the unrestrained swing of the individual's personality, our maxim of "every man for himself." The idea of perfection as an *harmonious* expansion of human nature is at variance with our want of flexibility, with our inaptitude for seeing more than one side of a thing, with our intense energetic absorption in the particular pursuit we happen to be following. So culture has a rough task to achieve in this country, and its preachers have, and are likely long to have, a hard time of it, and they will much oftener be regarded, for a great while to come, as elegant or spurious Jeremiahs, than as friends and benefactors. That, however, will not prevent their doing in the end good service if they persevere; and meanwhile, the mode of action they have to pursue, and the sort of habits they must fight against, should be made quite clear to every one who may be willing to look at the matter attentively and dispassionately.

16

Faith in machinery is, I said, our besetting danger; often in machinery most absurdly disproportioned to the end which this machinery, if it is to do any good at all, is to serve; but always in machinery, as if it had a value in and for itself. What is freedom but machinery? what is population but machinery? what is coal but machinery? what are railroads but machinery? what is wealth but machinery? what are religious organisations but machinery? Now almost every voice in England is accustomed to speak of these things as if they were precious ends in themselves, and therefore had some of the characters of perfection indisputably joined to them. I have once before noticed Mr. Roebuck's stock argument for proving the greatness and happiness of England as she is, and for quite stopping the mouths of all gainsayers. Mr. Roebuck is never weary of reiterating this argument of his, so I do not know why I should be weary of noticing it. "May not every man in England say what he likes?"—Mr. Roebuck perpetually asks; and that, he thinks, is quite sufficient, and when every man may say what he likes, our aspirations ought to be satisfied. But the aspirations of culture, which is the study of perfection, are not satisfied, unless what men say, when they may say what they like, is worth saying,—has good in it, and more good than bad. In the same way *The Times,* replying to some foreign strictures on the dress, looks, and behaviour of the English abroad, urges that the English ideal is that every one should be free to do and to look just as he likes. But culture indefatigably tries, not to make what each

17

raw person may like, the rule by which he fashions himself; but to draw 18
ever nearer to a sense of what is indeed beautiful, graceful, and becoming,
and to get the raw person to like that. And in the same way with respect to
railroads and coal. Every one must have observed the strange language
current during the late discussions as to the possible failure of our supplies
of coal. Our coal, thousands of people were saying, is the real basis of our
national greatness; if our coal runs short, there is an end of the greatness of
England. But what *is* greatness?—culture makes us ask. Greatness is a
spiritual condition worthy to excite love, interest, and admiration; and the
outward proof of possessing greatness is that we excite love, interest, and
admiration. If England were swallowed up by the sea to-morrow, which of
the two, a hundred years hence, would most excite the love, interest, and
admiration of mankind,—would most, therefore, show the evidences of
having possessed greatness,—the England of the last twenty years, or the
England of Elizabeth, of a time of splendid spiritual effort, but when our
coal, and our industrial operations depending on coal, were very little
developed? Well then, what an unsound habit of mind it must be which
makes us talk of things like coal or iron as constituting the greatness of 19
England, and how salutary a friend is culture, bent on seeing things as they
are, and thus dissipating delusions of this kind and fixing standards of
perfection that are real!

Wealth, again, that end to which our prodigious works for material
advantage are directed,—the commonest of commonplaces tells us how
men are always apt to regard wealth as a precious end in itself; and
certainly they have never been so apt thus to regard it as they are in
England at the present time. Never did people believe anything more
firmly, than nine Englishmen out of ten at the present day believe that our
greatness and welfare are proved by our being so very rich. Now, the use
of culture is that it helps us, by means of its spiritual standard of perfection, to regard wealth as but machinery, and not only to say as a matter of
words that we regard wealth as but machinery, but really to perceive and
feel that it is so. If it were not for this purging effect wrought upon our
minds by culture, the whole world, the future as well as the present, would
inevitably belong to the Philistines. The people who believe most that our
greatness and welfare are proved by our being very rich, and who most 20
give their lives and thoughts to becoming rich, are just the very people
whom we call the Philistines. Culture says: "Consider these people, then,
their way of life, their habits, their manners, the very tones of their voice;
look at them attentively; observe the literature they read, the things which
give them pleasure, the words which come forth out of their mouths, the

thoughts which make the furniture of their minds; would any amount of wealth be worth having with the condition that one was to become just like these people by having it?" And thus culture begets a dissatisfaction which is of the highest possible value in stemming the common tide of men's thoughts in a wealthy and industrial community, and which saves the future, as one may hope, from being vulgarised, even if it cannot save the present.

Population, again, and bodily health and vigour, are things which are nowhere treated in such an unintelligent, misleading, exaggerated way as in England. Both are really machinery; yet how many people all around us do we see rest in them and fail to look beyond them! Why, I have heard
21 people, fresh from reading certain articles of *The Times* on the Registrar-General's returns of marriages and births in this country, who would talk of large families in quite a solemn strain, as if they had something in itself beautiful, elevating, and meritorious in them; as if the British Philistine would have only to present himself before the Great Judge with his twelve children, in order to be received among the sheep as a matter of right! But bodily health and vigour, it may be said, are not to be classed with wealth and population as mere machinery; they have a more real and essential value. True; but only as they are more intimately connected with a perfect spiritual condition than wealth or population are. The moment we disjoin them from the idea of a perfect spiritual condition, and pursue them, as we do pursue them, for their own sake and as ends in themselves, our worship of them becomes as mere worship of machinery, as our worship of wealth or population, and as unintelligent and vulgarising a worship as that is. Every one with anything like an adequate idea of human perfection has distinctly marked this subordination to higher and spiritual ends of the
22 cultivation of bodily vigour and activity. "Bodily exercise profiteth little; but godliness is profitable unto all things," says the author of the Epistle to Timothy. And the utilitarian Franklin says just as explicitly:—"Eat and drink such an exact quantity as suits the constitution of thy body, *in reference to the services of the mind*." But the point of view of culture, keeping the mark of human perfection simply and broadly in view, and not assigning to this perfection, as religion or utilitarianism assign to it, a special and limited character,—this point of view, I say, of culture is best given by these words of Epictetus:—"It is a sign of ἀφυΐα," says he,—that is, of a nature not finely tempered,—"to give yourselves up to things which relate to the body; to make, for instance, a great fuss about exercise, a great fuss about eating, a great fuss about drinking, a great fuss about walking, a great fuss about riding. All these things ought to be done

merely *by the way:* the formation of the spirit and character must be our real concern." This is admirable; and, indeed, the Greek words ἀφυΐα, εὐφυΐα, a finely tempered nature, a coarsely tempered nature, give exactly the notion of perfection as culture brings us to conceive of it: a perfection in which the characters of beauty and intelligence are both 23 present, which unites, "the two noblest of things,"—as Swift, who of one of the two, at any rate, had himself all too little, most happily calls them in his *Battle of the Books,*—"the two noblest of things, *sweetness and light.*" The εὐφυής is the man who tends towards sweetness and light; the ἀφυής is precisely our Philistine. The immense spiritual significance of the Greeks is due to their having been inspired with this central and happy idea of the essential character of human perfection; and Mr. Bright's misconception of culture, as a smattering of Greek and Latin, comes itself, after all, from this wonderful significance of the Greeks having affected the very machinery of our education, and is in itself a kind of homage to it.

It is by thus making sweetness and light to be characters of perfection, that culture is of like spirit with poetry, follows one law with poetry. I have called religion a more important manifestation of human nature than poetry, because it has worked on a broader scale for perfection, and with greater masses of men. But the idea of beauty and of a human nature perfect on all its sides, which is the dominant idea of poetry, is a true and invaluable idea, though it has not yet had the success that the idea of 24 conquering the obvious faults of our animality, and of a human nature perfect on the moral side, which is the dominant idea of religion, has been enabled to have; and it is destined, adding to itself the religious idea of a devout energy, to transform and govern the other. The best art and poetry of the Greeks, in which religion and poetry are one, in which the idea of beauty and of a human nature perfect on all sides adds to itself a religious and devout energy, and works in the strength of that, is on this account of such surpassing interest and instructiveness for us, though it was,—as, having regard to the human race in general, and, indeed, having regard to the Greeks themselves, we must own,—a premature attempt, an attempt which for success needed the moral and religious fibre in humanity to be more braced and developed than it had yet been. But Greece did not err in having the idea of beauty, harmony, and complete human perfection, so present and paramount; it is impossible to have this idea too present and paramount; only the moral fibre must be braced too. And we, because we have braced the moral fibre, are not on that account in the right way, if at the same time the idea of beauty, harmony, and complete human perfec- 25 tion, is wanting or misapprehended amongst us; and evidently it *is* wanting or misapprehended at present. And when we rely as we do on our religious organisations, which in themselves do not and cannot give us this idea, and think we have done enough if we make them spread and prevail, then, I say, we fall into our common fault of overvaluing machinery.

Nothing is more common than for people to confound the inward peace and satisfaction which follows the subduing of the obvious faults of our animality with what I may call absolute inward peace and satisfaction,— the peace and satisfaction which are reached as we draw near to complete spiritual perfection, and not merely to moral perfection, or rather to relative moral perfection. No people in the world have done more and struggled more to attain this relative moral perfection than our English race has; for no people in the world has the command to *resist the Devil,* to *overcome the Wicked One,* in the nearest and most obvious sense of those words, had such a pressing force and reality. And we have had our reward, not only in the great worldly prosperity which our obedience to this command has brought us, but also, and far more, in great inward peace and satisfaction. But to me few things are more pathetic than to see people, on the strength of the inward peace and satisfaction which their rudimentary efforts towards perfection have brought them, use, concerning their incomplete perfection and the religious organisations within which they have found it, language which properly applies only to complete perfection, and is a far-off echo of the human soul's prophecy of it. Religion itself, I need hardly say, supplies in abundance this grand language, which is really the severest criticism of such an incomplete perfection as alone we have yet reached through our religious organisations.

The impulse of the English race towards moral development and self-conquest has nowhere so powerfully manifested itself as in Puritanism; nowhere has Puritanism found so adequate an expression as in the religious organisation of the Independents. The modern Independents have a newspaper, the *Nonconformist,* written with great sincerity and ability. The motto, the standard, the profession of faith which this organ of theirs carries aloft, is: "The Dissidence of Dissent and the Protestantism of the Protestant religion." There is sweetness and light, and an ideal of complete harmonious human perfection! One need not go to culture and poetry to find language to judge it. Religion, with its instinct for perfection, supplies language to judge it: "Finally, be of one mind, united in feeling," says St. Peter. There is an ideal which judges the Puritan ideal—"The Dissidence of Dissent and the Protestantism of the Protestant religion!" And religious organisations like this are what people believe in, rest in, would give their lives for! Such, I say, is the wonderful virtue of even the beginnings of perfection, of having conquered even the plain faults of our animality, that the religious organisation which has helped us to do it can seem to us something precious, salutary, and to be propagated, even when it wears such a brand of imperfection on its forehead as this. And men have got such a habit of giving to the language of religion a special application, of making it a mere jargon, that for the condemnation which religion itself passes on the shortcomings of their religious organisations they have no ear; they are sure to cheat themselves and to explain this condemnation 28 away. They can only be reached by the criticism which culture, like poetry, speaking a language not to be sophisticated, and resolutely testing these organisations by the ideal of a human perfection complete on all sides, applies to them.

But men of culture and poetry, it will be said, are again and again failing, and failing conspicuously, in the necessary first stage to perfection, in the subduing of the great obvious faults of our animality, which it is the glory of these religious organisations to have helped us to subdue. True, they do often so fail: they have often been without the virtues as well as the faults of the Puritan; it has been one of their dangers that they so felt the Puritan's faults that they too much neglected the practice of his virtues. I will not, however, exculpate them at the Puritan's expense; they have often failed in morality, and morality is indispensable; they have been punished for their failure, as the Puritan has been rewarded for his performance. They have been punished wherein they erred; but their ideal of beauty and sweetness and light, and a human nature complete on all its sides, remains the true ideal of perfection still; just as the Puritan's ideal of 29 perfection remains narrow and inadequate, although for what he did well he has been richly rewarded. Notwithstanding the mighty results of the Pilgrim Fathers' voyage, they and their standard of perfection are rightly judged when we figure to ourselves Shakespeare or Virgil,—souls in whom sweetness and light, and all that in human nature is most humane, were eminent,—accompanying them on their voyage, and think what intolerable company Shakespeare and Virgil would have found them! In the same way let us judge the religious organisations which we see all around us. Do not let us deny the good and the happiness which they have accomplished; but do not let us fail to see clearly that their idea of human perfection is narrow and inadequate, and that the Dissidence of Dissent and the Protestantism of the Protestant religion will never bring humanity to its true goal. As I said with regard to wealth,—let us look at the life of those who live in and for it;—so I say with regard to the religious orga-

nisations. Look at the life imagined in such a newspaper as the *Noncon-formist;*—a life of jealousy of the Establishment, disputes, tea-meetings,
30 openings of chapels, sermons; and then think of it as an ideal of a human life completing itself on all sides, and aspiring with all its organs after sweetness, light, and perfection!

Another newspaper, representing, like the *Nonconformist,* one of the religious organisations of this country, was a short time ago giving an account of the crowd at Epsom on the Derby day, and of all the vice and hideousness which was to be seen in that crowd; and then the writer turned suddenly round upon Professor Huxley, and asked him how he proposed to cure all this vice and hideousness without religion. I confess I felt dis-posed to ask the asker this question: And how do you propose to cure it with such a religion as yours? How is the ideal of a life so unlovely, so unattractive, so narrow, so far removed from a true and satisfying ideal of human perfection, as is the life of your religious organisation as you yourself image it, to conquer and transform all this vice and hideousness? Indeed, the strongest plea for the study of perfection as pursued by cul-ture, the clearest proof of the actual inadequacy of the idea of perfection held by the religious organisations,—expressing, as I have said, the most
31 wide-spread effort which the human race has yet made after perfection,— is to be found in the state of our life and society with these in possession of it, and having been in possession of it I know not how many hundred years. We are all of us included in some religious organisation or other; we all call ourselves, in the sublime and aspiring language of religion which I have before noticed, *children of God.* Children of God;—it is an immense pretension!—and how are we to justify it? By the works which we do, and the words which we speak. And the work which we collective children of God do, our grand centre of life, our *city* which we have builded for us to dwell in, is London! London, with its unutterable external hideousness, and with its internal canker of *publicé egestas, privatim opulentia,*—to use the words which Sallust puts into Cato's mouth about Rome,— unequalled in the world! The word, again, which we children of God speak, the voice which most hits our collective thought, the newspaper with the largest circulation in England, nay, with the largest circulation in the whole world, is the *Daily Telegraph!* I say that when our religious organisations,—which I admit to express the most considerable effort
32 after perfection that our race has yet made,—land us in no better result than this, it is high time to examine carefully their idea of perfection, to see whether it does not leave out of account sides and forces of human nature which we might turn to great use; whether it would not be more operative

if it were more complete. And I say that the English reliance on our religious organisations and on their ideas of human perfection just as they stand, is like our reliance on freedom, on *muscular Christianity, on population, on coal, on wealth,—mere belief in machinery, and unfruitful; and that it is wholesomely counteracted by culture, bent on seeing things as they are, and on drawing the human race onwards to a more complete perfection.

Culture, however, shows its single-minded love of perfection, its desire simply to make reason and the will of God prevail, its freedom from fanaticism, by its attitude towards all this machinery, even while it insists that it *is* machinery. Fanatics, seeing the mischief men do themselves by their blind belief in some machinery or other,—whether it is wealth and industrialism, or whether it is the cultivation of bodily strength and activity, or whether it is a political organisation, or whether it is a religious 33 organisation,—oppose with might and main the tendency to this or that political and religious organisation, or to games and athletic exercises, or to wealth and industrialism, and try violently to stop it. But the flexibility which sweetness and light give, and which is one of the rewards of culture pursued in good faith, enables a man to see that a tendency may be necessary, and even, as a preparation for something in the future, salutary, and yet that the generations or individuals who obey this tendency are sacrificed to it, that they fall short of the hope of perfection by following it; and that its mischiefs are to be criticised, lest it should take too firm a hold and last after it has served its purpose. Mr. Gladstone well pointed out, in a speech at Paris,—and others have pointed out the same thing,—how necessary is the present great movement towards wealth and industrialism, in order to lay broad foundations of material well-being for the society of the future. The worst of these justifications is, that they are generally addressed to the very people engaged, body and soul, in the movement in question; at all events, they are always seized with the 34 greatest avidity by these people, and taken by them as quite justifying their life; and that thus they tend to harden them in their sins. Now, culture admits the necessity of the movement towards fortune-making and exaggerated industrialism, readily allows that the future may derive benefit from it; but insists, at the same time, that the passing generations of industrialists,—forming, for the most part, the stout main body of Philistinism,—are sacrificed to it. In the same way, the result of all the games and sports which occupy the passing generation of boys and young men may be the establishment of a better and sounder physical type for the future to work with. Culture does not set itself against the games and

sports; it congratulates the future, and hopes it will make a good use of its improved physical basis; but it points out that our passing generation of boys and young men is, meantime, sacrificed. Puritanism was necessary to develop the moral fibre of the English race, Nonconformity to break the yoke of ecclesiastical domination over men's minds and to prepare the way for freedom of thought in the distant future; still, culture points out
35 that the harmonious perfection of generations of Puritans and Nonconformists have been in consequence, sacrificed. Freedom of speech is necessary for the society of the future, but the *young lions of the *Daily Telegraph* in the meanwhile are sacrificed. A voice for every man in his country's government is necessary for the society of the future, but meanwhile Mr. Beales and Mr. Bradlaugh are sacrificed.

Oxford, the Oxford of the past, has many faults; and she has heavily paid for them in defeat, in isolation, in want of hold upon the modern world. Yet we in Oxford, brought up amidst the beauty and sweetness of that beautiful place, have not failed to seize one truth:—the truth that beauty and sweetness are essential characters of a complete human perfection. When I insist on this, I am all in the faith and tradition of Oxford. I say boldly that this our sentiment for beauty and sweetness, our sentiment against hideousness and rawness, has been at the bottom of our attachment to so many beaten causes, of our opposition to so many triumphant movements. And the sentiment is true, and has never been wholly defeated, and has shown its power even in its defeat. We have not won our political
36 battles, we have not carried our main points, we have not stopped our adversaries' advance, we have not marched victoriously with the modern world; but we have told silently upon the mind of the country, we have prepared currents of feeling which sap our adversaries' position when it seems gained, we have kept up our own communications with the future. Look at the course of the great movement which shook Oxford to its centre some thirty years ago! It was directed, as any one who reads Dr. Newman's *Apology* may see, against what in one word may be called "liberalism." Liberalism prevailed; it was the appointed force to do the work of the hour; it was necessary, it was inevitable that it should prevail. The Oxford movement was broken, it failed; our wrecks are scattered on every shore:

*Quæ regio in terris nostri non plena laboris?

But what was it, this liberalism, as Dr. Newman saw it, and as it really broke the Oxford movement? It was the great middle-class liberalism, which had for the cardinal points of its belief the Reform Bill of 1832, and local self-government, in politics; in the social sphere, free-trade, unrestricted competition, and the making of large industrial fortunes; in the religious sphere, the Dissidence of Dissent and the Protestantism of the Protestant religion. I do not say that other and more intelligent forces than this were not opposed to the Oxford movement: but this was the force which really beat it; this was the force which Dr. Newman felt himself fighting with; this was the force which till only the other day seemed to be the paramount force in this country, and to be in possession of the future; this was the force whose achievements fill Mr. Lowe with such inexpressible admiration, and whose rule he was so horror-struck to see threatened. And where is this great force of Philistinism now? It is thrust into the second rank, it is become a power of yesterday, it has lost the future. A new power has suddenly appeared, a power which it is impossible yet to judge fully, but which is certainly a wholly different force from middle-class liberalism; different in its cardinal points of belief, different in its tendencies in every sphere. It loves and admires neither the legislation of middle-class Parliaments, nor the local self-government of middle-class vestries, nor the unrestricted competition of middle-class industrialists, nor the dissidence of middle-class Dissent and the Protestantism of middle-class Protestant religion. I am not now praising this new force, or saying that its own ideals are better; all I say is, that they are wholly different. And who will estimate how much the currents of feeling created by Dr. Newman's movement, the keen desire for beauty and sweetness which it nourished, the deep aversion it manifested to the hardness and vulgarity of middle-class liberalism, the strong light it turned on the hideous and grotesque illusions of middle-class Protestantism,—who will estimate how much all these contributed to swell the tide of secret dissatisfaction which has mined the ground under the self-confident liberalism of the last thirty years, and has prepared the way for its sudden collapse and supersession? It is in this manner that the sentiment of Oxford for beauty and sweetness conquers, and in this manner long may it continue to conquer!

In this manner it works to the same end as culture, and there is plenty of work for it yet to do. I have said that the new and more democratic force which is now superseding our old middle-class liberalism cannot yet be rightly judged. It has its main tendencies still to form. We hear promises of its giving us administrative reform, law reform, reform of education, and I know not what; but those promises come rather from its advocates, wishing to make a good plea for it and to justify it for superseding middle-class

37

38

39

liberalism, than from clear tendencies which it has itself yet developed. But meanwhile it has plenty of well-intentioned friends against whom culture may with advantage continue to uphold steadily its ideal of human perfection; that this is *an inward spiritual activity, having for its characters increased sweetness, increased light, increased life, increased sympathy.* Mr. Bright, who has a foot in both worlds, the world of middle-class liberalism and the world of democracy, but who brings most of his ideas from the world of middle-class liberalism in which he was bred, always inclines to inculcate that faith in machinery to which, as we have seen, Englishmen are so prone, and which has been the bane of middle-class liberalism. He complains with a sorrowful indignation of people who "appear to have no proper estimate of the value of the franchise;" he leads his disciples to believe,—what the Englishman is always too ready

40 to believe,—that the having a vote, like the having a large family, or a large business, or large muscles, has in itself some edifying and perfecting effect upon human nature. Or else he cries out to the democracy,—"the men," as he calls them, "upon whose shoulders the greatness of England rests,"—he cries out to them: "See what you have done! I look over this country and see the cities you have built, the railroads you have made, the manufactures you have produced, the cargoes which freight the ships of the greatest mercantile navy the world has ever seen! I see that you have converted by your labours what was once a wilderness, these islands, into a fruitful garden; I know that you have created this wealth, and are a nation whose name is a word of power throughout all the world." Why, this is just the very style of laudation with which Mr. Roebuck or Mr. Lowe debauch the minds of the middle classes, and make such Philistines of them. It is the same fashion of teaching a man to value himself not on what he *is,* not on his progress in sweetness and light, but on the number of the railroads he has constructed, or the bigness of the Tabernacle he has built. Only the

41 middle classes are told they have done it all with their energy, self-reliance, and capital, and the democracy are told they have done it all with their hands and sinews. But teaching the democracy to put its trust in achievements of this kind is merely training them to be Philistines to take the place of the Philistines whom they are superseding; and they too, like the middle class, will be encouraged to sit down at the banquet of the future without having on a wedding garment, and nothing excellent can then come from them. Those who know their besetting faults, those who have watched them and listened to them, or those who will read the instructive account recently given of them by one of themselves, the *Journeyman Engineer,* will agree that the idea which culture sets before us

of perfection,—an increased spiritual activity, having for its characters increased sweetness, increased light, increased life, increased sympathy,—is an idea which the new democracy needs far more than the idea of the blessedness of the franchise, or the wonderfulness of their own industrial performances.

Other well-meaning friends of this new power are for leading it, not in the old ruts of middle-class Philistinism, but in ways which are naturally alluring to the feet of democracy, though in this country they are novel and untried ways. I may call them the ways of Jacobinism. Violent indignation with the past, abstract systems of renovation applied wholesale, a new doctrine drawn up in black and white for elaborating down to the very smallest details a rational society for the future,—these are the ways of Jacobinism. Mr. Frederic Harrison and other disciples of Comte,—one of them, Mr. Congreve, is an old acquaintance of mine, and I am glad to have an opportunity of publicly expressing my respect for his talents and character,—are among the friends of democracy who are for leading it in paths of this kind. Mr. Frederic Harrison is very hostile to culture, and from a natural enough motive; for culture is the eternal opponent of the two things which are the signal marks of Jacobinism,—its fierceness, and its addiction to an abstract system. Culture is always assigning to system-makers and systems a smaller share in the bent of human destiny than their friends like. A current in people's minds sets towards new ideas; people are dissatisfied with their old narrow stock of Philistine ideas, Anglo-Saxon ideas, or any other; and some man, some Bentham or Comte, who has the real merit of having early and strongly felt and helped the new current, but who brings plenty of narrownesses and mistakes of his own into his feeling and help of it, is credited with being the author of the whole current, the fit person to be entrusted with its regulation and to guide the human race. The excellent German historian of the mythology of Rome, Preller, relating the introduction at Rome under the Tarquins of the worship of Apollo, the god of light, healing, and reconciliation, observes that it was not so much the Tarquins who brought to Rome the new worship of Apollo, as a current in the mind of the Roman people which set powerfully at that time towards a new worship of this kind, and away from the old run of Latin and Sabine religious ideas. In a similar way, culture directs our attention to the current in human affairs, and to its continual working, and will not let us rivet our faith upon any one man and his doings. It makes us see, not only his good side, but also how much in him was of necessity limited and transient; nay, it even feels a pleasure, a sense of an increased freedom and of an ampler future, in so doing. I remember, when I was

42

43

44

under the influence of a mind to which I feel the greatest obligations, the mind of a man who was the very incarnation of sanity and clear sense, a man the most considerable, it seems to me, whom America has yet produced,—Benjamin Franklin,—I remember the relief with which, after long feeling the sway of Franklin's imperturbable common-sense, I came upon a project of his for a new version of the Book of Job, to replace the old version, the style of which, says Franklin, has become obsolete, and thence less agreeable. "I give," he continues, "a few verses, which may serve as a sample of the kind of version I would recommend." We all recollect the famous verse in our translation: "Then Satan answered the Lord and said: 'Doth Job fear God for nought?'" Franklin makes this: "Does Your Majesty imagine that Job's good conduct is the effect of mere personal attachment and affection?" I well remember how when first I read that, I drew a deep breath of relief, and said to myself: "After all, there is a stretch of humanity beyond Franklin's victorious good sense!"

So, after hearing Bentham cried loudly up as the renovator of modern 45 society, and Bentham's mind and ideas proposed as the rulers of our future, I open the *Deontology*. There I read: "While Xenophon was writing his history and Euclid teaching geometry, Socrates and Plato were talking nonsense under pretence of talking wisdom and morality. This morality of theirs consisted in words; this wisdom of theirs was the denial of matters known to every man's experience." From the moment of reading that, I am delivered from the bondage of Bentham! the fanaticism of his adherents can touch me no longer; I feel the inadequacy of his mind and ideas for being the rule of human society, for perfection. Culture tends always thus to deal with the men of a system, of disciples, of a school; with men like Comte, or the late Mr. Buckle, or Mr. Mill. However much it may find to admire in these personages, or in some of them, it nevertheless remembers the text: *"Be not ye called Rabbi!" and it soon passes on from any Rabbi. But Jacobinism loves a Rabbi; it does not want to pass on from its Rabbi in pursuit of a future and still unreached perfection; it wants its Rabbi and his ideas to stand for perfection, that they may with the more 46 authority recast the world; and for Jacobinism, therefore, culture,— eternally passing onwards and seeking,—is an impertinence and an offence. But culture, just because it resists this tendency of Jacobinism to impose on us a man with limitations and errors of his own along with the true ideas of which he is the organ, really does the world and Jacobinism itself a service.

So, too, Jacobinism, in its fierce hatred of the past and of those whom it makes liable for the sins of the past, cannot away with culture,—culture

with its inexhaustible indulgence, its consideration of circumstances, its severe judgment of actions joined to its merciful judgment of persons. "The man of culture is in politics," cries Mr. Frederic Harrison, "one of the poorest mortals alive!" Mr. Frederic Harrison wants to be doing business, and he complains that the man of culture stops him with a "turn for small fault-finding, love of selfish ease, and indecision in action." Of what use is culture, he asks, except for "a critic of new books or a professor of *belles lettres?*" Why, it is of use because, in presence of the fierce exasperation which breathes, or rather, I may say, hisses, through the whole production in which Mr. Frederic Harrison asks that question, it   47
reminds us that the perfection of human nature is sweetness and light. It is of use because, like religion,—that other effort after perfection,—it testifies that, where bitter envying and strife are, there is confusion and every evil work.

The pursuit of perfection, then, is the pursuit of sweetness and light. He who works for sweetness works in the end for light also; he who works for light works in the end for sweetness also. But he who works for sweetness and light united, works to make reason and the will of God prevail. He who works for machinery, he who works for hatred, works only for confusion. Culture looks beyond machinery, culture hates hatred; culture has but one great passion, the passion for sweetness and light. Yes, it has one yet greater!—the passion for making them *prevail*. It is not satisfied till we *all* come to a perfect man; it knows that the sweetness and light of the few must be imperfect until the raw and unkindled masses of humanity are touched with sweetness and light. If I have not shrunk from saying that we must work for sweetness and light, so neither have I shrunk from saying that we must have a broad basis, must have sweetness and light for as many as possible. Again and again I have insisted how those   48
are the happy moments of humanity, how those are the marking epochs of a people's life, how those are the flowering times for literature and art and all the creative power of genius, when there is a *national* glow of life and thought, when the whole of society is in the fullest measure permeated by thought, sensible to beauty, intelligent and alive. Only it must be *real* thought and *real* beauty; *real* sweetness and *real* light. Plenty of people will try to give the masses, as they call them, an intellectual food prepared and adapted in the way they think proper for the actual condition of the masses. The ordinary popular literature is an example of this way of working on the masses. Plenty of people will try to indoctrinate the masses with the set of ideas and judgments constituting the creed of their own profession or party. Our religious and political organisations give an ex-

ample of this way of working on the masses. I condemn neither way; but culture works differently. It does not try to teach down to the level of inferior classes; it does not try to win them for this or that sect of its own, with
49   ready-made judgments and watchwords. It seeks to do away with classes; to make all live in an atmosphere of sweetness and light, and use ideas, as it uses them itself, freely,—to be nourished and not bound by them.

This is the *social idea;* and the men of culture are the true apostles of equality. The great men of culture are those who have had a passion for diffusing, for making prevail, for carrying from one end of society to the other, the best knowledge, the best ideas of their time; who have laboured to divest knowledge of all that was harsh, uncouth, difficult, abstract, professional, exclusive; to humanise it, to make it efficient outside the clique of the cultivated and learned, yet still remaining the *best* knowledge and thought of the time, and a true source, therefore, of sweetness and light. Such a man was Abelard in the Middle Ages, in spite of all his imperfections; and thence the boundless emotion and enthusiasm which Abelard excited. Such were Lessing and Herder in Germany, at the end of the last century; and their services to Germany were in this way inestimably precious. Generations will pass, and literary monuments will accumu-
50   late, and works far more perfect than the works of Lessing and Herder will be produced in Germany; and yet the names of these two men will fill a German with a reverence and enthusiasm such as the names of the most gifted masters will hardly awaken. Because they *humanised* knowledge; because they broadened the basis of life and intelligence; because they worked powerfully to diffuse sweetness and light, to make reason and the will of God prevail. With Saint Augustine they said: "Let us not leave Thee alone to make in the secret of thy knowledge, as thou didst before the creation of the firmament, the division of light from darkness; let the children of thy spirit, placed in their firmament, make their light shine upon the earth, mark the division of night and day, and announce the revolution of the times; for the old order is passed, and the new arises; the night is spent, the day is come forth; and thou shalt crown the year with thy blessing, when thou shalt send forth labourers into thy harvest sown by other hands than theirs; when thou shalt send forth new labourers to new seed-times, whereof the harvest shall be not yet."

51   # II. [Doing as One Likes]

I have been trying to show that culture is, or ought to be, the study and pursuit of perfection; and that of perfection as pursued by culture, beauty and intelligence, or, in other words, sweetness and light, are the main characters. But hitherto I have been insisting chiefly on beauty, or sweetness, as a character of perfection. To complete rightly my design, it evidently remains to speak also of intelligence, or light, as a character of perfection. First, however, I ought perhaps to notice that, both here and on the other side of the Atlantic, all sorts of objections are raised against the "religion of culture," as the objectors mockingly call it, which I am supposed to be promulgating. It is said to be a religion proposing parmaceti, or some scented salve or other, as a cure for human miseries; a religion breathing a spirit of cultivated inaction, making its believer refuse to lend a hand at uprooting the definite evils on all sides of us, and filling him with antipathy against the reforms and reformers which try to extir-   52 pate them. In general, it is summed up as being not practical, or,—as some critics more familiarly put it,—all moonshine. That Alcibiades, the editor of the *Morning Star,* taunts me, as its promulgator, with living out of the world and knowing nothing of life and men. That great austere toiler, the *editor of the *Daily Telegraph,* upbraids me,—but kindly, and more in sorrow than in anger,—for trifling with aesthetics and poetical fancies, while he himself, in that arsenal of his in Fleet Street, is bearing the burden and heat of the day. An intelligent American newspaper, the *Nation,* says that it is very easy to sit in one's study and find fault with the course of modern society, but the thing is to propose practical improvements for it. While, finally, Mr. Frederic Harrison, in a very good-tempered and witty satire, which makes me quite understand his having apparently achieved such a conquest of my young Prussian friend, Arminius, at last gets moved to an almost stern moral impatience, to behold, as he says, "Death, sin, cruelty stalk among us, filling their maws with innocence and youth," and me, in the midst of the general tribulation, handing out my pouncet-box.

It is impossible that all these remonstrances and reproofs should not   53 affect me, and I shall try my very best, in completing my design and in speaking of light as one of the characters of perfection, and of culture as giving us light, to profit by the objections I have heard and read, and to drive at practice as much as I can, by showing the communications and passages into practical life from the doctrine which I am inculcating.

It is said that a man with my theories of sweetness and light is full of antipathy against the rougher or coarser movements going on around him, that he will not lend a hand to the humble operation of uprooting evil by their means, and that therefore the believers in action grow impatient with them. But what if rough and coarse action, ill-calculated action, action with insufficient light, is, and has for a long time been, our bane? What if our urgent want now is, not to act at any price, but rather to lay in a stock of light for our difficulties? In that case, to refuse to lend a hand to the rougher and coarser movements going on round us, to make the primary need, both for oneself and others, to consist in enlightening ourselves and 54 qualifying ourselves to act less at random, is surely the best, and in real truth the most practical line, our endeavours can take. So that if I can show what my opponents call rough or coarse action, but what I would rather call random and ill-regulated action,—action with insufficient light, action pursued because we like to be doing something and doing it as we please, and do not like the trouble of thinking, and the severe constraint of any kind of rule,—if I can show this to be, at the present moment, a practical mischief and danger to us, then I have found a practical use for light in correcting this state of things, and have only to exemplify how, in cases which fall under everybody's observation, it may deal with it.

When I began to speak of culture, I insisted on our bondage to machinery, on our proneness to value machinery as an end in itself, without looking beyond it to the end for which alone, in truth, it is valuable. Freedom, I said, was one of those things which we thus worshipped in itself, without enough regarding the ends for which freedom is to be desired. In our common notions and talk about freedom, we eminently show our idolatry of machinery. Our prevalent notion is,—and I quoted a 55 number of instances to prove it,—that it is a most happy and important thing for a man merely to be able to do as he likes. On what he is to do when he is thus free to do as he likes, we do not lay so much stress. Our familiar praise of the British Constitution under which we live, is that it is a system of checks,—a system which stops and paralyses any power in interfering with the free action of individuals. To this effect Mr. Bright, who loves to walk in the old ways of the Constitution, said forcibly in one of his great speeches, what many other people are every day saying less forcibly, that the central idea of English life and politics is *the assertion of personal liberty.* Evidently this is so; but evidently, also, as feudalism, which with its ideas and habits of subordination was for many centuries silently behind the British Constitution, dies out, and we are left with nothing but our system of checks, and our notion of its being the great right and happiness of an Englishman to do as far as possible what he likes, we are in danger of drifting towards anarchy. We have not the notion, so familiar on the Continent and to antiquity, of *the State*—the nation, in its 56 collective and corporate character, entrusted with stringent powers for the general advantage, and controlling individual wills in the name of an interest wider than that of individuals. We say, what is very true, that this notion is often made instrumental to tyranny; we say that a State is in reality made up of the individuals who compose it, and that every individual is the best judge of his own interests. Our leading class is an aristocracy, and no aristocracy likes the notion of a State-authority greater than itself, with a stringent administrative machinery superseding the decorative inutilities of lord-lieutenancy, deputy-lieutenancy, and the *posse comitatûs,* which are all in its own hands. Our middle-class, the great representative of trade and Dissent, with its maxims of every man for himself in business, every man for himself in religion, dreads a powerful administration which might somehow interfere with it; and besides, it has its own decorative inutilities of vestrymanship and guardianship, which are to this class what lord-lieutenancy and the county magistracy are to the aristocratic class, and a stringent administration might either take these functions out of its hands, or prevent its exercising them in its own comfortable, independent manner, as at present.   57

Then as to our working-class. This class, pressed constantly by the hard daily compulsion of material wants, is naturally the very centre and stronghold of our national idea, that it is man's ideal right and felicity to do as he likes. I think I have somewhere related how Monsieur Michelet said to me of the people of France, that it was "a nation of barbarians civilised by the conscription." He meant that through their military service the idea of public duty and of discipline was brought to the mind of these masses, in other respects so raw and uncultivated. Our masses are quite as raw and uncultivated as the French; and, so far from their having the idea of public duty and of discipline, superior to the individual's self-will, brought to their mind by a universal obligation of military service, such as that of the conscription,—so far from their having this, the very idea of a conscription is so at variance with our English notion of the prime right and blessedness of doing as one likes, that I remember the manager of the Clay Cross works in Derbyshire told me during the Crimean war, when our   58
want of soldiers was much felt and some people were talking of a conscription, that sooner than submit to a conscription the population of that district would flee to the mines, and lead a sort of Robin Hood life under ground.

For a long time, as I have said, the strong feudal habits of subordination and deference continued to tell upon the working-class. The modern spirit has now almost entirely dissolved those habits, and the anarchical tendency of our worship of freedom in and for itself, of our superstitious faith, as I say, in machinery, is becoming very manifest. More and more, because of this our blind faith in machinery, because of our want of light to enable us to look beyond machinery to the end for which machinery is valuable, this and that man, and this and that body of men, all over the country, are beginning to assert and put in practice an Englishman's right to do what he likes; his right to march where he likes, meet where he likes, enter where he likes, hoot as he likes, threaten as he likes, smash as he likes. All this, I say, tends to anarchy; and though a number of excellent people, and particularly my friends of the liberal or progressive party, as they call themselves, are kind enough to reassure us by saying that these are trifles, that a few transient outbreaks of rowdyism signify nothing, that our system of liberty is one which itself cures all the evils which it works, that the educated and intelligent classes stand in overwhelming strength and majestic repose, ready, like our military force in riots, to act at a moment's notice,—yet one finds that one's liberal friends generally say this because they have such faith in themselves and their nostrums, when they shall return, as the public welfare requires, to place and power. But this faith of theirs one cannot exactly share, when one has so long had them and their nostrums at work, and sees that they have not prevented our coming to our present embarrassed condition; and one finds, also, that the outbreaks of rowdyism tend to become less and less of trifles, to become more frequent rather than less frequent; and that meanwhile our educated and intelligent classes remain in their majestic repose, and somehow or other, whatever happens, their overwhelming strength, like our military force in riots, never does act.

60   How, indeed, *should* their overwhelming strength act, when the *man who gives an inflammatory lecture, or *breaks down the Park railings, or *invades a Secretary of State's office, is only following an Englishman's impulse to do as he likes; and our own conscience tells us that we ourselves have always regarded this impulse as something primary and sacred? Mr. Murphy lectures at Birmingham, and showers on the Catholic population of that town "words," says Mr. Hardy, "only fit to be addressed to thieves or murderers." What then? Mr. Murphy has his own reasons of several kinds. He suspects the Roman Catholic Church of designs upon Mrs. Murphy; and he says, if mayors and magistrates do not care for their wives and daughters, he does. But, above all, he is doing as he likes, or, in worthier language, asserting his personal liberty. "I will carry out my lectures if they walk over my body as a dead corpse; and I say to the Mayor of Birmingham that he is my servant while I am in Birmingham, and as my servant he must do his duty and protect me." Touching and beautiful words, which find a sympathetic chord in every British bosom! The mo-

ment it is plainly put before us that a man is asserting his personal liberty, we are half disarmed; because we are believers in freedom, and not in some dream of a right reason to which the assertion of our freedom is to be subordinated. Accordingly, the Secretary of State had to say that although the lecturer's language was "only fit to be addressed to thieves or murderers," yet, "I do not think he is to be deprived, I do not think that anything I have said could justify the inference that he is to be deprived, of the right of protection in a place built by him for the purpose of these lectures; because the language was not language which afforded grounds for a criminal prosecution." No, nor to be silenced by Mayor, or Home Secretary, or any administrative authority on earth, simply on their notion of what is discreet and reasonable! This is in perfect consonance with our public opinion, and with our national love for the assertion of personal liberty.

In quite another department of affairs, an experienced and distinguished Chancery Judge relates an incident which is just to the same effect as this of Mr. Murphy. A testator bequeathed 300*l.* a year, to be for ever applied as a pension to some person who had been unsuccessful in literature, and whose duty should be to support and diffuse, by his writings, the testator's own views, as enforced in the testator's publications. This bequest was appealed against in the Court of Chancery, on the ground of its absurdity; but, being only absurd, it was upheld, and the so-called charity was established. Having, I say, at the bottom of our English hearts a very strong belief in freedom, and a very weak belief in right reason, we are soon silenced when a man pleads the prime right to do as he likes, because this is the prime right for ourselves too; and even if we attempt now and then to mumble something about reason, yet we have ourselves thought so little about this and so much about liberty, that we are in conscience forced, when our brother Philistine with whom we are meddling turns boldly round upon us and asks: *Have you any light?*—to shake our heads ruefully, and to let him go his own way after all.

There are many things to be said on behalf of this exclusive attention of ours to liberty, and of the relaxed habits of government which it has engendered. It is very easy to mistake or to exaggerate the sort of anarchy from which we are in danger through them. We are not in danger from Fenianism, fierce and turbulent as it may show itself; for against this our conscience is free enough to let us act resolutely and put forth our overwhelming strength the moment there is any real need for it. In the first place, it never was any part of our creed that the great right and blessedness of an Irishman, or, indeed, of anybody on earth except an Englishman, is to do as he likes; and we can have no scruple at all about abridging, if necessary, a non-Englishman's assertion of personal liberty. The British Constitution, its checks, and its prime virtues, are for Englishmen. We may extend them to others out of love and kindness; but we find no real divine law written on our hearts constraining us so to extend them. And then the difference between an Irish Fenian and an English rough is so immense, and the case, in dealing with the Fenian, so much more clear! He is so evidently desperate and dangerous, a man of a conquered race, a Papist, with centuries of ill-usage to inflame him against us, with an alien religion established in his country by us at his expense, with no admiration of our institutions, no love of our virtues, no talents for our business, no

64   turn for our comfort! Show him our symbolical Truss Manufactory on the finest site in Europe, and tell him that British industrialism and individualism can bring a man to that, and he remains cold! Evidently, if we deal tenderly with a sentimentalist like this, it is out of pure philanthropy. But with the Hyde Park rioter how different! He is our own flesh and blood; he is a Protestant; he is framed by nature to do as we do, hate what we hate, love what we love; he is capable of feeling the symbolical force of the Truss Manufactory; the question of questions, for him, is a wages' question. That beautiful sentence Sir Daniel Gooch quoted to the Swindon workmen, and which I treasure as Mrs. Gooch's Golden Rule, or the Divine Injunction "Be ye Perfect" done into British,—the sentence Sir Daniel Gooch's mother repeated to him every morning when he was a boy going to work: *"Ever remember, my dear Dan, that you should look forward to being some day manager of that concern!"*—this fruitful maxim is perfectly fitted to shine forth in the heart of the Hyde Park rough also, and to be his guiding-star through life. He has no visionary schemes of revolution and transformation, though of course he would like his class

65   to rule, as the aristocratic class like their class to rule, and the middle-class theirs. Meanwhile, our social machine is a little out of order; there are a good many people in our paradisiacal centres of industrialism and individualism taking the bread out of one another's mouths; the rioter has not yet quite found his groove and settled down to his work, and so he is just asserting his personal liberty a little, going where he likes, assembling where he likes, bawling as he likes, hustling as he likes. Just as the rest of us,—as the country squires in the aristocratic class, as the political dissenters in the middle-class,—he has no idea of a *State,* of the nation in its collective and corporate character controlling, as government, the free swing of this or that one of its members in the name of the higher reason of all of them, his own as well as that of others. He sees the rich, the

aristocratic class, in occupation of the executive government, and so if he is stopped from making Hyde Park a bear-garden or the streets impassable, he says he is being butchered by the aristocracy.

His apparition is somewhat embarrassing, because too many cooks spoil the broth; because, while the aristocratic and middle classes have long been doing as they like with great vigour, he has been too undeveloped and submissive hitherto to join in the game; and now, when he does come, he comes in immense numbers, and is rather raw and rough. But he does not break many laws, or not many at one time; and, as our laws were made for very different circumstances from our present (but always with an eye to Englishmen doing as they like), and as the clear letter of the law must be against our Englishman who does as he likes and not only the spirit of the law and public policy, and as Government must neither have any discretionary power nor act resolutely on its own interpretation of the law if any one disputes it, it is evident our laws give our playful giant, in doing as he likes, considerable advantage. Besides, even if he can be clearly proved to commit an illegality in doing as he likes, there is always the resource of not putting the law in force, or of abolishing it. So he has his way, and if he has his way he is soon satisfied for the time; however, he falls into the habit of taking it oftener and oftener, and at last begins to create by his operations a confusion of which mischievous people can take advantage, and which at any rate, by troubling the common course of business throughout the country tends to cause distress, and so to increase the sort of anarchy and social disintegration which had previously commenced. And thus that profound sense of settled order and security, without which a society like ours cannot live and grow at all, is beginning to threaten us with taking its departure.

Now, if culture, which simply means trying to perfect oneself, and one's mind as part of oneself, brings us light, and if light shows us that there is nothing so very blessed in merely doing as one likes, that the worship of the mere freedom to do as one likes is worship of machinery, that the really blessed thing is to like what right reason ordains, and to follow her authority, then we have got a practical benefit out of culture. We have got a much wanted principle, a principle of authority, to counteract the tendency to anarchy which seems to be threatening us.

But how to organise this authority, or to what hands to entrust the wielding of it? How to get your *State,* summing up the right reason of the community, and giving effect to it, as circumstances may require, with vigour? And here I think I see my enemies waiting for me with a hungry joy in their eyes. But I shall elude them.

The *State*, the power most representing the right reason of the nation, and most worthy, therefore, of ruling,—of exercising, when circumstances require it, authority over us all,—is for Mr. Carlyle the aristocracy. For Mr. Lowe, it is the middle-class with its incomparable Parliament. For the Reform League, it is the working-class, with its "brightest powers of sympathy and readiest powers of action." Now, culture, with its disinterested pursuit of perfection, culture, simply trying to see things as they are, in order to seize on the best and to make it prevail, is surely well fitted to help us to judge rightly, by all the aids of observing, reading, and thinking, the qualifications and titles to our confidence of these three candidates for authority, and can thus render us a practical service of no mean value.

So when Mr. Carlyle, a man of genius to whom we have all at one time or other been indebted for refreshment and stimulus, says we should give rule to the aristocracy, mainly because of its dignity and politeness, surely 69 culture is useful in reminding us, that in our idea of perfection the characters of beauty and intelligence are both of them present, and sweetness and light, the two noblest of things, are united. Allowing, therefore, with Mr. Carlyle, the aristocratic class to possess sweetness, culture insists on the necessity of light also, and shows us that aristocracies, being by the very nature of things inaccessible to ideas, unapt to see how the world is going, must be somewhat wanting in light, and must therefore be, at a moment when light is our great requisite, inadequate to our needs. Aristocracies, those children of the established fact, are for epochs of concentration. In epochs of expansion, epochs such as that in which we now live, epochs when always the warning voice is again heard: *Now is the judgment of this world*—in such epochs aristocracies, with their natural clinging to the established fact, their want of sense for the flux of things, for the inevitable transitoriness of all human institutions, are bewildered and helpless. Their serenity, their high spirit, their power of haughty resistance,—the great qualities of an aristocracy, and the secret of its distinguished man- 70 ners and dignity,—these very qualities, in an epoch of expansion, turn against their possessors. Again and again I have said how the refinement of an aristocracy may be precious and educative to a raw nation as a kind of shadow of true refinement; how its serenity and dignified freedom from petty cares may serve as a useful foil to set off the vulgarity and hideousness of that type of life which a hard middle-class tends to establish, and to help people to see this vulgarity and hideousness in their true colours. From such an ignoble spectacle as that of poor Mrs. Lincoln,—a spectacle to vulgarise a whole nation,—aristocracies undoubtedly preserve us. But the true grace and serenity is that of which Greece and Greek art suggest the admirable ideals of perfection,—a serenity which comes from having made order among ideas and harmonised them; whereas the serenity of aristocracies, at least the peculiar serenity of aristocracies of Teutonic origin, appears to come from their never having had any ideas to trouble them. And so, in a time of expansion like the present, a time for ideas, one gets, perhaps, in regarding an aristocracy, even more than the idea of serenity, the idea of futility and sterility. One has often wondered whether upon the whole earth there is anything so unintelligent, so unapt to per-   71 ceive how the world is really going, as an ordinary young Englishman of our upper class. Ideas he has not, and neither has he that seriousness of our middle-class, which is, as I have often said, the great strength of this class, and may become its salvation. Why, a man may hear a young Dives of the aristocratic class, when the whim takes him to sing the praises of wealth and material comfort, sing them with a cynicism from which the con- science of the veriest Philistine of our industrial middle-class would recoil in affright. And when, with the natural sympathy of aristocracies for firm dealing with the multitude, and his uneasiness at our feeble dealing with it at home, an unvarnished young Englishman of our aristocratic class ap- plauds the absolute rulers on the Continent, he in general manages com- pletely to miss the grounds of reason and intelligence which alone can give any colour of justification, any possibility of existence, to those rulers, and applauds them on grounds which it would make their own hair stand on end to listen to.

And all this time, we are in an epoch of expansion; and the essence of   72 an epoch of expansion is a movement of ideas, and the one salvation of an epoch of expansion is a harmony of ideas. The very principle of the authority which we are seeking as a defence against anarchy is right reason, ideas, light. The more, therefore, an aristocracy calls to its aid its innate forces,—its impenetrability, its high spirit, its power of haughty resistance,—to deal with an epoch of expansion, the graver is the danger, the greater the certainty of explosion, the surer the aristocracy's defeat; for it is trying to do violence to nature instead of working along with it. The best powers shown by the best men of an aristocracy at such an epoch are, it will be observed, non-aristocratical powers, powers of industry, powers of intelligence; and these powers, thus exhibited, tend really not to strengthen the aristocracy, but to take their owners out of it, to expose them to the dissolving agencies of thought and change, to make them men of the modern spirit and of the future. If, as sometimes happens, they add to their non-aristocratical qualities of labour and thought, a strong dose of

aristocratical qualities also,—of pride, defiance, turn for resistance—this
73 truly aristocratical side of them, so far from adding any strength to them really neutralises their force and makes them impracticable and ineffective.

Knowing myself to be indeed sadly to seek, as one of my many critics says, in "a philosophy with coherent, interdependent, subordinate and derivative principles," I continually have recourse to a plain man's expedient of trying to make what few simple notions I have, clearer, and more intelligible to myself, by means of example and illustration. And having been brought up at Oxford in the bad old times, when we were stuffed with Greek and Aristotle, and thought nothing of preparing ourselves,—as after Mr. Lowe's great speech at Edinburgh we shall do,—to fight the battle of life with the German waiters, my head is still full of a lumber of phrases we learnt at Oxford from Aristotle, about virtue being in a mean, and about excess and defect, and so on. Once when I had had the advantage of listening to the Reform debates in the House of Commons, having heard a number of interesting speakers, and among them Lord Elcho and Sir Thomas Bateson, I remember it struck me, applying Aristotle's ma-
74 chinery of the mean to my ideas about our aristocracy, that Lord Elcho was exactly the perfection, or happy mean, or virtue, of aristocracy, and Sir Thomas Bateson the excess; and I fancied that by observing these two we might see both the inadequacy of aristocracy to supply the principle of authority needful for our present wants, and the danger of its trying to supply it when it was not really competent for the business. On the one hand, in Lord Elcho, showing plenty of high spirit, but remarkable, far above and beyond his gift of high spirit, for the fine tempering of his high spirit, for ease, serenity, politeness,—the great virtues, as Mr. Carlyle says, of aristocracy,—in this beautiful and virtuous mean, there seemed evidently some insufficiency of light; while, on the other hand, Sir Thomas Bateson, in whom the high spirit of aristocracy, its impenetrability, defiant courage, and pride of resistance, were developed even in excess, was manifestly capable, if he had his way given him, of causing us great danger, and, indeed, of throwing the whole commonwealth into confusion. Then I reverted to that old fundamental notion of mine about
75 the grand merit of our race being really our honesty; and the very helplessness of our aristocratic or governing class in dealing with our perturbed social state gave me a sort of pride and satisfaction, because I saw they were, as a whole, too honest to try and manage a business for which they did not feel themselves capable.

Surely, now, it is no inconsiderable boon culture confers upon us, if in embarrassed times like the present it enables us to look at the ins and the outs of things in this way, without hatred and without partiality, and with a disposition to see the good in everybody all round. And I try to follow just the same course with our middle-class as with our aristocracy. Mr. Lowe talks to us of this strong middle part of the nation, of the unrivalled deeds of our liberal middle-class Parliament, of the noble, the heroic work it has performed in the last thirty years; and I begin to ask myself if we shall not, then, find in our middle-class the principle of authority we want, and if we had not better take administration as well as legislation away from the weak extreme which now administers for us, and commit both to the strong middle part. I observe, too, that the heroes of middle-class liberalism, such as we have hitherto known it, speak with a kind of prophetic 76 anticipation of the great destiny which awaits them, and as if the future was clearly theirs. The advanced party, the progressive party, the party in alliance with the future, are the names they like to give themselves. "The principles which will obtain recognition in the future," says Mr. Miall, a personage of deserved eminence among the political Dissenters, as they are called, who have been the backbone of middle-class liberalism—"the principles which will obtain recognition in the future are the principles for which I have long and zealously laboured. I qualified myself for joining in the work of harvest by doing to the best of my ability the duties of seed-time." These duties, if one is to gather them from the works of the great liberal party in the last thirty years, are, as I have elsewhere summed them up, the advocacy of free-trade, of parliamentary reform, of abolition of church-rates, of voluntaryism in religion and education, of non-interference of the State between employers and employed, and of marriage with one's deceased wife's sister.

Now I know, when I object that all this is machinery, the great liberal middle-class has by this time grown cunning enough to answer, that it 77 always meant more by these things than meets the eye; that it has had that within which passes show, and that we are soon going to see, in a Free Church and all manner of good things, what it was. But I have learned from Bishop Wilson (if Mr. Frederic Harrison will forgive my again quoting that poor old hierophant of a decayed superstition): "If we would really know our heart let us impartially view our actions;" and I cannot help thinking that if our liberals had had so much sweetness and light in their inner minds as they allege, more of it must have come out in their sayings and doings. An American friend of the English liberals says, indeed, that their Dissidence of Dissent has been a mere instrument of the political Dissenters for making reason and the will of God prevail (and no doubt he would say the same of marriage with one's deceased wife's sister); and that the abolition of a State Church is merely the Dissenter's means to this end, just as culture is mine. Another American defender of theirs says just the same of their industrialism and free-trade; indeed, this gentleman, taking the bull by the horns, proposes that we should for the

78 future call industrialism culture, and the industrialists the men of culture, and then of course there can be no longer any misapprehension about their true character; and besides the pleasure of being wealthy and comfortable, they will have authentic recognition as vessels of sweetness and light. All this is undoubtedly specious; but I must remark that the culture of which I talked was an endeavour to come at reason and the will of God by means of reading, observing, and thinking; and that whoever calls anything else culture, may, indeed, call it so if he likes, but then he talks of something quite different from what I talked of. And, again, as culture's way of working for reason and the will of God is by directly trying to know more about them, while the Dissidence of Dissent is evidently in itself no effort of this kind, nor is its Free Church, in fact, a church with worthier conceptions of God and the ordering of the world than the State Church professes, but with mainly the same conceptions of these as the State Church has, only that every man is to comport himself as he likes in professing them,—this being so, I cannot at once accept the Nonconformity any

79 more than the industrialism and the other great works of our liberal middle-class as proof positive that this class is in possession of light, and that here is the true seat of authority for which we are in search; but I must try a little further, and seek for other indications which may enable me to make up my mind.

Why should we not do with the middle-class as we have done with the aristocratic class,—find in it some representative men who may stand for the virtuous mean of this class, for the perfection of its present qualities and mode of being, and also for the excess of them. Such men must clearly not be men of genius like Mr. Bright; for, as I have formerly said, so far as a man has genius he tends to take himself out of the category of class altogether, and to become simply a man. Mr. Bright's brother, Mr. Jacob Bright, would, perhaps, be more to the purpose; he seems to sum up very well in himself, without disturbing influences, the general liberal force of the middle-class, the force by which it has done its great works of free-trade, parliamentary reform, voluntaryism, and so on, and the spirit in which it has done them. Now it is clear, from what has been already said,

80 that there has been at least an apparent want of light in the force and spirit through which these great works have been done, and that the works have

worn in consequence too much a look of machinery. But this will be clearer still if we take, as the happy mean of the middle-class, not Mr. Jacob Bright, but his colleague in the representation of Manchester, Mr. Bazley. Mr. Bazley sums up for us, in general, the middle-class, its spirit and its works, at least as well as Mr. Jacob Bright; and he has given us, moreover, a famous sentence, which bears directly on the resolution of our present question,—whether there is light enough in our middle-class to make it the proper seat of the authority we wish to establish. When there was a talk some little while ago about the state of middle-class education, Mr. Bazley, as the representative of that class, spoke some memorable words:—"There had been a cry that middle-class education ought to receive more attention. He confessed himself very much surprised by the clamour that was raised. He did not think that class need excite the sympathy either of the legislature or the public." Now this satisfaction of Mr. Bazley with the mental state of the middle-class was truly representative, 81 and enhances his claim (if that were necessary) to stand as the beautiful and virtuous mean of that class. But it is obviously at variance with our definition of culture, or the pursuit of light and perfection, which made light and perfection consist, not in resting and being, but in growing and becoming, in a perpetual advance in beauty and wisdom. So the middle-class is by its essence, as one may say, by its incomparable self-satisfaction decisively expressed through its beautiful and virtuous mean, self-excluded from wielding an authority of which light is to be the very soul.

Clear as this is, it will be made clearer still if we take some representative man as the excess of the middle-class, and remember that the middle-class, in general, is to be conceived as a body swaying between the qualities of its mean and of its excess, and on the whole, of course, as human nature is constituted, inclining rather towards the excess than the mean. Of its excess no better representative can possibly be imagined than the Rev. W. Cattle, a Dissenting minister from Walsall, who came before the public in connection with the proceedings at Birmingham of Mr. 82 Murphy, already mentioned. Speaking in the midst of an irritated population of Catholics, the Rev. W. Cattle exclaimed:—"I say, then, away with the mass! It is from the bottomless pit; and in the bottomless pit shall all liars have their part, in the lake that burneth with fire and brimstone." And again: "When all the praties were black in Ireland, why didn't the priests say the hocus-pocus over them, and make them all good again?" He shared, too, Mr. Murphy's fears of some invasion of his domestic happiness: "What I wish to say to you as Protestant husbands is, *Take care of your wives!*" And, finally, in the true vein of an Englishman doing as he likes, a vein of which I have at some length pointed out the present dangers, he recommended for imitation the example of some church-wardens at Dublin, among whom, said he, "there was a Luther and also a Melancthon," who had made very short work with some ritualist or other, handed him down from his pulpit, and kicked him out of church. Now it is manifest, as I said in the case of Sir Thomas Bateson, that if we let this excess of the sturdy English middle-class, this conscientious Protestant Dissenter, so strong, so self-reliant, so fully persuaded in his own mind, have his way, he would be capable, with his want of light—or, to use the language of the religious world, with his zeal without knowledge—of stirring up strife which neither he nor any one else could easily compose.

And then comes in, as it did also with the aristocracy, the honesty of our race, and by the voice of another middle-class man, Alderman Wilson, Alderman of the City of London and Colonel of the City of London Militia, proclaims that it has twinges of conscience, and that it will not attempt to cope with our social disorders, and to deal with a business which it feels to be too high for it. Every one remembers how this virtuous Alderman-Colonel, or Colonel-Alderman, led his militia through the London streets; how the bystanders gathered to see him pass; how the London roughs, asserting an Englishman's best and most blissful right of doing what he likes, robbed and beat the bystanders; and how the blame-less warrior-magistrate refused to let his troops interfere. "The crowd," he touchingly said afterwards, "was mostly composed of fine healthy strong men, bent on mischief; if he had allowed his soldiers to interfere they might have been overpowered, their rifles taken from them and used against them by the mob; a riot, in fact, might have ensued, and been attended with bloodshed, compared with which the assaults and loss of property that actually occurred would have been as nothing." Honest and affecting testimony of the English middle-class to its own inadequacy for the authoritative part one's admiration would sometimes incline one to assign to it! "Who are we," they say by the voice of their Alderman-Colonel, "that we should not be overpowered if we attempt to cope with social anarchy, our rifles taken from us and used against us by the mob, and we, perhaps, robbed and beaten ourselves? Or what light have we, beyond a free-born Englishman's impulse to do as he likes, which could justify us in preventing, at the cost of bloodshed, other free-born English-men from doing as they like, and robbing and beating us as much as they please?"

This distrust of themselves as an adequate centre of authority does not

mark the working-class, as was shown by their readiness the other day in   85
*Hyde Park to take upon themselves all the functions of government. But
this comes from the working-class being, as I have often said, still an
embryo, of which no one can yet quite foresee the final development; and
from its not having the same experience and self-knowledge as the aristocratic and middle classes. Honesty it no doubt has, just like the other
classes of Englishmen, but honesty in an inchoate and untrained state; and
meanwhile its powers of action, which are, as Mr. Frederic Harrison says,
exceedingly ready, easily run away with it. That it cannot at present have a
sufficiency of light which comes by culture,—that is, by reading, observing, and thinking,—is clear from the very nature of its condition; and,
indeed, we saw that Mr. Frederic Harrison, in seeking to make a free stage
for its bright powers of sympathy and ready powers of action, had to begin
by throwing overboard culture, and flouting it as only fit for a professor of
belles lettres. Still, to make it perfectly manifest that no more in the
working-class than in the aristocratic and middle classes can one find an
adequate centre of authority,—that is, as culture teaches us to conceive
our required authority, of light,—let us again follow, with this class, the   86
method we have followed with the aristocratic and middle classes, and try
to bring before our minds representative men, who may figure to us its
virtue and its excess. We must not take, of course, Colonel Dickson or Mr.
Beales; because Colonel Dickson, by his martial profession and dashing
exterior, seems to belong properly, like Julius Cæsar and Mirabeau and
other great popular leaders, to the aristocratic class, and to be carried into
the popular ranks only by his ambition or his genius; while Mr. Beales
belongs to our solid middle-class, and, perhaps, if he had not been a great
popular leader, would have been a Philistine. But Mr. Odger, whose
speeches we have all read, and of whom his friends relate, besides, much
that is favourable, may very well stand for the beautiful and virtuous mean
of our present working-class; and I think everybody will admit that in Mr.
Odger, as in Lord Elcho, there is manifestly, with all his good points,
some insufficiency of light. The excess of the working-class, in its present
state of development, is perhaps best shown in Mr. Bradlaugh, the icono-
clast, who seems to be almost for baptizing us all in blood and fire into his
new social dispensation, and to whose reflections, now that I have once   87
been set going on Bishop Wilson's track, I cannot forbear commending
this maxim of the good old man: "Intemperance in talk makes a dreadful
havoc in the heart." Mr. Bradlaugh, like Sir Thomas Bateson and the Rev.
W. Cattle, is evidently capable, if he had his head given him, of running us
all into great dangers and confusion. I conclude, therefore,—what, in-

deed, few of those who do me the honour to read this disquisition are likely to dispute,—that we can as little find in the working-class as in the aristocratic or in the middle class our much-wanted source of authority, as culture suggests it to us.

Well, then, what if we tried to rise above the idea of class to the idea of the whole community, *the State,* and to find our centre of light and authority there? Every one of us has the idea of country, as a sentiment; hardly any one of us has the idea of *the State,* as a working power. And why? Because we habitually live in our ordinary selves, which do not carry us beyond the ideas and wishes of the class to which we happen to belong. And we are all afraid of giving to the State too much power, because we only conceive of the State as something equivalent to the class in occupation of the executive government, and are afraid of that class abusing power to its own purposes. If we strengthen the State with the aristocratic class in occupation of the executive government, we imagine we are delivering ourselves up captive to the ideas and wishes of Sir Thomas Bateson; if with the middle-class in occupation of the executive government, to those of the Rev. W. Cattle; if with the working-class, to those of Mr. Bradlaugh. And with much justice; owing to the exaggerated notion which we English, as I have said, entertain of the right and blessedness of the mere doing as one likes, of the affirming oneself, and oneself just as it is. People of the aristocratic class want to affirm their ordinary selves, their likings and dislikings; people of the middle-class the same, people of the working-class the same. By our everyday selves, however, we are separate, personal, at war; we are only safe from one another's tyranny when no one has any power; and this safety, in its turn, cannot save us from anarchy. And when, therefore, anarchy presents itself as a danger to us, we know not where to turn.

88

89

But by our *best self* we are united, impersonal, at harmony. We are in no peril from giving authority to this, because it is the truest friend we all of us can have; and when anarchy is a danger to us, to this authority we may turn with sure trust. Well, and this is the very self which culture, or the study of perfection, seeks to develop in us; at the expense of our old untransformed self, taking pleasure only in doing what it likes or is used to do, and exposing us to the risk of clashing with every one else who is doing the same! So that our poor culture, which is flouted as so unpractical, leads us to the very ideas capable of meeting the great want of our present embarrassed times! We want an authority, and we find nothing but jealous classes, checks, and a dead-lock; culture suggests the idea of *the State.* We find no basis for a firm State-power in our ordinary selves; culture suggests one to us in our *best self.*

It cannot but acutely try a tender conscience to be accused, in a practical country like ours, of keeping aloof from the work and hope of a multitude of earnest-hearted men, and of merely toying with poetry and aesthetics. So it is with no little sense of relief that I find myself thus in the 90 position of one who makes a contribution in aid of the practical necessities of our times. The great thing, it will be observed, is to find our *best* self, and to seek to affirm nothing but that; not,—as we English with our overvalue for merely being free and busy have been so accustomed to do,— resting satisfied with a self which comes uppermost long before our best self, and affirming that with blind energy. In short,—to go back yet once more to Bishop Wilson,—of these two excellent rules of Bishop Wilson's for a man's guidance: "Firstly, never go against the best light you have; secondly, take care that your light be not darkness," we English have followed with praiseworthy zeal the first rule, but we have not given so much heed to the second. We have gone manfully, the Rev. W. Cattle and the rest of us, according to the best light we have; but we have not taken enough care that this should be really the best light possible for us, that it should not be darkness. And, our honesty being very great, conscience has whispered to us that the light we were following, our ordinary self, was, indeed, perhaps, only an inferior self, only darkness; and that it 91 would not do to impose this seriously on all the world.

But our best self inspires faith, and is capable of affording a serious principle of authority. For example. We are on our way to what the late Duke of Wellington, with his strong sagacity, foresaw and admirably described as "a revolution by due course of law." This is undoubtedly,—if we are still to live and grow, and this famous nation is not to stagnate and dwindle away on the one hand, or, on the other, to perish miserably in mere anarchy and confusion,—what we are on the way to. Great changes there must be, for a revolution cannot accomplish itself without great changes; yet order there must be, for without order a revolution cannot accomplish itself by due course of law. So whatever brings risk of tumult and disorder, multitudinous processions in the streets of our crowded towns, multitudinous meetings in their public places and parks,— demonstrations perfectly unnecessary in the present course of our affairs,—our best self, or right reason, plainly enjoins us to set our faces against. It enjoins us to encourage and uphold the occupants of the executive power, whoever they may be, in firmly prohibiting them. But it does 92 this clearly and resolutely, and is thus a real principle of authority, because it does it with a free conscience; because in thus provisionally strengthening the executive power, it knows that it is not doing this merely to enable Sir Thomas Bateson to affirm himself as against Mr. Bradlaugh, or the Rev. W. Cattle to affirm himself as against both. It knows that it is stablishing *the State,* or organ of our collective best self, of our national right reason; and it has the testimony of conscience that it is stablishing the State on behalf of whatever great changes are needed, just as much as on behalf of order; stablishing it to deal just as stringently, when the time comes, with Sir Thomas Bateson's Protestant ascendency, or with the Rev. W. Cattle's sorry education of his children, as it deals with Mr. Bradlaugh's street-processions.

93 III. [Barbarians, Philistines, Populace]

From a man without a philosophy no one can expect philosophical completeness. Therefore I may observe without shame, that in trying to get a distinct notion of our aristocratic, our middle, and our working class, with a view of testing the claims of each of these classes to become a centre of authority, I have omitted, I find, to complete the old-fashioned analysis which I had the fancy of applying, and have not shown in these classes, as well as the virtuous mean and the excess, the defect also. I do not know that the omission very much matters; still as clearness is the one merit which a plain, unsystematic writer, without a philosophy, can hope to have, and as our notion of the three great English classes may perhaps be made clearer if we see their distinctive qualities in the defect, as well as in the excess and in the mean, let us try, before proceeding further, to remedy this omission.

It is manifest, if the perfect and virtuous mean of that fine spirit which
94   is the distinctive quality of aristocracies, is to be found in Lord Elcho's chivalrous style, and its excess in Sir Thomas Bateson's turn for resistance, that its defect must lie in a spirit not bold and high enough, and in an excessive and pusillanimous unaptness for resistance. If, again, the perfect and virtuous mean of that force by which our middle-class has done its great works, and of that self-reliance with which it contemplates itself and them, is to be seen in the performances and speeches of Mr. Bazley, and the excess of that force and that self-reliance in the performances and speeches of the Rev. W. Cattle, then it is manifest that their defect must lie in a helpless inaptitude for the great works of the middle-class, and in a poor and despicable lack of its self-satisfaction. To be chosen to exemplify

the happy mean of a good quality, or set of good qualities, is evidently a praise to a man; nay, to be chosen to exemplify even their excess, is a kind of praise. Therefore I could have no hesitation in taking Lord Elcho and Mr. Bazley, the Rev. W. Cattle and Sir Thomas Bateson, to exemplify, respectively, the mean and the excess of aristocratic and middle-class qualities. But perhaps there might be a want of urbanity in singling out this 95 or that personage as the representative of defect. Therefore I shall leave the defect of aristocracy unillustrated by any representative man. But with oneself one may always, without impropriety, deal quite freely; and, indeed, this sort of plain-dealing with oneself has in it, as all the moralists tell us, something very wholesome. So I will venture to humbly offer myself as an illustration of defect in those forces and qualities which make our middle-class what it is. The too well-founded reproaches of my opponents declare how little I have lent a hand to the great works of the middle-class; for it is evidently these works, and my slackness at them, which are meant, when I am said to "refuse to lend a hand to the humble operation of uprooting certain definite evils" (such as church-rates and others), and that therefore "the believers in action grow impatient" with me. The line, again, of a still unsatisfied seeker which I have followed, the idea of self-transformation, of growing towards some measure of sweetness and light not yet reached, is evidently at clean variance with the perfect self-satisfaction current in my class, the middle-class, and may serve to indi- 96 cate in me, therefore, the extreme defect of this feeling. But these confessions, though salutary, are bitter and unpleasant.

To pass, then, to the working-class. The defect of this class would be the falling short in what Mr. Frederic Harrison calls those "bright powers of sympathy and ready powers of action," of which we saw in Mr. Odger the virtuous mean, and in Mr. Bradlaugh the excess. The working-class is so fast growing and rising at the present time, that instances of this defect cannot well be now very common. Perhaps Canning's "Needy Knife-grinder" (who is dead, and therefore cannot be pained at my taking him for an illustration) may serve to give us the notion of defect in the essential quality of a working-class; or I might even cite (since, though he is alive in the flesh, he is dead to all heed of criticism) my poor old poaching friend, Zephaniah Diggs, who, between his haresnaring and his gin-drinking, has got his powers of sympathy quite dulled and his powers of action in any great movement of his class hopelessly impaired. But examples of this defect belong, as I have said, to a bygone age rather than to the present.

The same desire for clearness, which has led me thus to extend a little 97 my first analysis of the three great classes of English society, prompts me also to make my nomenclature for them a little fuller, with a view to making it thereby more clear and manageable. It is awkward and tiresome to be always saying the aristocratic class, the middle-class, the working-class. For the middle-class, for that great body which, as we know, "has done all the great things that have been done in all departments," and which is to be conceived as chiefly moving between its two cardinal points of Mr. Bazley and the Rev. W. Cattle, but inclining, in the mass, rather towards the latter than the former—for this class we have a designation which now has become pretty well known, and which we may as well still keep for them, the designation of Philistines. What this term means I have so often explained that I need not repeat it here. For the aristocratic class, conceived mainly as a body moving between the two cardinal points of Lord Elcho and Sir Thomas Bateson, but as a whole nearer to the latter

98   than the former, we have as yet got no special designation. Almost all my attention has naturally been concentrated on my own class, the middle-class, with which I am in closest sympathy, and which has been, besides, the great power of our day, and has had its praises sung by all speakers and newspapers. Still the aristocratic class is so important in itself, and the weighty functions which Mr. Carlyle proposes at the present critical time to commit to it must add so much to its importance, that it seems neglect-ful, and a strong instance of that want of coherent philosophic method for which Mr. Frederic Harrison blames me, to leave the aristocratic class so much without notice and denomination. It may be thought that the charac-teristic which I have occasionally mentioned as proper to aristocracies,— their natural inaccessibility, as children of the established fact, to ideas,— points to our extending to this class also the designation of Philistines; the Philistine being, as is well known, the enemy of the children of light, or servants of the idea. Nevertheless, there seems to be an inconvenience in thus giving one and the same designation to two very different classes; and besides, if we look into the thing closely, we shall find that the term

99   Philistine conveys a sense which makes it more peculiarly appropriate to our middle class than to our aristocratic. For *Philistine* gives the notion of something particularly stiff-necked and perverse in the resistance to light and its children, and therein it specially suits our middle-class, who not only do not pursue sweetness and light, but who prefer to them that sort of machinery of business, chapels, tea meetings, and addresses from Mr. Murphy and the Rev. W. Cattle, which makes up the dismal and illiberal life on which I have so often touched. But the aristocratic class has actually, as we have seen, in its well-known politeness, a kind of image or shadow of sweetness; and as for light, if it does not pursue light, it is not

that it perversely cherishes some dismal and illiberal existence in preference to light, but it is seduced from following light by those mighty and
eternal seducers of our race which weave for this class their most irresistible charms,—by worldly splendour, security, power and pleasure. These
seducers are exterior goods, but they are goods; and he who is hindered by
them from caring for light and ideas, is not so much doing what is perverse
as what is natural.

Keeping this in view, I have in my own mind often indulged myself   100
with the fancy of putting side by side with the idea of our aristocratic class,
the idea of *the Barbarians*. The Barbarians, to whom we all owe so much,
and who reinvigorated and renewed our worn-out Europe, had, as is well-
known, eminent merits; and in this country, where we are for the most part
sprung from the Barbarians, we have never had the prejudice against them
which prevails among the races of Latin origin. The Barbarians brought
with them that staunch individualism, as the modern phrase is, and that
passion for doing as one likes, for the assertion of personal liberty, which
appears to Mr. Bright the central idea of English life, and of which we
have, at any rate, a very rich supply. The stronghold and natural seat of this
passion was in the nobles of whom our aristocratic class are the inheritors;
and this class, accordingly, have signally manifested it, and have done
much by their example to recommend it to the body of the nation, who
already, indeed, had it in their blood. The Barbarians, again, had the
passion for field-sports; and they have handed it on to our aristocratic
class, who of this passion too, as of the passion for asserting one's personal liberty, are the great natural stronghold. The care of the Barbarians   101
for the body, and for all manly exercises; the vigour, good looks, and fine
complexion which they acquired and perpetuated in their families by these
means,—all this may be observed still in our aristocratic class. The chivalry of the Barbarians, with its characteristics of high spirit, choice manners, and distinguished bearing,—what is this but the beautiful commencement of the politeness of our aristocratic class? In some Barbarian
noble, no doubt, one would have admired, if one could have been then
alive to see it, the rudiments of Lord Elcho. Only, all this culture (to call it
by that name) of the Barbarians was an exterior culture mainly: it consisted
principally in outward gifts and graces, in looks, manners, accomplishments, prowess; the chief inward gifts which had part in it were the most
exterior, so to speak, of inward gifts, those which come nearest to outward
ones: they were courage, a high spirit, self-confidence. Far within, and
unawakened, lay a whole range of powers of thought and feeling, to which
these interesting productions of nature had, from the circumstances of

102   their life, no access. Making allowances for the difference of the times, surely we can observe precisely the same thing now in our aristocratic class. In general its culture is exterior chiefly; all the exterior graces and accomplishments, and the more external of the inward virtues, seem to be principally its portion. It now, of course, cannot but be often in contact with those studies by which, from the world of thought and feeling, true culture teaches us to fetch sweetness and light; but its hold upon these very studies appears remarkably external, and unable to exert any deep power upon its spirit. Therefore the one insufficiency which we noted in the perfect mean of this class, Lord Elcho, was an insufficiency of light. And owing to the same causes, does not a subtle criticism lead us to make, even on the good looks and politeness of our aristocratic class, the one qualifying remark, that in these charming gifts there should perhaps be, for ideal perfection, a shade more *soul?*

      I often, therefore, when I want to distinguish clearly the aristocratic class from the Philistines proper, or middle-class, name the former, in my own mind, *the Barbarians:* and when I go through the country, and see

103   this and that beautiful and imposing seat of theirs crowning the landscape, "There," I say to myself, "is a great fortified post of the Barbarians."

      It is obvious that that part of the working-class which, working diligently by the light of Mrs. Gooch's Golden Rule, looks forward to the happy day when it will sit on thrones with Mr. Bazley and other middle-class potentates, to survey, as Mr. Bright beautifully says, "the cities it has built, the railroads it has made, the manufactures it has produced, the cargoes which freight the ships of the greatest mercantile navy the world has ever seen,"—it is obvious, I say, that this part of the working-class is, or is in a fair way to be, one in spirit with the industrial middle-class. It is notorious that our middle-class liberals have long looked forward to this consummation, when the working-class shall join forces with them, aid them heartily to carry forward their great works, go in a body to their tea-meetings, and, in short, enable them to bring about their millennium. That part of the working-class, therefore, which does really seem to lend itself to these great aims, may, with propriety, be numbered by us among the

104   Philistines. That part of it, again, which so much occupies the attention of philanthropists at present,—the part which gives all its energies to organising itself, through trades' unions and other means, so as to constitute, first, a great working-class power, independent of the middle and aristocratic classes, and then, by dint of numbers, give the law to them, and itself reign absolutely,—this lively and interesting part must also, according to our definition, go with the Philistines; because it is its class and its

class-instinct which it seeks to affirm, its ordinary self not its best self; and it is a machinery, an industrial machinery, and power and pre-eminence and other external goods which fill its thoughts, and not an inward perfection. It is wholly occupied, according to Plato's subtle expression, with the things of itself and not its real self, with the things of the State and not the real State. But that vast portion, lastly, of the working-class which, raw and half-developed, has long lain half-hidden amidst its poverty and squalor, and is now issuing from its hiding-place to assert an Englishman's heaven-born privilege of doing as he likes, and is beginning to perplex us by marching where it likes, meeting where it likes, bawling what it likes, breaking what it likes,—to this vast residuum we may with great propriety 105
give the name of *Populace.*

Thus we have got three distinct terms, *Barbarians, Philistines, Populace,* to denote roughly the three great classes into which our society is divided; and though this humble attempt at a scientific nomenclature falls, no doubt, very far short in precision of what might be required from a writer equipped with a complete and coherent philosophy, yet, from a notoriously unsystematic and unpretending writer, it will, I trust, be accepted as sufficient.

But in using this new, and, I hope, convenient division of English society, two things are to be borne in mind. The first is, that since, under all our class divisions, there is a common basis of human nature, therefore, in every one of us, whether we be properly Barbarians, Philistines, or Populace, there exists, sometimes only in germ and potentially, sometimes more or less developed, the same tendencies and passions which have made our fellow-citizens of other classes what they are. This consideration is very important, because it has great influence in begetting that spirit of indulgence which is a necessary part of sweetness, and which, 106
indeed, when our culture is complete, is, as I have said, inexhaustible. Thus, an English Barbarian who examines himself, will, in general, find himself to be not so entirely a Barbarian but that he has in him, also, something of the Philistine, and even something of the Populace as well. And the same with Englishmen of the two other classes. This is an experience which we may all verify every day. For instance, I myself (I again take myself as a sort of *corpus vile* to serve for illustration in a matter where serving for illustration may not by every one be thought agreeable), I myself am properly a Philistine,—Mr. Swinburne would add, the son of a Philistine,—and though, through circumstances which will perhaps one day be known, if ever the affecting history of my conversion comes to be written, I have, for the most part, broken with the ideas and the tea-

meetings of my own class, yet I have not, on that account, been brought much the nearer to the ideas and works of the Barbarians or of the Populace. Nevertheless, I never take a gun or a fishing-rod in my hands without feeling that I have in the ground of my nature the self-same seeds which, 107 fostered by circumstances, do so much to make the Barbarian; and that, with the Barbarian's advantages, I might have rivalled him. Place me in one of his great fortified posts, with these seeds of a love for field-sports sown in my nature, with all the means of developing them, with all pleasures at my command, with most whom I met deferring to me, every one I met smiling on me, and with every appearance of permanence and security before me and behind me,—then I too might have grown, I feel, into a very passable child of the established fact, of commendable spirit and politeness, and, at the same time, a little inaccessible to ideas and light; not, of course, with either the eminent fine spirit of Lord Elcho, or the eminent power of resistance of Sir Thomas Bateson, but, according to the measure of the common run of mankind, something between the two. And as to the Populace, who, whether he be Barbarian or Philistine, can look at them without sympathy, when he remembers how often,—every time that we snatch up a vehement opinion in ignorance and passion, every time that we long to crush an adversary by sheer violence, every time that 108 we are envious, every time that we are brutal, every time that we adore mere power or success, every time that we add our voice to swell a blind clamour against some unpopular personage, every time that we trample savagely on the fallen,—he has found in his own bosom the eternal spirit of the Populace, and that there needs only a little help from circumstances to make it triumph in him untameably?

The second thing to be borne in mind I have indicated several times already. It is this. All of us, so far as we are Barbarians, Philistines, or Populace, imagine happiness to consist in doing what one's ordinary self likes. What one's ordinary self likes differs according to the class to which one belongs, and has its severer and its lighter side; always, however, remaining machinery, and nothing more. The graver self of the Barbarian likes honours and consideration; his more relaxed self, field-sports and pleasure. The graver self of one kind of Philistine likes business and money-making; his more relaxed self, comfort and tea-meetings. Of another kind of Philistine, the graver self likes trades' unions; the relaxed self, deputations, or hearing Mr. Odger speak. The sterner self of the 109 Populace likes bawling, hustling, and smashing; the lighter self, beer. But in each class there are born a certain number of natures with a curiosity about their best self, with a bent for seeing things as they are, for disentan-

gling themselves from machinery, for simply concerning themselves with reason and the will of God, and doing their best to make these prevail;— for the pursuit, in a word, of perfection. To certain manifestations of this love for perfection mankind have accustomed themselves to give the name of genius; implying, by this name, something original and heaven-bestowed in the passion. But the passion is to be found far beyond those manifestations of it to which the world usually gives the name of genius, and in which there is, for the most part, a *talent* of some kind or other, a special and striking faculty of execution, informed by the heaven-bestowed ardour, or genius. It is to be found in many manifestations besides these, and may best be called, as we have called it, the love and pursuit of perfection; culture being the true nurse of the pursuing love, and sweetness and light the true character of the pursued perfection. Natures with this bent emerge in all classes,—among the Barbarians, among the Philistines, among the Populace. And this bent always tends, as I have   110
said, to take them out of their class, and to make their distinguishing characteristic not their Barbarianism or their Philistinism, but their *humanity*. They have, in general, a rough time of it in their lives; but they are sown more abundantly than one might think, they appear where and when one least expects it, they set up a fire which enfilades, so to speak, the class with which they are ranked; and, in general, by the extrication of their best self as the self to develope, and by the simplicity of the ends fixed by them as paramount, they hinder the unchecked predominance of that class-life which is the affirmation of our ordinary self, and seasonably disconcert mankind in their worship of machinery.

Therefore, when we speak of ourselves as divided into Barbarians, Philistines, and Populace, we must be understood always to imply that within each of these classes there are a certain number of *aliens*, if we may so call them,—persons who are mainly led, not by their class spirit, but by a general *humane* spirit, by the love of human perfection; and that this number is capable of being diminished or augmented. I mean, the number of those who will succeed in developing this happy instinct will be greater   111
or smaller, in proportion both to the force of the original instinct within them, and to the hindrance or encouragement which it meets with from without. In almost all who have it, it is mixed with some infusion of the spirit of an ordinary self, some quantity of class-instinct, and even, as has been shown, of more than one class-instinct at the same time; so that, in general, the extrication of the best self, the predominance of the *humane* instinct, will very much depend upon its meeting, or not, with what is fitted to help and elicit it. At a moment, therefore, when it is agreed that

[Barbarians, Philistines, Populace]   73 we want a source of authority, and when it seems probable that the right source is our best self, it becomes of vast importance to see whether or not the things around us are, in general, such as to help and elicit our best self, and if they are not, to see why they are not, and the most promising way of mending them.

Now, it is clear that the very absence of any powerful authority amongst us, and the prevalent doctrine of the duty and happiness of doing as one likes, and asserting our personal liberty, must tend to prevent the erection of any very strict standard of excellence, the belief in any very paramount authority of right reason, the recognition of our best self as anything very recondite and hard to come at. It may be, as I have said, a proof of our honesty that we do not attempt to give to our ordinary self, as we have it in action, predominant authority, and to impose its rule upon other people; but it is evident, also, that it is not easy, with our style of proceeding, to get beyond the notion of an ordinary self at all, or to get the paramount authority of a commanding best self, or right reason, recognised. The learned Martinus Scriblerus well says:—"The taste of the bathos is implanted by nature itself in the soul of man; till, perverted by custom or example, he is taught, or rather compelled, to relish the sublime." But with us everything seems directed to prevent any such perversion of us by custom or example as might compel us to relish the sublime; by all means we are encouraged to keep our natural taste for the bathos unimpaired. I have formerly pointed out how in literature the absence of any authoritative centre, like an Academy, tends to do this; each section of the public has its own literary organ, and the mass of the public is without any suspicion that the value of these organs is relative to their being nearer a certain ideal centre of correct information, taste, and intelligence, or farther away from it. I have said that within certain limits, which any one who is likely to read this will have no difficulty in drawing for himself, my old adversary, the *Saturday Review,* may, on matters of literature and taste, be fairly enough regarded, relatively to a great number of newspapers which treat these matters, as a kind of organ of reason. But I remember once conversing with a company of Nonconformist admirers of some lecturer who had let off a great fire-work, which the *Saturday Review* said was all noise and false lights, and feeling my way as tenderly as I could about the effect of this unfavourable judgment upon those with whom I was conversing. "Oh," said one who was their spokesman, with the most tranquil air of conviction, "it is true the *Saturday Review* abuses the lecture, but the *British Banner*" (I am not quite sure it was the *British Banner,* but it was some newspaper of that stamp) "says that the *Saturday*

Review is quite wrong." The speaker had evidently no notion that there was a scale of value for judgments on these topics, and that the judgments of the *Saturday Review* ranked high on this scale, and those of the *British* 114 *Banner* low; the taste of the bathos implanted by nature in the literary judgments of man had never, in my friend's case, encountered any let or hindrance.

Just the same in religion as in literature. We have most of us little idea of a high standard to choose our guides by, of a great and profound spirit, which is an authority, while inferior spirits are none; it is enough to give importance to things that this or that person says them decisively, and has a large following of some strong kind when he says them. This habit of ours is very well shown in that able and interesting work of Mr. Hepworth Dixon's, which we were all reading lately, *The Mormons, by One of Themselves.* Here, again, I am not quite sure that my memory serves me as to the exact title, but I mean the well-known book in which Mr. Hepworth Dixon described the Mormons, and other similar religious bodies in America, with so much detail and such warm sympathy. In this work it seems enough for Mr. Dixon that this or that doctrine has its Rabbi, who talks big to him, has a staunch body of disciples, and, above all, has plenty of rifles. That there are any further stricter tests to be applied to a doctrine, 115 before it is pronounced important, never seems to occur to him. "It is easy to say," he writes of the Mormons, "that these saints are dupes and fanatics, to laugh at Joe Smith and his church, but what then? *The great facts remain.* Young and his people are at Utah; a church of 200,000 souls; an army of 20,000 rifles." But if the followers of a doctrine are really dupes, or worse, and its promulgators are really fanatics, or worse, it gives the doctrine no seriousness or authority the more that there should be found 200,000 souls,—200,000 of the innumerable multitude with a natural taste for the bathos,—to hold it, and 20,000 rifles to defend it. And again, of another religious organisation in America: "A fair and open field is not to be refused when hosts so mighty throw down wager of battle on behalf of what they hold to be true, however strange their faith may seem." A fair and open field is not to be refused to any speaker; but this solemn way of heralding him is quite out of place unless he has, for the best reason and spirit of man, some significance. "Well, but," says Mr. Hepworth Dixon, "a theory which has been accepted by men like Judge Edmonds, Dr. Hare, 116 Elder Frederick, and Professor Bush!" And again: "Such are, in brief, the bases of what Newman Weeks, Sarah Horton, Deborah Butler, and the associated brethren, proclaimed in Rolt's Hall as the new covenant!" If he was summing up an account of the teaching of Plato or St. Paul, Mr.

Hepworth Dixon could not be more earnestly reverential. But the question is, have personages like Judge Edmonds, and Newman Weeks, and Elderess Polly, and Elderess Antoinette, and the rest of Mr. Hepworth Dixon's heroes and heroines, anything of the weight and significance for the best reason and spirit of man that Plato and St. Paul have? Evidently they, at present, have not; and a very small taste of them and their doctrines ought to have convinced Mr. Hepworth Dixon that they never could have. "But," says he, "the magnetic power which Shakerism is exercising on American thought would of itself compel us,"—and so on. Now as far as real thought is concerned,—thought which affects the best reason and spirit of man, the scientific thought of the world, the only thought which deserves speaking of in this solemn way,—America has up to the present time been hardly more than a province of England, and even now would not herself claim to be more than abreast of England; and of this only real human thought, English thought itself is not just now, as we must all admit, one of the most significant factors. Neither, then, can American thought be; and the magnetic power which Shakerism exercises on American thought is about as important, for the best reason and spirit of man, as the magnetic power which Mr. Murphy exercises on Birmingham Protestantism. And as we shall never get rid of our natural taste for the bathos in religion,—never get access to a best self and right reason which may stand as a serious authority,—by treating Mr. Murphy as his own disciples treat him, seriously, and as if he was as much an authority as any one else: so we shall never get rid of it while our able and popular writers treat their Joe Smiths and Deborah Butlers, with their so many thousand souls and so many thousand rifles, in the like exaggerated and misleading manner, and so do their best to confirm us in a bad mental habit to which we are already too prone.

117

118   If our habits make it hard for us to come at the idea of a high best self, of a paramount authority, in literature or religion, how much more do they make this hard in the sphere of politics! In other countries, the governors, not depending so immediately on the favour of the governed, have everything to urge them, if they know anything of right reason (and it is at least supposed that governors should know more of this than the mass of the governed), to set it authoritatively before the community. But our whole scheme of government being representative, every one of our governors has all possible temptation, instead of setting up before the governed who elect him, and on whose favour he depends, a high standard of right reason, to accommodate himself as much as possible to their natural taste for the bathos; and even if he tries to go counter to it, to proceed in this with

so much flattering and coaxing, that they shall not suspect their ignorance and prejudices to be anything very unlike right reason, or their natural taste for the bathos to differ much from a relish for the sublime. Every one is thus in every possible way encouraged to trust in his own heart; but "he that trusteth in his own heart," says the Wise Man, "is a fool;" and at any rate this, which Bishop Wilson says, is undeniably true: "The number of those who need to be awakened is far greater than that of those who need comfort." But in our political system everybody is comforted. Our guides and governors who have to be elected by the influence of the Barbarians, and who depend on their favour, sing the praises of the Barbarians, and say all the smooth things that can be said of them. With Mr. Tennyson, they celebrate "the great broad-shouldered genial Englishman," with his "sense of duty," his "reverence for the laws," and his "patient force," who saves us from the "revolts, republics, revolutions, most no graver than a schoolboy's barring out," which upset other and less broad-shouldered nations. Our guides who are chosen by the Philistines and who have to look to their favour, tell the Philistines how "all the world knows that the great middle-class of this country supplies the mind, the will, and the power requisite for all the great and good things that have to be done," and congratulate them on their "earnest good sense, which penetrates through sophisms, ignores commonplaces, and gives to conventional illusions their true value." Our guides who look to the favour of the Populace, tell them that "theirs are the brightest powers of sympathy, and the readiest powers of action." Harsh things are said too, no doubt, against all the great classes of the community; but these things so evidently come from a hostile class, and are so manifestly dictated by the passions and prepossessions of a hostile class, and not by right reason, that they make no serious impression on those at whom they are launched, but slide easily off their minds. For instance, when the Reform League orators inveigh against our cruel and bloated aristocracy, these invectives so evidently show the passions and point of view of the Populace, that they do not sink into the minds of those at whom they are addressed, or awaken any thought or self-examination in them. Again, when Sir Thomas Bateson describes the Philistines and the Populace as influenced with a kind of hideous mania for emasculating the aristocracy, that reproach so clearly comes from the wrath and excited imagination of the Barbarians, that it does not much set the Philistines and the Populace thinking. Or when Mr. Lowe calls the Populace drunken and venal, he so evidently calls them this in an agony of apprehension for his Philistine or middle-class Parliament, which has done so many great and heroic works, and is now threatened with mixture

119

120

121

[Barbarians, Philistines, Populace]

and debasement, that the Populace do not lay his words seriously to heart. So the voice which makes a permanent impression on each of our classes is the voice of its friends, and this is from the nature of things, as I have said, a comforting voice. The Barbarians remain in the belief that the great broad-shouldered genial Englishman may be well satisfied with himself; the Philistines remain in the belief that the great middle-class of this country, with its earnest common-sense penetrating through sophisms and ignoring commonplaces, may be well satisfied with itself: the Populace, that the working-man with his bright powers of sympathy and ready powers of action, may be well satisfied with himself. What hope, at this rate, of extinguishing the taste of the bathos implanted by nature itself in the soul of man, or of inculcating the belief that excellence dwells among high and steep rocks, and can only be reached by those who sweat blood to reach her?

122   But it will be said, perhaps, that candidates for political influence and leadership, who thus caress the self-love of those whose suffrages they desire, know quite well that they are not saying the sheer truth as reason sees it, but that they are using a sort of conventional language, or what we call clap-trap, which is essential to the working of representative institutions. And therefore, I suppose, we ought rather to say with *Figaro: *Qui est-ce qu'on trompe ici?* Now, I admit that often, but not always, when our governors say smooth things to the self-love of the class whose political support they want, they know very well that they are overstepping, by a long stride, the bounds of truth and soberness; and while they talk, they in a manner, no doubt, put their tongue in their cheek. Not always; because, when a Barbarian appeals to his own class to make him their representative and give him political power, he, when he pleases their self-love by extolling broad-shouldered genial Englishmen with their sense of duty, reverence for the laws, and patient force, pleases his own self-love and extols himself, and is, therefore, himself ensnared by his own smooth words. And so, too, when a Philistine wants to represent his brother
123   Philistines, and extols the earnest good sense which characterises Manchester, and supplies the mind, the will, and the power, as the *Daily News* eloquently says, requisite for all the great and good things that have to be done, he intoxicates and deludes himself as well as his brother Philistines who hear him. But it is true that a Barbarian often wants the political support of the Philistines; and he unquestionably, when he flatters the self-love of Philistinism, and extols, in the approved fashion, its energy, enterprise, and self-reliance, knows that he is talking clap-trap, and, so to say, puts his tongue in his cheek. On all matters where Nonconformity and

its catchwords are concerned, this insincerity of Barbarians needing Nonconformist support, and, therefore, flattering the self-love of Nonconformity and repeating its catchwords without the least real belief in them, is very noticeable. When the Nonconformists, in a transport of blind zeal, threw out Sir James Graham's useful Education Clauses in 1843, one-half of their parliamentary representatives, no doubt, who cried aloud against "trampling on the religious liberty of the Dissenters by taking the money of Dissenters to teach the tenets of the Church of England," put their   124
tongue in their cheek while they so cried out. And perhaps there is even a sort of motion of Mr. Frederic Harrison's tongue towards his cheek when he talks of the "shriek of superstition," and tells the working-class that theirs are the brightest powers of sympathy and the readiest powers of action. But the point on which I would insist is, that this involuntary tribute to truth and soberness on the part of certain of our governors and guides never reaches at all the mass of us governed, to serve as a lesson to us, to abate our self-love, and to awaken in us a suspicion that our favourite prejudices may be, to a higher reason, all nonsense. Whatever by-play goes on among the more intelligent of our leaders, we do not see it; and we are left to believe that, not only in our own eyes, but in the eyes of our representative and ruling men, there is nothing more admirable than our ordinary self, whatever our ordinary self happens to be,—Barbarian, Philistine, or Populace.

Thus everything in our political life tends to hide from us that there is anything wiser than our ordinary selves, and to prevent our getting the notion of a paramount right reason. Royalty itself, in its idea the expres-   125
sion of the collective nation, and a sort of constituted witness to its best mind, we try to turn into a kind of grand advertising van, to give publicity and credit to the inventions, sound or unsound, of the ordinary self of individuals. I remember, when I was in North Germany, having this very strongly brought to my mind in the matter of schools and their institution. In Prussia, the best schools are Crown patronage schools, as they are called; schools which have been established and endowed (and new ones are to this day being established and endowed) by the Sovereign himself out of his own revenues, to be under the direct control and management of him or of those representing him, and to serve as types of what schools should be. The Sovereign, as his position raises him above many prejudices and littlenesses, and as he can always have at his disposal the best advice, has evident advantages over private founders in well planning and directing a school; while at the same time his great means and his great influence secure, to a well-planned school of his, credit and authority.

This is what, in North Germany, the governors do, in the matter of educa-
126 tion, for the governed; and one may say that they thus give the governed a
lesson, and draw out in them the idea of a right reason higher than the
suggestions of an ordinary man's ordinary self. But in England how different is the part which in this matter our governors are accustomed to play!
The Licensed Victuallers or the Commercial Travellers propose to make a
school for their children; and I suppose, in the matter of schools, one may
call the Licensed Victuallers or the Commercial Travellers ordinary men,
with their natural taste for the bathos still strong; and a Sovereign with the
advice of men like Wilhelm von Humboldt or Schleiermacher may, in this
matter, be a better judge, and nearer to right reason. And it will be
allowed, probably, that right reason would suggest that, to have a sheer
school of Licensed Victuallers' children, or a sheer school of Commercial
Travellers' children, and to bring them all up, not only at home but at
school too, in a kind of odour of licensed victualism or of bagmanism, is
not a wise training to give to these children. And in Germany, I have said,
the action of the national guides or governors is to suggest and provide a
127 better. But, in England, the action of the national guides or governors is,
for a Royal Prince or a great Minister to go down to the opening of the
Licensed Victuallers' or of the Commercial Travellers' school, to take the
chair, to extol the energy and self-reliance of the Licensed Victuallers or
the Commercial Travellers, to be all of their way of thinking, to predict
full success to their schools, and never so much as to hint to them that they
are doing a very foolish thing, and that the right way to go to work with
their children's education is quite different. And it is the same in almost
every department of affairs. While, on the Continent, the idea prevails that
it is the business of the heads and representatives of the nation, by virtue of
their superior means, power, and information, to set an example and to
provide suggestions of right reason, among us the idea is that the business
of the heads and representatives of the nation is to do nothing of the kind,
but to applaud the natural taste for the bathos showing itself vigorously in
any part of the community, and to encourage its works.

Now I do not say that the political system of foreign countries has not
inconveniences which may outweigh the inconveniences of our own polit-
128 ical system; nor am I the least proposing to get rid of our own political
system and to adopt theirs. But a sound centre of authority being what, in
this disquisition, we have been led to seek, and right reason, or our best
self, appearing alone to offer such a sound centre of authority, it is necessary to take note of the chief impediments which hinder, in this country,

the extrication or recognition of this right reason as a paramount authority, with a view to afterwards trying in what way they can best be removed. This being borne in mind, I proceed to remark how not only do we get no suggestions of right reason, and no rebukes of our ordinary self, from our governors, but a kind of philosophical theory is widely spread among us to the effect that there is no such thing at all as a best self and a right reason having claim to paramount authority, or, at any rate, no such thing ascertainable and capable of being made use of; and that there is nothing but an infinite number of ideas and works of our ordinary selves, and suggestions of our natural taste for the bathos, pretty equal in value, which are doomed either to an irreconcileable conflict, or else to a perpetual give 129 and take; and that wisdom consists in choosing the give and take rather than the conflict, and in sticking to our choice with patience and good humour. And, on the other hand, we have another philosophical theory rife among us, to the effect that without the labour of perverting ourselves by custom or example to relish right reason, but by continuing all of us to follow freely our natural taste for the bathos, we shall, by the mercy of Providence, and by a kind of natural tendency of things, come in due time to relish and follow right reason. The great promoters of these philosophical theories are our newspapers, which, no less than our parliamentary representatives, may be said to act the part of guides and governors to us; and these favourite doctrines of theirs I call,—or should call, if the doctrines were not preached by authorities I so much respect,—the first, a peculiarly British form of Atheism, the second, a peculiarly British form of Quietism. The first-named melancholy doctrine is preached in *The Times* with great clearness and force of style; indeed, it is well known, from the example of the poet Lucretius and others, what great masters of style the atheistic doctrine has always counted among its promulgators. "It 130 is of no use," says *The Times,* "for us to attempt to force upon our neighbours our several likings and dislikings. We must take things as they are. Everybody has his own little vision of religious or civil perfection. Under the evident impossibility of satisfying everybody, we agree to take our stand on equal laws and on a system as open and liberal as is possible. The result is that everybody has more liberty of action and of speaking here than anywhere else in the Old World." We come again here upon Mr. Roebuck's celebrated definition of happiness, on which I have so often commented: "I look around me and ask what is the state of England? Is not every man able to say what he likes? I ask you whether the world over, or in past history, there is anything like it? Nothing. I pray that our unrivalled happiness may last." This is the old story of our system of checks and every Englishman doing as he likes, which we have already seen to have been convenient enough so long as there were only Barbarians and the Philistines to do what they liked, but to be getting inconvenient, and 131 productive of anarchy, now that the Populace wants to do what it likes too. But for all that, I will not at once dismiss this famous doctrine, but will first quote another passage from *The Times,* applying the doctrine to a matter of which we have just been speaking,—education. "The difficulty here" (in providing a national system of education), says *The Times,* "does not reside in any removeable arrangements. It is inherent and native in the actual and inveterate state of things in this country. All these powers and personages, all these conflicting influences and varieties of character, exist, and have long existed among us; they are fighting it out, and will long continue to fight it out, without coming to that happy consummation when some one element of the British character is to destroy or to absorb all the rest." There it is; the various promptings of the natural taste for the bathos in this man and that amongst us are fighting it out; and the day will never come (and, indeed, why should we wish it to come?) when one man's particular sort of taste for the bathos shall tyrannise over another man's; nor when right reason (if that may be called an element of the 132 British character) shall absorb and rule them all. "The whole system of this country, like the constitution we boast to inherit, and are glad to uphold, is made up of established facts, prescriptive authorities, existing usages, powers that be, persons in possession, and communities or classes that have won dominion for themselves, and will hold it against all comers." Every force in the world, evidently, except the one reconciling force, right reason! Sir Thomas Bateson here, the Rev. W. Cattle on this side, Mr. Bradlaugh on that!—pull devil, pull baker! Really, presented with the mastery of style of our leading journal, the sad picture, as one gazes upon it, assumes the iron and inexorable solemnity of tragic Destiny.

After this, the milder doctrine of our other philosophical teacher, the *Daily News,* has, at first, something very attractive and assuaging. The *Daily News* begins, indeed, in appearance, to weave the iron web of necessity round us like *The Times.* "The alternative is between a man's doing what he likes and his doing what some one else, probably not one whit wiser than himself, likes." This points to the tacit compact, men- 133 tioned in my last paper, between the Barbarians and the Philistines, and into which it is hoped that the Populace will one day enter; the compact, so creditable to English honesty, that no class, if it exercise power, having only the ideas and aims of its ordinary self to give effect to, shall treat its ordinary self too seriously, or attempt to impose it on others; but shall let these others,—the Rev. W. Cattle, for instance, in his Papist-baiting, and Mr. Bradlaugh in his Hyde Park anarchy-mongering,—have their fling. But then the *Daily News* suddenly lights up the gloom of necessitarianism with bright beams of hope. "No doubt," it says, "the common reason of society ought to check the aberrations of individual eccentricity." This common reason of society looks very like our best self or right reason, to which we want to give authority, by making the action of the *State,* or nation in its collective character, the expression of it. But of this project of ours, the *Daily News,* with its subtle dialectics, makes havoc. "Make the State the organ of the common reason?"—it says. "You may make it the organ of something or other, but how can you be certain that reason will be 134 the quality which will be embodied in it?" You cannot be certain of it, undoubtedly, if you never try to bring the thing about; but the question is, the action of the State being the action of the collective nation, and the action of the collective nation carrying naturally great publicity, weight, and force of example with it, whether we should not try to put into the action of the State as much as possible of right reason, or our best self, which may, in this manner, come back to us with new force and authority, may have visibility, form, and influence, and help to confirm us, in the many moments when we are tempted to be our ordinary selves merely, in resisting our natural taste of the bathos rather than in giving way to it?

But no! says our teacher: "it is better there should be an infinite variety of experiments in human action, because, as the explorers multiply, the true track is more likely to be discovered. The common reason of society can check the aberrations of individual eccentricity only by acting on the individual reason; and it will do so in the main sufficiently, if left to this natural operation." This is what I call the specially British form of Qui- 135 etism, or a devout, but excessive, reliance on an over-ruling Providence. Providence, as the moralists are careful to tell us, generally works in human affairs by human means; so when we want to make right reason act on individual reason, our best self on our ordinary self, we seek to give it more power of doing so by giving it public recognition and authority, and embodying it, so far as we can, in the State. It seems too much to ask of Providence, that while we, on our part, leave our congenital taste for the bathos to its natural operation and its infinite variety of experiments, Providence should mysteriously guide it into the true track, and compel it to relish the sublime. At any rate, great men and great institutions have hitherto seemed necessary for producing any considerable effect of this kind. No doubt we have an infinite variety of experiments, and an ever-multiplying multitude of explorers; even in this short paper I have enumerated many: the *British Banner,* Judge Edmonds, Newman Weeks, Deborah Butler, Elderess Polly, Brother Noyes, the Rev. W. Cattle, the Licensed Victuallers, the Commercial Travellers, and I know not how many more; and the numbers of this noble army are swelling every day. But what a depth of Quietism, or rather, what an over-bold call on the direct interposition of Providence, to believe that these interesting explorers will discover the true track, or at any rate, "will do so in the main sufficiently" (whatever that may mean) if left to their natural operation; that is, by going on as they are! Philosophers say, indeed, that we learn virtue by performing acts of virtue; but to say that we shall learn virtue by performing any acts to which our natural taste for the bathos carries us, that the Rev. W. Cattle comes at his best self by Papist-baiting, or Newman Weeks and Deborah Butler at right reason by following their noses, this certainly does appear over-sanguine.

It is true, what we want is to make right reason act on individual reason, the reason of individuals; all our search for authority has that for its end and aim. The *Daily News* says, I observe, that all my argument for authority "has a non-intellectual root;" and from what I know of my own mind and its inertness, I think this so probable, that I should be inclined easily to admit it, if it were not that, in the first place, nothing of this kind, perhaps, should be admitted without examination; and, in the second, a way of accounting for this charge being made, in this particular instance, without full grounds, appears to present itself. What seems to me to account here, perhaps, for the charge, is the want of flexibility of our race, on which I have so often remarked. I mean, it being admitted that the conformity of the individual reason of the Rev. W. Cattle or Mr. Bradlaugh with right reason is our true object, and not the mere restraining them, by the strong arm of the State, from Papist-baiting or railing-breaking,— admitting this, we have so little flexibility that we cannot readily perceive that the State's restraining them from these indulgences may yet fix clearly in their minds that, to the collective nation, these indulgences appear irrational and unallowable, may make them pause and reflect, and may contribute to bringing, with time, their individual reason into harmony with right reason. But in no country, owing to the want of intellectual flexibility above mentioned, is the leaning which is our natural one, and, therefore, needs no recommending to us, so sedulously recommended, and the leaning which is not our natural one, and, therefore, does not need dispraising to us, so sedulously dispraised, as in ours. To rely on the individual being, with us, the natural leaning, we will hear of nothing but the good of relying on the individual; to act through the collective nation on the individual being not our natural leaning, we will hear nothing in recommendation of it. But the wise know that we often need to hear most of that to which we are least inclined, and even to learn to employ, in certain circumstances, that which is capable, if employed amiss, of being a danger to us.

Elsewhere this is certainly better understood than here. In a recent number of the *Westminster Review,* an able writer, but with precisely our national want of flexibility of which I have been speaking, has unearthed, I see, for our present needs, an English translation, published some years ago, of Wilhelm von Humboldt's book, *The Sphere and Duties of Government.* Humboldt's object in this book is to show that the operation of government ought to be severely limited to what directly and immediately relates to the security of person and property. Wilhelm von Humboldt, one of the most beautiful and perfect souls that have ever existed, used to say 139 that one's business in life was, first, to perfect oneself by all the means in one's power, and, secondly, to try and create in the world around one an aristocracy, the most numerous that one possibly could, of talents and characters. He saw, of course, that, in the end, everything comes to this,—that the individual must act for himself, and must be perfect in himself; and he lived in a country, Germany, where people were disposed to act too little for themselves, and to rely too much on the Government. But even thus, such was his flexibility, so little was he in bondage to a mere abstract maxim, that he saw very well that for his purpose itself, of enabling the individual to stand perfect on his own foundations and to do without the State, the action of the State would for long, long years be necessary; and soon after he wrote his book on *The Sphere and Duties of Government,* Wilhelm von Humboldt became Minister of Education in Prussia, and from his ministry all the great reforms which give the control of Prussian education to the State,—the transference of the management of public schools from their old boards of trustees to the State, the obliga- 140 tory State-examination for schools, the obligatory State-examination for schoolmasters, and the foundation of the great State University of Berlin,—take their origin. This his English reviewer says not a word of. But, writing for a people whose dangers lie, as we have seen, on the side of their unchecked and unguided individual action, whose dangers none of them lie on the side of an over-reliance on the State, he quotes just so much of Wilhelm von Humboldt's example as can flatter them in their propensities, and do them no good; and just what might make them think, and be of use to them, he leaves on one side. This precisely recalls the manner, it will be observed, in which we have seen that our royal and noble personages proceed with the Licensed Victuallers.

In France the action of the State on individuals is yet more preponderant than in Germany; and the need which friends of human perfection feel to enable the individual to stand perfect on his own foundations is all the stronger. But what says one of the staunchest of these friends, Monsieur Renan, on State action, and even State action in that very sphere where in France it is most excessive, the sphere of education? Here are his words:—"A liberal believes in liberty, and liberty signifies the non-intervention of the State. *But such an ideal is still a long way off from us, and the very means to remove it to an indefinite distance would be precisely the State's withdrawing its action too soon.*" And this, he adds, is even truer of education than of any other department of public affairs.

141

We see, then, how indispensable to that human perfection which we seek is, in the opinion of good judges, some public recognition and establishment of our best self, or right reason. We see how our habits and practice oppose themselves to such a recognition, and the many inconveniences which we therefore suffer. But now let us try to go a little deeper, and to find, beneath our actual habits and practice, the very ground and cause out of which they spring.

142 ## IV. [Hebraism and Hellenism]

This fundamental ground is our preference of doing to thinking. Now this preference is a main element in our nature, and as we study it we find ourselves opening up a number of large questions on every side.

Let me go back for a moment to what I have already quoted from Bishop Wilson:—"First, never go against the best light you have; secondly, take care that your light be not darkness." I said we show, as a nation, laudable energy and persistence in walking according to the best light we have, but are not quite careful enough, perhaps, to see that our light be not darkness. This is only another version of the old story that energy is our strong point and favourable characteristic, rather than intelligence. But we may give to this idea a more general form still, in which it will have a yet larger range of application. We may regard this energy driving at practice, this paramount sense of the obligation of duty, self-control, and work, this earnestness in going manfully with the best light we have as one force. And we may regard the intelligence driving at those ideas which are, after all, the basis of right practice, the ardent sense for all

143

the new and changing combinations of them which man's development brings with it, the indomitable impulse to know and adjust them perfectly, as another force. And these two forces we may regard as in some sense rivals,—rivals not by the necessity of their own nature, but as exhibited in man and his history,—and rivals dividing the empire of the world between them. And to give these forces names from the two races of men who have supplied the most signal and splendid manifestations of them, we may call them respectively the forces of Hebraism and Hellenism. Hebraism and Hellenism,—between these two points of influence moves our world. At one time it feels more powerfully the attraction of one of them, at another time of the other; and it ought to be, though it never is, evenly and happily balanced between them.

The final aim of both Hellenism and Hebraism, as of all great spiritual disciplines, is no doubt the same: man's perfection or salvation. The very language which they both of them use in schooling us to reach this aim is   144
often identical. Even when their language indicates by variation,— sometimes a broad variation, often a but slight and subtle variation,—the different courses of thought which are uppermost in each discipline, even then the unity of the final end and aim is still apparent. To employ the actual words of that discipline with which we ourselves are all of us most familiar, and the words of which, therefore, come most home to us, that final end and aim is "that we might be partakers of the divine nature." These are the words of a Hebrew apostle, but of Hellenism and Hebraism alike this is, I say, the aim. When the two are confronted, as they very often are confronted, it is nearly always with what I may call a rhetorical purpose; the speaker's whole design is to exalt and enthrone one of the two, and he uses the other only as a foil and to enable him the better to give effect to his purpose. Obviously, with us, it is usually Hellenism which is thus reduced to minister to the triumph of Hebraism. There is a sermon on Greece and the Greek spirit by a man never to be mentioned without interest and respect, Frederick Robertson, in which this rhetorical use of Greece and the Greek spirit, and the inadequate exhibition of them neces-   145
sarily consequent upon this, is almost ludicrous, and would be censurable if it were not to be explained by the exigences of a sermon. On the other hand, Heinrich Heine, and other writers of his sort, give us the spectacle of the tables completely turned, and of Hebraism brought in just as a foil and contrast to Hellenism, and to make the superiority of Hellenism more manifest. In both these cases there is injustice and misrepresentation. The aim and end of both Hebraism and Hellenism is, as I have said, one and the same, and this aim and end is august and admirable.

Still, they pursue this aim by very different courses. The uppermost idea with Hellenism is to see things as they really are; the uppermost idea with Hebraism is conduct and obedience. Nothing can do away with this ineffaceable difference; the Greek quarrel with the body and its desires is, that they hinder right thinking, the Hebrew quarrel with them is, that they hinder right acting. "He that keepeth the law, happy is he;" "There is nothing sweeter than to take heed unto the commandments of the Lord;"—that is the Hebrew notion of felicity; and, pursued with passion and tenacity, this notion would not let the Hebrew rest till, as is well known, he had, at last, got out of the law a network of prescriptions to enwrap his whole life, to govern every moment of it, every impulse, every action. The Greek notion of felicity, on the other hand, is perfectly conveyed in these words of a great French moralist: *"C'est le bonheur des hommes"*—when? when they abhor that which is evil?—no; when they exercise themselves in the law of the Lord day and night?—no; when they die daily?—no; when they walk about the New Jerusalem with palms in their hands?—no; but when they think aright, when their thought hits,— *"quand ils pensent juste."* At the bottom of both the Greek and the Hebrew notion is the desire, native in man, for reason and the will of God, the feeling after the universal order,—in a word, the love of God. But, while Hebraism seizes upon certain plain, capital intimations of the universal order, and rivets itself, one may say, with unequalled grandeur of earnestness and intensity on the study and observance of them, the bent of Hellenism is to follow, with flexible activity, the whole play of the universal order, to be apprehensive of missing any part of it, of sacrificing one part to another, to slip away from resting in this or that intimation of it, however capital. An unclouded clearness of mind, an unimpeded play of thought, is what this bent drives at. The governing idea of Hellenism is *spontaneity of consciousness;* that of Hebraism, *strictness of conscience.*

Christianity changed nothing in this essential bent of Hebraism to set doing above knowing. Self-conquest, self-devotion, the following not our own individual will, but the will of God, *obedience,* is the fundamental idea of this form, also, of the discipline to which we have attached the general name of Hebraism. Only, as the old law and the network of prescriptions with which it enveloped human life were evidently a motive power not driving and searching enough to produce the result aimed at,— patient continuance in well doing, self-conquest,—Christianity substituted for them boundless devotion to that inspiring and affecting pattern of self-conquest offered by Christ; and by the new motive power, of which the essence was this, though the love and admiration of Christian churches

have for centuries been employed in varying, amplifying, and adorning   148
the plain description of it, Christianity, as St. Paul truly says, "establishes
the law," and in the strength of the ampler power which she has thus
supplied to fulfil it, has accomplished the miracles, which we all see, of
her history.

So long as we do not forget that both Hellenism and Hebraism are
profound and admirable manifestations of man's life, tendencies, and
powers, and that both of them aim at a like final result, we can hardly insist
too strongly on the divergence of line and of operation with which they
proceed. It is a divergence so great that it most truly, as the prophet
Zechariah says, "has raised up thy sons, O Zion, against thy sons, O
Greece!" The difference whether it is by doing or by knowing that we set
most store, and the practical consequences which follow from this difference, leave their mark on all the history of our race and of its development.
Language may be abundantly quoted from both Hellenism and Hebraism
to make it seem that one follows the same current as the other towards the
same goal. They are, truly, borne towards the same goal; but the currents
which bear them are infinitely different. It is true, Solomon will praise
knowing: "Understanding is a well-spring of life unto him that hath it."   149
And in the New Testament, again, Christ is a "light," and "truth makes us
free." It is true, Aristotle will undervalue knowing: "In what concerns
virtue," says he, "three things are necessary,—knowledge, deliberate
will, and perseverance; but, whereas the two last are all important, the first
is a matter of little importance." It is true that with the same impatience
with which St. James enjoins a man to be not a forgetful hearer, but a *doer
of the work,* Epictetus exhorts us to *do* what we have demonstrated to
ourselves we ought to do; or he taunts us with futility, for being armed at
all points to prove that lying is wrong, yet all the time continuing to lie. It
is true, Plato, in words which are almost the words of the New Testament
or the Imitation, calls life a learning to die. But underneath the superficial
agreement the fundamental divergence still subsists. The understanding
of Solomon is "the walking in the way of the commandments;" this is "the
way of peace," and it is of this that blessedness comes. In the New
Testament, the truth which gives us the peace of God and makes us free, is
the love of Christ constraining us to crucify, as he did, and with a like   150
purpose of moral regeneration, the flesh with its affections and lusts, and
thus establishing, as we have seen, the law. To St. Paul it appears possible
to "hold the truth in unrighteousness," which is just what Socrates judged
impossible. The moral virtues, on the other hand, are with Aristotle but
the porch and access to the intellectual, and with these last is blessedness.

That partaking of the divine life, which both Hellenism and Hebraism, as we have said, fix as their crowning aim, Plato expressly denies to the man of practical virtue merely, of self-conquest with any other motive than that of perfect intellectual vision; he reserves it for the lover of pure knowledge, of seeing things as they really are, the φιλομαθής.

Both Hellenism and Hebraism arise out of the wants of human nature, and address themselves to satisfying those wants. But their methods are so different, they lay stress on such different points, and call into being by their respective disciplines such different activities, that the face which human nature presents when it passes from the hands of one of them to those of the other, is no longer the same. To get rid of one's ignorance, to see things as they are, and by seeing them as they are to see them in their beauty, is the simple and attractive ideal which Hellenism holds out before human nature; and from the simplicity and charm of this ideal, Hellenism, and human life in the hands of Hellenism, is invested with a kind of aerial ease, clearness, and radiancy; they are full of what we call sweetness and light. Difficulties are kept out of view, and the beauty and rationalness of the ideal have all our thoughts. "The best man is he who most tries to perfect himself, and the happiest man is he who most feels that he *is* perfecting himself,"—this account of the matter by Socrates, the true Socrates of the *Memorabilia,* has something so simple, spontaneous, and unsophisticated about it, that it seems to fill us with clearness and hope when we hear it. But there is a saying which I have heard attributed to Mr. Carlyle about Socrates,—a very happy saying, whether it is really Mr. Carlyle's or not,—which excellently marks the essential point in which Hebraism differs from Hellenism. *"Socrates," this saying goes, "is terribly *at ease in Zion.*" Hebraism,—and here is the source of its wonderful strength,—has always been severely preoccupied with an awful sense of the impossibility of being at ease in Zion; of the difficulties which oppose themselves to man's pursuit or attainment of that perfection of which Socrates talks so hopefully, and, as from this point of view one might almost say, so glibly. It is all very well to talk of getting rid of one's ignorance, of seeing things in their reality, seeing them in their beauty; but how is this to be done when there is something which thwarts and spoils all our efforts? This something is *sin;* and the space which sin fills in Hebraism, as compared with Hellenism, is indeed prodigious. This obstacle to perfection fills the whole scene, and perfection appears remote and rising away from earth, in the background. Under the name of sin, the difficulties of knowing oneself and conquering oneself which impede man's passage to perfection, become, for Hebraism, a positive, active entity

hostile to man, a mysterious power which I heard Dr. Pusey the other day, in one of his impressive sermons, compare to a hideous hunchback seated on our shoulders, and which it is the main business of our lives to hate and oppose. The discipline of the Old Testament may be summed up as a   153
discipline teaching us to abhor and flee from sin; the discipline of the New Testament, as a discipline teaching us to die to it. As Hellenism speaks of thinking clearly, seeing things in their essence and beauty, as a grand and precious feat for man to achieve, so Hebraism speaks of becoming conscious of sin, of awakening to a sense of sin, as a feat of this kind. It is obvious to what wide divergence these differing tendencies, actively followed, must lead. As one passes and repasses from Hellenism to Hebraism, from Plato to St. Paul, one feels inclined to rub one's eyes and ask oneself whether man is indeed a gentle and simple being, showing the traces of a noble and divine nature; or an unhappy chained captive, labouring with groanings that cannot be uttered to free himself from the body of this death.

Apparently it was the Hellenic conception of human nature which was unsound, for the world could not live by it. Absolutely to call it unsound, however, is to fall into the common error of its Hebraising enemies; but it was unsound at that particular moment of man's development, it was premature. The indispensable basis of conduct and self-control, the plat-   154
form upon which alone the perfection aimed at by Greece can come into bloom, was not to be reached by our race so easily; centuries of probation and discipline were needed to bring us to it. Therefore the bright promise of Hellenism faded, and Hebraism ruled the world. Then was seen that astonishing spectacle, so well marked by the often quoted words of the prophet Zechariah, when men of all languages of the nations took hold of the skirt of him that was a Jew, saying:—*"We will go with you, for we have heard that God is with you."* And the Hebraism which thus received and ruled a world all gone out of the way and altogether become unprofitable, was, and could not but be, the later, the more spiritual, the more attractive development of Hebraism. It was Christianity; that is to say, Hebraism aiming at self-conquest and rescue from the thrall of vile affections, not by obedience to the letter of a law, but by conformity to the image of a self-sacrificing example. To a world stricken with moral enervation Christianity offered its spectacle of an inspired self-sacrifice; to men who refused themselves nothing, it showed one who refused himself everything:—   155
"my Saviour banished joy!" says George Herbert. When the *alma Venus,* the life-giving and joy-giving power of nature, so fondly cherished by the Pagan world, could not save her followers from self-dissatisfaction and

ennui, the severe words of the apostle came bracingly and refreshingly: "Let no man deceive you with vain words, for because of these things cometh the wrath of God upon the children of disobedience." Throughout age after age, and generation after generation, our race, or all that part of our race which was most living and progressive, was *baptized into a death;* and endeavoured, by suffering in the flesh, to cease from sin. Of this endeavour, the animating labours and afflictions of early Christianity, the touching asceticism of mediæval Christianity, are the great historical manifestations. Literary monuments of it, each, in its own way, incomparable, remain in the Epistles of St. Paul, in St. Augustine's Confessions, and in the two original and simplest books of the Imitation.†

156   Of two disciplines laying their main stress, the one, on clear intelligence, the other, on firm obedience; the one, on comprehensively knowing the grounds of one's duty, the other, on diligently practising it; the one on taking all possible care (to use Bishop Wilson's words again) that the light we have be not darkness, the other, that according to the best light we have we diligently walk,—the priority naturally belongs to that discipline which braces man's moral powers, and founds for him an indispensable basis of character. And, therefore, it is justly said of the Jewish people, who were charged with setting powerfully forth that side of the divine order to which the words *conscience* and *self-conquest* point, that they were "entrusted with the oracles of God;" as it is justly said of Christianity, which followed Judaism and which set forth this side with a much deeper effectiveness and a much wider influence, that the wisdom of the old Pagan world was foolishness compared to it. No words of devotion and admiration can be too strong to render thanks to these beneficent forces which have so borne forward humanity in its appointed work of coming to

157   the knowledge and possession of itself; above all, in those great moments when their action was the wholesomest and the most necessary.

But the evolution of these forces, separately and in themselves, is not the whole evolution of humanity,—their single history is not the whole history of man; whereas their admirers are always apt to make it stand for the whole history. Hebraism and Hellenism are, neither of them, the *law* of human development, as their admirers are prone to make them; they are, each of them, *contributions* to human development,—august contributions, invaluable contributions; and each showing itself to us more august, more invaluable, more preponderant over the other, according to the moment in which we take them, and the relation in which we stand to

---

† The two first books.

them. The nations of our modern world, children of that immense and salutary movement which broke up the Pagan world, inevitably stand to Hellenism in a relation which dwarfs it, and to Hebraism in a relation which magnifies it. They are inevitably prone to take Hebraism as the law of human development, and not as simply a contribution to it, however precious. And yet the lesson must perforce be learned, that the human 158 spirit is wider than the most priceless of the forces which bear it onward, and that to the whole development of man Hebraism itself is, like Hellenism, but a contribution.

Perhaps we may help ourselves to see this clearer by an illustration drawn from the treatment of a single great idea which has profoundly engaged the human spirit, and has given it eminent opportunities for showing its nobleness and energy. It surely must be perceived that the idea of the immortality of the soul, as this idea rises in its generality before the human spirit, is something grander, truer, and more satisfying, than it is in the particular forms by which St. Paul, in the famous fifteenth chapter of the Epistle to the Corinthians, and Plato, in the *Phœdo,* endeavour to develope and establish it. Surely we cannot but feel, that the argumentation with which the Hebrew apostle goes about to expound this great idea is, after all, confused and inconclusive; and that the reasoning, drawn from analogies of likeness and equality, which is employed upon it by the Greek philosopher, is over-subtle and sterile? Above and beyond the inadequate solutions which Hebraism and Hellenism here attempt, extends the immense and august problem itself, and the human spirit which 159 gave birth to it. And this single illustration may suggest to us how the same thing happens in other cases also.

But meanwhile, by alternations of Hebraism and Hellenism, of man's intellectual and moral impulses, of the effort to see things as they really are, and the effort to win peace by self-conquest, the human spirit proceeds, and each of these two forces has its appointed hours of culmination and seasons of rule. As the great movement of Christianity was a triumph of Hebraism and man's moral impulses, so the great movement which goes by the name of the Renascence† was an uprising and re-instatement of man's intellectual impulses and of Hellenism. We in England, the devoted children of Protestantism, chiefly know the Renascence by its

---

† I have ventured to give to the foreign word *Renaissance,* destined to become of more common use amongst us as the movement which it denotes comes, as it will come, increasingly to interest us, an English form.

subordinate and secondary side of the Reformation. The Reformation has been often called a Hebraising revival, a return to the ardour and sincereness of primitive Christianity. No one, however, can study the development of Protestantism and of Protestant churches without feeling that into the Reformation too,—Hebraising child of the Renascence and offspring of its fervour, rather than its intelligence, as it undoubtedly was,—the subtle Hellenic leaven of the Renascence found its way, and that the exact respective parts in the Reformation, of Hebraism and of Hellenism, are not easy to separate. But what we may with truth say is, that all which Protestantism was to itself clearly conscious of, all which it succeeded in clearly setting forth in words, had the characters of Hebraism rather than of Hellenism. The Reformation was strong, in that it was an earnest return to the Bible and to doing from the heart the will of God as there written; it was weak, in that it never consciously grasped or applied the central idea of the Renascence,—the Hellenic idea of pursuing, in all lines of activity, the law and science, to use Plato's words, of things as they really are. Whatever direct superiority, therefore, Protestantism had over Catholicism was a moral superiority, a superiority arising out of its greater sincerity and earnestness,—at the moment of its apparition at any rate,—in dealing with the heart and conscience; its pretensions to an intellectual superiority are in general quite illusory. For Hellenism, for the thinking side in man as distinguished from the acting side, the attitude of mind of Protestantism towards the Bible in no respect differs from the attitude of mind of Catholicism towards the Church. The mental habit of him who imagines that Balaam's ass spoke, in no respect differs from the mental habit of him who imagines that a Madonna of wood or stone winked; and the one, who says that God's Church makes him believe what he believes, and the other, who says that God's Word makes him believe what he believes, are for the philosopher perfectly alike in not really and truly knowing, when they say *God's Church* and *God's Word*, what it is they say, or whereof they affirm.

In the sixteenth century, therefore, Hellenism re-entered the world, and again stood in presence of Hebraism,—a Hebraism renewed and purged. Now, it has not been enough observed, how, in the seventeenth century, a fate befell Hellenism in some respects analogous to that which befell it at the commencement of our era. The Renascence, that great reawakening of Hellenism, that irresistible return of humanity to nature and to seeing things as they are, which in art, in literature, and in physics, produced such splendid fruits, had, like the anterior Hellenism of the Pagan world, a side of moral weakness, and of relaxation or insensibility of the moral fibre, which in Italy showed itself with the most startling plainness, but which in France, England, and other countries was very apparent too. Again this loss of spiritual balance, this exclusive preponderance given to man's perceiving and knowing side, this unnatural defect of his feeling and acting side, provoked a reaction. Let us trace that reaction where it most nearly concerns us.

Science has now made visible to everybody the great and pregnant elements of difference which lie in race, and in how signal a manner they make the genius and history of an *Indo-European people vary from those of a Semitic people. Hellenism is of Indo-European growth, Hebraism is of Semitic growth; and we English, a nation of Indo-European stock, seem to belong naturally to the movement of Hellenism. But nothing more strongly marks the essential unity of man than the affinities we can per- 163 ceive, in this point or that, between members of one family of peoples and members of another; and no affinity of this kind is more strongly marked than that likeness in the strength and prominence of the moral fibre, which, notwithstanding immense elements of difference, knits in some special sort the genius and history of us English, and of our American descendants across the Atlantic, to the genius and history of the Hebrew people. Puritanism, which has been so great a power in the English nation, and in the strongest part of the English nation, was originally the reaction, in the seventeenth century, of the conscience and moral sense of our race, against the moral indifference and lax rule of conduct which in the sixteenth century came in with the Renascence. It was a reaction of Hebraism against Hellenism; and it powerfully manifested itself, as was natural, in a people with much of what we call a Hebraising turn, with a signal affinity for the bent which was the master-bent of Hebrew life. Eminently Indo-European by its *humour,* by the power it shows, through this gift, of imaginatively acknowledging the multiform aspects of the problem of life, and of thus getting itself unfixed from its own over-certainty, of smil- 164 ing at its own over-tenacity, our race has yet (and a great part of its strength lies here), in matters of practical life and moral conduct, a strong share of the assuredness, the tenacity, the intensity of the Hebrews. This turn manifested itself in Puritanism, and has had a great part in shaping our history for the last two hundred years. Undoubtedly it checked and changed amongst us that movement of the Renascence which we see producing in the reign of Elizabeth such wonderful fruits; undoubtedly it stopped the prominent rule and direct development of that order of ideas which we call by the name of Hellenism, and gave the first rank to a different order of ideas. Apparently, too, as we said of the former defeat of

Hellenism, if Hellenism was defeated, this shows that Hellenism was imperfect, and that its ascendency at that moment would not have been for the world's good.

Yet there is a very important difference between the defeat inflicted on Hellenism by Christianity eighteen hundred years ago, and the check given to the Renascence by Puritanism. The greatness of the difference is well measured by the difference in force, beauty, significance and useful-165 ness, between primitive Christianity and Protestantism. Eighteen hundred years ago it was altogether the hour of Hebraism; primitive Christianity was legitimately and truly the ascendent force in the world at that time, and the way of mankind's progress lay through its full development. Another hour in man's development began in the fifteenth century, and the main road of his progress then lay for a time through Hellenism. Puritan- ism was no longer the central current of the world's progress, it was a side stream crossing the central current and checking it. The cross and the check may have been necessary and salutary, but that does not do away with the essential difference between the main stream of man's advance and a cross or side stream. For more than two hundred years the main stream of man's advance has moved towards knowing himself and the world, seeing things as they are, spontaneity of consciousness; the main impulse of a great part, and that the strongest part, of our nation, has been towards strictness of conscience. They have made the secondary the prin- cipal at the wrong moment, and the principal they have at the wrong 166 moment treated as secondary. This contravention of the natural order has produced, as such contravention always must produce, a certain confusion and false movement, of which we are now beginning to feel, in almost every direction, the inconvenience. In all directions our habitual courses of action seem to be losing efficaciousness, credit, and control, both with others and even with ourselves; everywhere we see the beginnings of confusion, and we want a clue to some sound order and authority. This we can only get by going back upon the actual instincts and forces which rule our life, seeing them as they really are, connecting them with other in- stincts and forces, and enlarging our whole view and rule of life.

V. [Porro Unum Est Necessarium]

The matter here opened is so large, and the trains of thought to which it gives rise are so manifold, that we must be careful to limit ourselves scrupulously to what has a direct bearing upon our actual discussion. We 167 have found that at the bottom of our present unsettled state, so full of the

seeds of trouble, lies the notion of its being the prime right and happiness, for each of us, to affirm himself, and his ordinary self; to be doing, and to be doing freely and as he likes. We have found at the bottom of it the disbelief in right reason as a lawful authority. It was easy to show from our practice and current history that this is so; but it was impossible to show why it is so without taking a somewhat wider sweep and going into things a little more deeply. Why, in fact, should good, well-meaning, energetic, sensible people, like the bulk of our countrymen, come to have such light belief in right reason, and such an exaggerated value for their own independent doing, however crude? The answer is: because of an exclusive and excessive development in them, without due allowance for time, place, and circumstance, of that side of human nature, and that group of human forces, to which we have given the general name of Hebraism. Because they have thought their real and only important homage was owed to a power concerned with their obedience rather than with their intelligence, a power interested in the moral side of their nature almost exclusively. Thus they have been led to regard in themselves, as the one   168
thing needful, *strictness of conscience,* the staunch adherence to some fixed law of doing we have got already, instead of *spontaneity of consciousness,* which tends continually to enlarge our whole law of doing. They have fancied themselves to have in their religion a sufficient basis for the whole of their life fixed and certain for ever, a full law of conduct and a full law of thought, so far as thought is needed, as well; whereas what they really have is a law of conduct, a law of unexampled power for enabling them to war against the law of sin in their members and not to serve it in the lusts thereof. The book which contains this invaluable law they call the Word of God, and attribute to it, as I have said, and as, indeed, is perfectly well known, a reach and sufficiency co-extensive with all the wants of human nature. This might, no doubt, be so, if humanity were not the composite thing it is, if it had only, or in quite overpowering eminence, a moral side, and the group of instincts and powers which we call moral. But it has besides, and in notable eminence, an intellectual side, and the group of instincts and powers which we call intellectual. No doubt, mankind makes in general its progress in a fashion which gives at one time full   169
swing to one of these groups of instincts, at another time to the other; and man's faculties are so intertwined, that when his moral side, and the current of force which we call Hebraism, is uppermost, this side will manage somehow to provide, or appear to provide, satisfaction for his intellectual needs; and when his moral side, and the current of force which we call Hellenism, is uppermost, this, again, will provide, or appear to

provide, satisfaction for men's moral needs. But sooner or later it becomes manifest that when the two sides of humanity proceed in this fashion of alternate preponderance, and not of mutual understanding and balance, the side which is uppermost does not really provide in a satisfactory manner for the needs of the side which is undermost, and a state of confusion is, sooner or later, the result. The Hellenic half of our nature, bearing rule, makes a sort of provision for the Hebrew half, but it turns out to be an inadequate provision; and again the Hebrew half of our nature bearing rule makes a sort of provision for the Hellenic half, but this, too, turns out to be an inadequate provision. The true and smooth order of 170 humanity's development is not reached in either way. And therefore, while we willingly admit with the Christian apostle that the world by wisdom,—that is, by the isolated preponderance of its intellectual impulses,—knew not God, or the true order of things, it is yet necessary, also, to set up a sort of converse to this proposition, and to say likewise (what is equally true) that the world by Puritanism knew not God. And it is on this converse of the apostle's proposition that it is particularly needful to insist in our own country just at present.

Here, indeed, is the answer to many criticisms which have been addressed to all that we have said in praise of sweetness and light. Sweetness and light evidently have to do with the bent or side in humanity which we call Hellenic. Greek intelligence has obviously for its essence the instinct for what Plato calls the true, firm, intelligible law of things; the love of light, of seeing things as they are. Even in the natural sciences, where the Greeks had not time and means adequately to apply this instinct, and where we have gone a great deal further than they did, it is this instinct 171 which is the root of the whole matter and the ground of all our success; and this instinct the world has mainly learnt of the Greeks, inasmuch as they are humanity's most signal manifestation of it. Greek art, again, Greek beauty, have their root in the same impulse to see things as they really are, inasmuch as Greek art and beauty rest on fidelity to nature,—the *best* nature,—and on a delicate discrimination of what this best nature is. To say we work for sweetness and light, then, is only another way of saying that we work for Hellenism. But, oh! cry many people, sweetness and light are not enough; you must put strength or energy along with them, and make a kind of trinity of strength, sweetness and light, and then, perhaps, you may do some good. That is to say, we are to join Hebraism, strictness of the moral conscience, and manful walking by the best light we have, together with Hellenism, inculcate both, and rehearse the praises of both.

Or, rather, we may praise both in conjunction, but we must be careful to praise Hebraism most. "Culture," says an acute, though somewhat rigid critic, Mr. Sidgwick, "diffuses sweetness and light. I do not undervalue these blessings, but religion gives fire and strength, and the world wants fire and strength even more than sweetness and light." By religion, let me explain, Mr. Sidgwick here means particularly that Puritanism on the insufficiency of which I have been commenting and to which he says I am unfair. Now, no doubt, it is possible to be a fanatical partisan of light and the instincts which push us to it, a fanatical enemy of strictness of moral conscience and the instincts which push us to it. A fanaticism of this sort deforms and vulgarises the well-known work, in some respects so remarkable, of the late Mr. Buckle. Such a fanaticism carries its own mark with it, in lacking sweetness; and its own penalty, in that, lacking sweetness, it comes in the end to lack light too. And the Greeks,—the great exponents of humanity's bent for sweetness and light united, of its perception that the truth of things must be at the same time beauty,—singularly escaped the fanaticism which we moderns, whether we Hellenise or whether we Hebraise, are so apt to show, and arrived,—though failing, as has been said, to give adequate practical satisfaction to the claims of man's moral side,—at the idea of a comprehensive adjustment of the claims of both the sides in man, the moral as well as the intellectual, of a full estimate of both, and of a reconciliation of both; an idea which is philosophically of the greatest value, and the best of lessons for us moderns. So we ought to have no difficulty in conceding to Mr. Sidgwick that manful walking by the best light one has,—fire and strength as he calls it,—has its high value as well as culture, the endeavour to see things in their truth and beauty, the pursuit of sweetness and light. But whether at this or that time, and to this or that set of persons, one ought to insist most on the praises of fire and strength, or on the praises of sweetness and light, must depend, one would think, on the circumstances and needs of that particular time and those particular persons. And all that we have been saying, and indeed any glance at the world around us, shows that with us, with the most respectable and strongest part of us, the ruling force is now, and long has been, a Puritan force, the care for fire and strength, strictness of conscience, Hebraism, rather than the care for sweetness and light, spontaneity of consciousness, Hellenism.

Well, then, what is the good of our now rehearsing the praises of fire and strength to ourselves, who dwell too exclusively on them already? When Mr. Sidgwick says so broadly, that the world wants fire and strength even more than sweetness and light, is he not carried away by a turn from powerful generalisation? does he not forget that the world is not all of one

172

173

174

piece, and every piece with the same needs at the same time? It may be true that the Roman world at the beginning of our era, or Leo the Tenth's Court at the time of the Reformation, or French society in the eighteenth century, needed fire and strength even more than sweetness and light. But can it be said that the Barbarians who overran the empire, needed fire and strength even more than sweetness and light; or that the Puritans needed them more; or that Mr. Murphy, the Birmingham lecturer, and the Rev. W. Cattle and his friends, need them more?

The Puritan's great danger is that he imagines himself in possession of a rule telling him the *unum necessarium,* or one thing needful, and that he then remains satisfied with a very crude conception of what this rule really is and what it tells him, thinks he has now knowledge and henceforth needs only to act, and, in this dangerous state of assurance and self-satisfaction, proceeds to give full swing to a number of the instincts of his ordinary self. Some of the instincts of his ordinary self he has, by the help of his rule of life, conquered; but others which he has not conquered by this help he is so far from perceiving to need subjugation, and to be instincts of an inferior self, that he even fancies it to be his right and duty, in virtue of having conquered a limited part of himself, to give unchecked swing to the remainder. He is, I say, a victim of Hebraism, of the tendency to cultivate strictness of conscience rather than spontaneity of consciousness. And what he wants is a larger conception of human nature, showing him the number of other points at which his nature must come to its best, besides the points which he himself knows and thinks of. There is no *unum necessarium,* or one thing needful, which can free human nature from the obligation of trying to come to its best at all these points. The real *unum necessarium* for us is to come to our best at all points. Instead of our "one thing needful," justifying in us vulgarity, hideousness, ignorance, violence,—our vulgarity, hideousness, ignorance, violence, are really so many touchstones which try our one thing needful, and which prove that in the state, at any rate, in which we ourselves have it, it is not all we want. And as the force which encourages us to stand staunch and fast by the rule and ground we have is Hebraism, so the force which encourages us to go back upon this rule, and to try the very ground on which we appear to stand, is Hellenism,—a turn for giving our consciousness free play and enlarging its range. And what I say is, not that Hellenism is always for everybody more wanted than Hebraism, but that for the Rev. W. Cattle at this particular moment, and for the great majority of us his fellow-countrymen, it is more wanted.

Nothing is more striking than to observe in how many ways a limited conception of human nature, the notion of a one thing needful, a one side in us to be made uppermost, the disregard of a full and harmonious development of ourselves, tells injuriously on our thinking and acting. In the first place, our hold upon the rule or standard to which we look for our one thing needful, tends to become less and less near and vital, our conception of it more and more mechanical, and unlike the thing itself as it 177 was conceived in the mind where it originated. The dealings of Puritanism with the writings of St. Paul afford a noteworthy illustration of this. Nowhere so much as in the writings of St. Paul, and in that great apostle's greatest work, the Epistle to the Romans, has Puritanism found what seemed to furnish it with the one thing needful, and to give it canons of truth absolute and final. Now all writings, as has been already said, even the most precious writings and the most fruitful, must inevitably, from the very nature of things, be but contributions to human thought and human development, which extend wider than they do. Indeed, St. Paul, in the very Epistle of which we are speaking, shows, when he asks, "Who hath known the mind of the Lord?"—who hath known, that is, the true and divine order of things in its entirety,—that he himself acknowledges this fully. And we have already pointed out in another Epistle of St. Paul a great and vital idea of the human spirit,—the idea of the immortality of the soul,—transcending and overlapping, so to speak, the expositor's power to give it adequate definition and expression. But quite distinct from the question whether St. Paul's expression, or any man's expression, can be a 178 perfect and final expression of truth, comes the question whether we rightly seize and understand his expression as it exists. Now, perfectly to seize another man's meaning, as it stood in his own mind, is not easy; especially when the man is separated from us by such differences of race, training, time, and circumstances as St. Paul. But there are degrees of nearness in getting at a man's meaning; and though we cannot arrive quite at what St. Paul had in his mind, yet we may come near it. And who, that comes thus near it, must not feel how terms which St. Paul employs in trying to follow, with his analysis of such profound power and originality, some of the most delicate, intricate, obscure, and contradictory workings and states of the human spirit, are detached and employed by Puritanism, not in the connected and fluid way in which St. Paul employs them, and for which alone words are really meant, but in an isolated, fixed, mechanical way, as if they were talismans; and how all trace and sense of St. Paul's true movement of ideas, and sustained masterly analysis, is thus lost? Who, I say, that has watched Puritanism,—the force which so strongly 179 Hebraises, which so takes St. Paul's writings as something absolute and final, containing the one thing needful,—handle such terms as *grace, faith, election, righteousness,* but must feel, not only that these terms have for the mind of Puritanism a sense false and misleading, but also that this sense is the most monstrous, and grotesque caricature of the sense of St. Paul, and that his true meaning is by these worshippers of his words altogether lost?

Or to take another eminent example, in which not Puritanism only, but, one may say, the whole religious world, by their mechanical use of St. Paul's writings, can be shown to miss or change his real meaning. The whole religious world, one may say, use now the word *resurrection,*—a word which is so often in their thoughts and on their lips, and which they find so often in St. Paul's writings,—in one sense only. They use it to mean a rising again after the physical death of the body. Now it is quite true that St. Paul speaks of resurrection in this sense, that he tries to describe and explain it, and that he condemns those who doubt and deny it. But it is true, also, that in nine cases out of ten where St. Paul thinks and
180   speaks of resurrection, he thinks and speaks of it in a sense different from this; in the sense of a rising to a new life before the physical death of the body, and not after it. The idea on which we have already touched, the profound idea of being baptized into the death of the great exemplar of self-devotion and self-annulment, of repeating in our own person, by virtue of identification with our exemplar, his course of self-devotion and self-annulment, and of thus coming, within the limits of our present life, to a new life, in which, as in the death going before it, we are identified with our exemplar,—this is the fruitful and original conception of being *risen with Christ* which possesses the mind of St. Paul, and this is the central point around which, with such incomparable emotion and elo-quence, all his teaching moves. For him, the life after our physical death is really in the main but a consequence and continuation of the inexhaustible energy of the new life thus originated on this side the grave. This grand Pauline idea of Christian resurrection is worthily rehearsed in one of the noblest collects of the Prayer-Book, and is destined, no doubt, to fill a more and more important place in the Christianity of the future; but almost
181   as signal as is the essentialness of this characteristic idea in St. Paul's teaching, is the completeness with which the worshippers of St. Paul's words, as an absolute final expression of saving truth, have lost it, and have substituted for the apostle's living and near conception of a resur-rection now, their mechanical and remote conception of a resurrection hereafter!

In short, so fatal is the notion of possessing, even in the most precious words or standards, the one thing needful, of having in them, once for all, a full and sufficient measure of light to guide us, and of there being no duty left for us except to make our practice square exactly with them,—so fatal, I say, is this notion to the right knowledge and comprehension of the very words or standards we thus adopt, and to such strange distortions and perversions of them does it inevitably lead, that whenever we hear that commonplace which Hebraism, if we venture to inquire what a man knows, is so apt to bring out against us in disparagement of what we call culture, and in praise of a man's sticking to the one thing needful,—*he knows,* says Hebraism, *his Bible!*—whenever we hear this said, we may, without any elaborate defence of culture, content ourselves with answer- 182 ing simply: "No man, who knows nothing else, knows even his Bible."

Now the force which we have so much neglected, Hellenism, may be liable to fail in moral force and earnestness, but by the law of its nature,—the very same law which makes it sometimes deficient in intensity when intensity is required,—it opposes itself to the notion of cutting our being in two, of attributing to one part the dignity of dealing with the one thing needful, and leaving the other part to take its chance, which is the bane of Hebraism. Essential in Hellenism is the impulse to the development of the whole man, to connecting and harmonising all parts of him, perfecting all, leaving none to take their chance; because the characteristic bent of Helle-nism, as has been said, is to find the intelligible law of things, and there is no intelligible law of things, things cannot really appear intelligible, un-less they are also beautiful.† The body is not intelligible, is not seen in its true nature and as it really is, unless it is seen as beautiful; behaviour is not intelligible, does not account for itself to the mind and show the reason for its existing, unless it is beautiful. The same with discourse, the same with 183 song, the same with worship, the same with all the modes in which man proves his activity and expresses himself. To think that when one shows what is mean, or vulgar, or hideous, one can be permitted to plead that one has that within which passes show; to suppose that the possession of what

---

† The final lines of this sentence, as they stand in the first edition, do not make sense; I give them here as they are printed in the original text, with what seems to me the required emendation in brackets: "because the characteristic bent of Hellenism, as has been said, is to find the intelligible law of things, and there is no intelligible law of things, [and] things cannot really appear intelligible, unless they are also beautiful." In Wilson's recension, though based on Arnold's first edition, the corresponding passage from the third edition, much changed by Arnold, is inserted without any other explana-tion than that there is "some confusion" in the original text [Wilson 233]—ED.

benefits and satisfies one part of our being can make allowable either discourse like Mr. Murphy's and the Rev. W. Cattle's, or poetry like the hymns we all hear, or places of worship like the chapels we all see,—this it is abhorrent to the nature of Hellenism to concede. And to be, like our honoured and justly honoured Faraday, a great natural philosopher with one side of his being and a Sandemanian with the other, would to Archimedes have been impossible. It is evident to what a many-sided perfecting of man's powers and activities this demand of Hellenism for satisfaction to be given to the mind by everything which we do, is calculated to impel our race. It has its dangers, as has been fully granted; the notion of this sort of equipollency in man's modes of activity may lead to moral relaxation, what we do not make our one thing needful we may come to treat not

184   enough as if it were needful, though it is indeed very needful and at the same time very hard. Still, what side in us has not its dangers, and which of our impulses can be a talisman to give us perfection outright, and not merely a help to bring us towards it? Has not Hebraism, as we have shown, its dangers as well as Hellenism; and have we used so excessively the tendencies in ourselves to which Hellenism makes appeal, that we are now suffering from it? Are we not, on the contrary, now suffering because we have not enough used these tendencies as a help towards perfection?

    For we see whither it has brought us, the long exclusive predominance of Hebraism,—the insisting on perfection in one part of our nature and not in all; the singling out the moral side, the side of obedience and action, for such intent regard; making strictness of the moral conscience so far the principal thing, and putting off for hereafter and for another world the care for being complete at all points, the full and harmonious development of our humanity. Instead of watching and following on its ways the desire which, as Plato says, "for ever through all the universe tends towards that

185   which is lovely," we think that the world has settled its accounts with this desire, knows what this desire wants of it, and that all the impulses of our ordinary self which do not conflict with the terms of this settlement, in our narrow view of it, we may follow unrestrainedly, under the sanction of some such text as "Not slothful in business," or "Whatsoever thy hand findeth to do, do it with all thy might," or something else of the same kind. And to any of these impulses we soon come to give that same character of a mechanical, absolute law, which we give to our religion; we regard it, as we do our religion, as an object for strictness of conscience, not for spontaneity of consciousness; for unremitting adherence on its own account, not for going back upon, viewing in its connection with other things, and adjusting to a number of changing circumstances; we treat it,

in short, just as we treat our religion,—as machinery. It is in this way that the Barbarians treat their bodily exercises, the Philistines their business, Mr. Spurgeon his voluntaryism, Mr. Bright the assertion of personal liberty, Mr. Beales the right of meeting in Hyde Park. In all those cases what is needed is a freer play of consciousness upon the object of pursuit; and in all of them Hebraism, the valuing staunchness and earnestness more than this free play, the entire subordination of thinking to doing, has led to a mistaken and misleading treatment of things.

186

The newspapers a short time ago contained an account of the suicide of a Mr. Smith, secretary to some insurance company, who, it was said, "laboured under the apprehension that he would come to poverty, and that he was eternally lost." And when I read these words, it occurred to me that the poor man who came to such a mournful end was, in truth, a kind of type, by the selection of his two grand objects of concern, by their isola-tion from everything else, and their juxtaposition to one another, of all the strongest, most respectable, and most representative part of our nation. "He laboured under the apprehension that he would come to poverty, and that he was eternally lost." The whole middle-class have a conception of things,—a conception which makes us call them Philistines,—just like that of this poor man; though we are seldom, of course, shocked by seeing it take the distressing, violently morbid, and fatal turn, which it took with him. But how generally, with how many of us, are the main concerns of life limited to these two,—the concern for making money, and the concern for saving our souls! And how entirely does the narrow and mechanical conception of our secular business proceed from a narrow and mechanical conception of our religious business! What havoc do the united concep-tions make of our lives! It is because the second-named of these two master-concerns presents to us the one thing needful in so fixed, narrow, and mechanical a way, that so ignoble a fellow master-concern to it as the first-named becomes possible; and, having been once admitted, takes the same rigid and absolute character as the other. Poor Mr. Smith had sin-cerely the nobler master-concern as well as the meaner,—the concern for saving his soul (according to the narrow and mechanical conception which Puritanism has of what the salvation of the soul is), and the concern for making money. But let us remark how many people there are, especially outside the limits of the serious and conscientious middle-class to which Mr. Smith belonged, who take up with a meaner master-concern,— whether it be pleasure, or field-sports, or bodily exercises, or business, or popular agitation,—who take up with one of these exclusively, and ne-glect Mr. Smith's nobler master-concern, because of the mechanical form

187

188

which Hebraism has given to this nobler master-concern, making it stand, as we have said, as something talismanic, isolated, and all-sufficient, justifying our giving our ordinary selves free play in amusement, or business, or popular agitation, if we have made our accounts square with this master-concern; and, if we have not, rendering other things indifferent, and our ordinary self all we have to follow, and to follow with all the energy that is in us, till we do. Whereas the idea of perfection at all points, the encouraging in ourselves spontaneity of consciousness, the letting a free play of thought live and flow around all our activity, the indisposition to allow one side of our activity to stand as so all-important and all-sufficing that it makes other sides indifferent,—this bent of mind in us may not only check us in following unreservedly a mean master-concern of any kind, but may even, also, bring new life and movement into that side of us with which alone Hebraism concerns itself, and awaken a

189   healthier and less mechanical activity there. Hellenism may thus actually serve to further the designs of Hebraism.

Undoubtedly it thus served in the first days of Christianity. Christianity, as has been said, occupied itself, like Hebraism, with the moral side of man exclusively, with his moral affections and moral conduct; and so far it was but a continuation of Hebraism. But it transformed and renewed Hebraism by going back upon a fixed rule, which had become mechanical, and had thus lost its vital motive-power; by letting the thought play freely around this old rule, and perceive its inadequacy; by developing a new motive-power, which men's moral consciousness could take living hold of, and could move in sympathy with. What was this but an importation of Hellenism, as we have defined it, into Hebraism? And as St. Paul used the contradiction between the Jew's profession and practice, his shortcomings on that very side of moral affection and moral conduct which the Jew and St. Paul, both of them, regarded as all in all—("Thou that sayest a man should not steal, dost thou steal? thou that sayest a man

190   should not commit adultery, dost thou commit adultery?")—for a proof of the inadequacy of the old rule of life, in the Jew's mechanical conception of it, and tried to rescue him by making his consciousness play freely around this rule,—that is, by a, so far, Hellenic treatment of it,—even so, when we hear so much said of the growth of commercial immorality in our serious middle-class, of the melting away of habits of strict probity before the temptation to get quickly rich and to cut a figure in the world; when we see, at any rate, so much confusion of thought and of practice in this great representative class of our nation, may we not be disposed to say that this confusion shows that his new motive-power of grace and imputed righ-

teousness has become to the Puritan as mechanical, and with as ineffective a hold upon his practice, as the old motive-power of the law was to the Jew? and that the remedy is the same as that which St. Paul employed,— an importation of what we have called Hellenism into his Hebraism, a making his consciousness flow freely round his petrified rule of life and renew it? Only with this difference: that whereas St. Paul imported Hellenism within the limits of our moral part only, this part being still treated by him as all in all; and whereas he exhausted, one may say, and used to the very uttermost, the possibilities of fruitfully importing it on that side exclusively; we ought to try and import it,—guiding ourselves by the ideal of a human nature harmoniously perfect at all points,—into all the lines of our activity, and only by so doing can we rightly quicken, refresh, and renew those very instincts, now so much baffled, to which Hebraism makes appeal.

191

But if we will not be warned by the confusion visible enough at present in our thinking and acting, that we are in a false line in having developed our Hebrew side so exclusively, and our Hellenic side so feebly and at random, in loving fixed rules of action so much more than the intelligible law of things, let us listen to a remarkable testimony which the opinion of the world around us offers. All the world now sets great and increasing value on three objects which have long been very dear to us, and pursues them in its own way, or tries to pursue them. These three objects are industrial enterprise, bodily exercises, and freedom. Certainly we have, before and beyond our neighbours, given ourselves to these three things with ardent passion and with high success. And this our neighbours cannot but acknowledge; and they must needs, when they themselves turn to these things, have an eye to our example, and take something of our practice. Now, generally, when people are interested in an object of pursuit, they cannot help feeling an enthusiasm for those who have already laboured successfully at it, and for their success; not only do they study them, they also love and admire them. In this way a man who is interested in the art of war not only acquaints himself with the performance of great generals, but he has an admiration and enthusiasm for them. So, too, one who wants to be a painter or a poet cannot help loving and admiring the great painters or poets who have gone before him and shown him the way. But it is strange with how little of love, admiration, or enthusiasm, the world regards us and our freedom, our bodily exercises, and our industrial prowess, much as these things themselves are beginning to interest it. And is not the reason because we follow each of these things in a mechanical manner, as an end in and for itself, and not in reference to a general end of

192

193   human perfection? and this makes our pursuit of them uninteresting to humanity, and not what the world truly wants? It seems to them mere machinery that we can, knowingly, teach them to worship,—a mere fetish. British freedom, British industry, British muscularity, we work for each of these three things blindly, with no notion of giving each its due proportion and prominence, because we have no ideal of harmonious human perfection before our minds, to set our work in motion, and to guide it. So the rest of the world, desiring industry, or freedom, or bodily strength, yet desiring these not, as we do, absolutely, but as means to something else, imitate, indeed, of our practice what seems useful for them, but us, whose practice they imitate, they seem to entertain neither love nor admiration for. Let us observe, on the other hand, the love and enthusiasm excited by others who have laboured for these very things. Perhaps of what we call industrial enterprise it is not easy to find examples in former times; but let us consider how Greek freedom and Greek gymnastics have attracted the love and praise of mankind, who give so little

194   love and praise to ours. And what can be the reason of this difference? Surely because the Greeks pursued freedom and pursued gymnastics not mechanically, but with constant reference to some ideal of complete human perfection and happiness. And therefore, in spite of faults and failures, they interest and delight by their pursuit of them all the rest of mankind, who instinctively feel that only as things are pursued with reference to this ideal are they valuable.

    Here again, therefore, as in the confusion into which the thought and action of even the steadiest class amongst us is beginning to fall, we seem to have an admonition that we have fostered our Hebraising instincts, our preference of earnestness of doing to delicacy and flexibility of thinking, too exclusively, and have been landed by them in a mechanical and unfruitful routine. And again we seem taught that the development of our Hellenising instincts, seeking skilfully the intelligible law of things, and making a stream of fresh thought play freely about our stock notions and habits, is what is most wanted by us at present.

    Well, then, from all sides, the more we go into the matter, the currents

195   seem to converge, and together to bear us along towards culture. If we look at the world outside us we find a disquieting absence of sure authority; we discover that only in right reason can we get a source of sure authority, and culture brings us towards right reason. If we look at our own inner world, we find all manner of confusion arising out of the habits of unintelligent routine and one-sided growth, to which a too exclusive worship of fire, strength, earnestness, and action has brought us. What we

want is a fuller harmonious development of our humanity, a free play of thought upon our routine notions, spontaneity of consciousness, sweetness and light; and these are just what culture generates and fosters. Proceeding from this idea of the harmonious perfection of our humanity, and seeking to help itself up towards this perfection by knowing and spreading the best which has been reached in the world—an object not to be gained without books and reading—culture has got its name touched, in the fancies of men, with a sort of air of bookishness and pedantry, cast upon it from the follies of the many bookmen who forget the end in the means, and use their books with no real aim at perfection. We will not stickle for a name, and the name of culture one might easily give up, if 196 only those who decry the frivolous and pedantic sort of culture, but wish at bottom for the same things as we do, would be careful on their part, not, in disparaging and discrediting the false culture, to unwittingly disparage and discredit, among a people with little natural reverence for it, the true also. But what we are concerned for is the thing, not the name; and the thing, call it by what name we will, is simply the enabling ourselves, whether by reading, observing, or thinking, to come as near as we can to the firm intelligible law of things, and thus to get a basis for a less confused action and a more complete perfection than we have at present.

And now, therefore, when we are accused of preaching up a spirit of cultivated inaction, of provoking the earnest lovers of action, of refusing to lend a hand at uprooting certain definite evils, of despairing to find any lasting truth to minister to the diseased spirit of our time, we shall not be so much confounded and embarrassed what to answer for ourselves. We shall say boldly that we do not at all despair of finding some lasting truth to minister to the diseased spirit of our time; but that we have discovered the 197 best way of finding this to be, not so much by lending a hand to our friends and countrymen in their actual operations for the removal of certain definite evils, but rather in getting our friends and countrymen to seek culture, to let their consciousness play freely round their present operations and the stock notions on which they are founded, show what these are like, and how related to the intelligible law of things, and auxiliary to true human perfection.

VI. [Our Liberal Practitioners]

But an unpretending writer, without a philosophy based on interdependent, subordinate, and coherent principles, must not presume to indulge himself too much in generalities, but he must keep close to the level ground of common fact, the only safe ground for understandings without a scientific equipment. Therefore I am bound to take, before concluding, some of the practical operations in which my friends and countrymen are at this moment engaged, and to make these, if I can, show the truth of what I have advanced. Probably I could hardly give a greater proof of my confessed inexpertness in reasoning and arguing, than by taking, for my first example of an operation of this kind, the proceedings for the disestablishment of the Irish Church, which we are now witnessing. It seems so clear that this is surely one of those operations for the uprooting of a certain definite evil in which one's Liberal friends engage, and have a right to complain and to get impatient and to reproach one with delicate Conservative scepticism and cultivated inaction if one does not lend a hand to help them. This does, indeed, seem evident; and yet this operation comes so prominently before us just at this moment,—it so challenges everybody's regard,—that one seems cowardly in blinking it. So let us venture to try and see whether this conspicuous operation is one of those round which we need to let our consciousness play freely and reveal what manner of spirit we are of in doing it; or whether it is one which by no means admits the application of this doctrine of ours, and one to which we ought to lend a hand immediately.

Now it seems plain that the present Church establishment in Ireland is contrary to reason and justice, in so far as the Church of a very small minority of the people there takes for itself all the Church property of the Irish people. And one would think, that property assigned for the purpose of providing for a people's religious worship when that worship was one, the State should, when that worship is split into several forms, apportion between those several forms, with due regard to circumstances, taking account only of great differences, which are likely to be lasting, and of considerable communions, which are likely to represent profound and widespread religious characteristics; and overlooking petty differences, which have no serious reason for lasting, and inconsiderable communions, which can hardly be taken to express any broad and necessary religious lineaments of our common nature. This is just in accordance with that maxim about the State which we have more than once used: *The State is of the religion of all its citizens, without the fanaticism of any of them.* Those who deny this, either think so poorly of the State that they do not like to see religion condescend to touch the State, or they think so poorly of religion that they do not like to see the State condescend to touch religion; but no good statesman will easily think thus unworthily either of the State or of religion, and our statesmen of both parties were inclined,

one may say, to follow the natural line of the State's duty, and to make in Ireland some fair apportionment of Church property between large and radically divided religious communions in that country. But then it was discovered that in Great Britain the national mind, as it is called, is grown averse to endowments for religion and will make no new ones; and though this in itself looks general and solemn enough, yet there were found political philosophers, like Mr. Baxter and Mr. Charles Buxton, to give it a look of more generality and more solemnity still, and to elevate, by their dexterous command of powerful and beautiful language, this supposed edict of the British national mind into a sort of formula for expressing a great law of religious transition and progress for all the world. But we, who, having no coherent philosophy, must not let ourselves philosophise, only see that the English and Scotch Nonconformists have a great horror of establishments and endowments for religion, which, they assert, were   201
forbidden by Christ when he said: "My kingdom is not of this world;" and that the Nonconformists will be delighted to aid statesmen in disestablishing any church, but will suffer none to be established or endowed if they can help it. Then we see that the Nonconformists make the strength of the Liberal majority in the House of Commons, and that, therefore, the leading Liberal statesmen, to get the support of the Nonconformists, forsake the notion of fairly apportioning Church property in Ireland among the chief religious communions, declare that the national mind has decided against new endowments, and propose simply to disestablish and disendow the present establishment in Ireland without establishing or endowing any other. The actual power, in short, by virtue of which the Liberal party in the House of Commons is now trying to disestablish the Irish Church, is not the power of reason and justice, it is the power of the Nonconformists' antipathy to Church establishments. Clearly it is this; because Liberal statesmen, relying on the power of reason and justice to help them, proposed something quite different from what they now propose; and they proposed what they now propose, and talked of the decision of the national   202
mind, because they had to rely on the English and Scotch Nonconformists. And clearly the Nonconformists are actuated by antipathy to establishments, not by antipathy to the injustice and irrationality of the present appropriation of Church property in Ireland; because Mr. Spurgeon, in his eloquent and memorable letter, expressly avowed that he would sooner leave things as they are in Ireland, that is, he would sooner let the injustice and irrationality of the present appropriation continue, than do anything to set up the Roman image, that is, than give the Catholics their fair and reasonable share of Church property. Most indisputably, therefore, we

may affirm that the real moving power by which the Liberal party are now operating the overthrow of the Irish establishment is the antipathy of the Nonconformists to Church establishments, and not the sense of reason or justice, except so far as reason and justice may be contained in this antipathy. And thus the matter stands at present.

Now surely we must all see many inconveniences in performing the operation of uprooting this evil, the Irish Church establishment, in this particular way. As was said about industry and freedom and gymnastics, we shall never awaken love and gratitude by this mode of operation; for it is pursued, not in view of reason and justice and human perfection and all that enkindles the enthusiasm of men, but it is pursued in view of a certain stock notion, or fetish, of the Nonconformists, which proscribes Church establishments. And yet, evidently, one of the main benefits to be got by operating on the Irish Church is to win the affections of the Irish people. Besides this, an operation performed in virtue of a mechanical rule, or fetish, like the supposed decision of the English national mind against new endowments, does not easily inspire respect in its adversaries, and make their opposition feeble and hardly to be persisted in, as an operation evidently done in virtue of reason and justice might. For reason and justice have in them something persuasive and irresistible; but a fetish or mechanical maxim, like this of the Nonconformists, has in it nothing at all to conciliate either the affections or the understanding; nay, it provokes the counter-employment of other fetishes or mechanical maxims on the opposite side, by which the confusion and hostility already prevalent are heightened. Only in this way can be explained the apparition of such fetishes as are beginning to be set up on the Conservative side against the fetish of the Nonconformists:—*The Constitution in danger! The bulwarks of British freedom menaced! The lamp of the Reformation put out! No Popery!*—and so on. To elevate these against an operation relying on reason and justice to back it is not so easy, or so tempting to human infirmity, as to elevate them against an operation relying on the Nonconformists' antipathy to Church establishments to back it; for after all, *No Popery!* is a rallying cry which touches the human spirit quite as vitally as *No Church establishments!*—that is to say, neither the one nor the other, in themselves, touch the human spirit vitally at all.

Ought the believers in action, then, to be so impatient with us, if we say, that even for the sake of this operation of theirs itself and its satisfactory accomplishment, it is more important to make our consciousness play freely round the stock notion or habit on which their operation relies for aid, than to lend a hand to it straight away? Clearly they ought not; because nothing is so effectual for operating as reason and justice, and a free play of thought will either disengage the reason and justice lying hid in the Nonconformist fetish, and make them effectual, or else it will help to get this fetish out of the way, and to let statesmen go freely where reason and justice take them.

So, suppose we take this absolute rule, this mechanical maxim of Mr. Spurgeon and the Nonconformists, that Church establishments are bad things because Christ said: "My kingdom is not of this world." Suppose we try and make our consciousness bathe and float this piece of petrifaction,—for such it now is,—and bring it within the stream of the vital movement of our thought, and into relation with the whole intelligible law of things. An enemy and a disputant might probably say that much machinery which Nonconformists themselves employ, the Liberation Society which exists already, and the *Nonconformist Union which Mr. Spurgeon desires to see existing, come within the scope of Christ's words as well as Church establishments. This, however, is merely a negative and contentious way of dealing with the Nonconformist maxim; whereas what 206 we desire is to bring this maxim within the positive and vital movement of our thought. We say, therefore, that Christ's words mean that his religion is a force of inward persuasion acting on the soul, and not a force of outward constraint acting on the body; and if the Nonconformist maxim against Church establishments and Church endowments has warrant given to it from what Christ thus meant, then their maxim is good, even though their own practice in the matter of the Liberation Society may be at variance with it.

And here we cannot but remember what we have formerly said about religion, Miss Cobbe, and the British College of Health in the New Road. In religion there are two parts, the part of thought and speculation, and the part of worship and devotion. Christ certainly meant his religion, as a force of inward persuasion acting on the soul, to employ both parts as perfectly as possible. Now thought and speculation is eminently an individual matter, and worship and devotion is eminently a collective matter. It does not help me to think a thing more clearly that thousands of other people are thinking the same; but it does help me to worship with more 207 emotion that thousands of other people are worshipping with me. The consecration of common consent, antiquity, public establishment, long-used rites, national edifices, is everything for religious worship. "Just what makes worship impressive," says Joubert, "is its publicity, its external manifestation, its sound, its splendour, its observance universally and visibly holding its way through all the details both of our outward and of our inward life." Worship, therefore, should have in it as little as possible of what divides us, and should be as much as possible a common and public act; as Joubert says again: "The best prayers are those which have nothing distinct about them, and which are thus of the nature of simple adoration." For, "The same devotion," as he says in another place, "unites men far more than the same thought and knowledge." Thought and knowledge, as we have said before, is eminently something individual, and of our own; the more we possess it as strictly of our own, the more power it has on us. Man worships best, therefore, with the community; he philoso-

208 phises best alone. So it seems that whoever would truly give effect to Christ's declaration that his religion is a force of inward persuasion acting on the soul, would leave our thought on the intellectual aspects of Christianity as individual as possible, but would make Christian worship as collective as possible. Worship, then, appears to be eminently a matter for public and national establishment; for even Mr. Bright, who, when he stands in Mr. Spurgeon's great Tabernacle is so ravished with admiration, will hardly say that the great Tabernacle and its worship are in themselves, as a temple and service of religion, so impressive and affecting as the public and national Westminster Abbey, or Notre Dame, with their worship. And when, very soon after the great Tabernacle, one comes plump down to the mass of private and individual establishments of religious worship, establishments falling, like the British College of Health in the New Road, conspicuously short of what a public and national establishment might be, then one cannot but feel that Christ's command to make his religion a force of persuasion to the soul, is, so far as one main source of persuasion is concerned, altogether set at nought.

209 But perhaps the Nonconformists worship so unimpressively because they philosophise so keenly; and one part of religion, the part of public national worship, they have subordinated to the other part, the part of individual thought and knowledge? This, however, their organisation in congregations forbids us to admit. They are members of congregations, not isolated thinkers; and a true play of individual thought is at least as much impeded by membership of a small congregation as by membership of a great church; thinking by batches of fifties is to the full as fatal to free thought as thinking by batches of thousands. Accordingly, we have had occasion already to notice that Nonconformity does not at all differ from the Established Church by having worthier or more philosophical ideas about God and the ordering of the world than the Established Church has; it has very much the same ideas about these as the Established Church has, but it differs from the Established Church in that its worship is a much less

collective and national affair. So Mr. Spurgeon and the Nonconformists seem to have misapprehended the true meaning of Christ's words, *My kingdom is not of this world;* because, by these words, Christ meant that his religion was to work on the soul; and of the two parts of the soul on which religion works,—the thinking and speculative part, and the feeling and imaginative part,—Nonconformity satisfies the first no better than the Established Churches, which Christ by these words is supposed to have condemned, satisfy it; and the second part it satisfies much worse than the Established Churches. And thus the balance of advantage seems to rest with the Established Churches; and they seem to have apprehended and applied Christ's words, if not with perfect adequacy, at least less inadequately than the Nonconformists.

Might it not, then, be urged with great force that the way to do good, in presence of this operation for uprooting the Church establishment in Ireland by the power of the Nonconformists' antipathy to publicly establishing or endowing religious worship, is not by lending a hand straight away to the operation, and Hebraising,—that is, in this case, taking an uncritical interpretation of certain Bible words as our absolute rule of conduct,— with the Nonconformists. It may be very well for born Hebraisers, like Mr. Spurgeon, to Hebraise; but for Liberal statesmen to Hebraise is surely unsafe, and to see poor old Liberal hacks Hebraising, whose real self belongs to a kind of negative Hellenism,—a state of moral indifferency without intellectual ardour,—is even painful. And when, by our Hebraising, we neither do what the better mind of statesmen prompted them to do, nor win the affections of the people we want to conciliate, nor yet reduce the opposition of our adversaries but rather heighten it, surely it may be not unreasonable to Hellenise a little, to let our thought and consciousness play freely about our proposed operation and its motives, dissolve these motives if they are unsound, which certainly they have some appearance, at any rate, of being, and create in their stead, if they are, a set of sounder and more persuasive motives conducting to a more solid operation. May not the man who promotes this be giving the best help towards finding some lasting truth to minister to the diseased spirit of his time, and does he really deserve that the believers in action should grow impatient with him?

But now to take another operation which does not at this moment so excite people's feelings as the disestablishment of the Irish Church, but which, I suppose, would also be called exactly one of those operations of simple, practical, common-sense reform, aiming at the removal of some particular abuse, and rigidly restricted to that object, to which a Liberal ought to lend a hand, and deserves that other Liberals should grow impatient with him if he does not. This operation I had the great advantage of with my own ears hearing discussed in the House of Commons, and recommended by a powerful speech from that famous speaker, Mr. Bright; so that the effeminate horror which, it is alleged, I have of practical reforms of this kind, was put to a searching test; and if it survived, it must have, one would think, some reason or other to support it, and can hardly quite merit the stigma of its present name. The operation I mean was that which the Real Estate Intestacy Bill aimed at accomplishing, and the discussion on this bill I heard in the House of Commons. The bill proposed, as every one knows, to prevent the land of a man who dies intestate from going, as it goes now, to his eldest son, and was thought, by its

213   friends and by its enemies, to be a step towards abating the now almost exclusive possession of the land of this country by the people whom we call the Barbarians. Mr. Bright, and other speakers on his side, seemed to hold that there is a kind of natural law or fitness of things which assigns to all a man's children a right to equal shares in the enjoyment of his property after his death; and that if, without depriving a man of an Englishman's prime privilege of doing what he likes by making what will he chooses, you provide that when he makes none his land shall be divided among his family, then you give the sanction of the law to the natural fitness of things, and inflict a sort of check on the present violation of this by the Barbarians. It occurred to me, when I saw Mr. Bright and his friends proceeding in this way, to ask myself a question. If the almost exclusive possession of the land of this country by the Barbarians is a bad thing, is this practical operation of the Liberals, and the stock notion, on which it seems to rest, about the right of children to share equally in the enjoyment of their father's property after his death, the best and most effective means

214   of dealing with it? Or is it best dealt with by letting one's thought and consciousness play freely and naturally upon the Barbarians, this Liberal operation, and the stock notion at the bottom of it, and trying to get as near as we can to the intelligible law of things as to each of them?

Now does any one, if he simply and naturally reads his consciousness, discover that he has any rights at all? For my part, the deeper I go in my own consciousness, and the more simply I abandon myself to it, the more it seems to tell me that I have no rights at all, only duties; and that men get this notion of rights from a process of abstract reasoning, inferring that the obligations they are conscious of towards others, others must be conscious of towards them, and not from any direct witness of consciousness at all. But it is obvious that the notion of a right, arrived at in this way, is likely to stand as a formal and petrified thing, deceiving and misleading us; and that the notions got directly from our consciousness ought to be brought to bear upon it, and to control it. So it is unsafe and misleading to say that our children have rights against us; what is true and safe to say is, that we have duties towards our children. But who will find among these natural duties, 215 set forth to us by our consciousness, the obligation to leave to all our children an equal share in the enjoyment of our property? or, though consciousness tells us we ought to provide for our children's welfare, whose consciousness tells him that the enjoyment of property is in itself welfare? Whether our children's welfare is best served by their all sharing equally in our property depends on circumstances and on the state of the community in which we live. With this equal sharing, society could not, for example, have organised itself afresh out of the chaos left by the fall of the Roman Empire, and to have an organised society to live in is more for a child's welfare than to have an equal share of his father's property. So we see how little convincing force the stock notion on which the Real Estate Intestacy Bill was based,—the notion that in the nature and fitness of things all a man's children have a right to an equal share in the enjoyment of what he leaves,—really has; and how powerless, therefore, it must of necessity be to persuade and win any one who has habits and interests which disincline him to it. On the other hand, the practical operation 216 proposed relies entirely, if it is to be effectual in altering the present practice of the Barbarians, on the power of truth and persuasiveness in the notion which it seeks to consecrate; for it leaves to the Barbarians full liberty to continue their present practice, to which all their habits and interests incline them, unless the promulgation of a notion, which we have seen to have no vital efficacy and hold upon our consciousness, shall hinder them.

Are we really to adorn an operation of this kind, merely because it proposes to do something, with all the favourable epithets of simple, practical, common-sense, definite; to enlist on its side all the zeal of the believers in action, and to call indifference to it a really effeminate horror of useful reforms? It seems to me quite easy to show that a free disinterested play of thought on the Barbarians and their land-holding is a thousand times more really practical, a thousand times more likely to lead to some effective result, than an operation such as that of which we have been now speaking. For if, casting aside the impediments of stock notions and mechanical action, we try to find the intelligible law of things respect- 217 ing a great land-owning class such as we have in this country, does not our consciousness readily tell us that whether the perpetuation of such a class is for its own real welfare and for the real welfare of the community, depends on the actual circumstances of this class and of the community? Does it not readily tell us that wealth, power, and consideration are, and above all when inherited and not earned, in themselves trying and dangerous things? as Bishop Wilson excellently says: "Riches are almost always abused without a very extraordinary grace." But this extraordinary grace was in great measure supplied by the circumstances of the feudal epoch, out of which our landholding class, with its rules of inheritance, sprang. The labour and contentions of a rude, nascent, and struggling society supplied it; these perpetually were trying, chastising, and forming the class whose predominance was then needed by society to give it points of cohesion, and was not so harmful to themselves because they were thus sharply tried and exercised. But in a luxurious, settled, and easy society, where wealth offers the means of enjoyment a thousand times more, and the temptation to abuse them is thus made a thousand times greater, the exercising discipline is at the same time taken away, and the feudal class is left exposed to the full operation of the natural law well put by the French moralist: *Pouvoir sans savoir est fort dangereux*. And, for my part, when I regard the young people of this class, it is above all by the trial and shipwreck made of their own welfare by the circumstances in which they live that I am struck; how far better it would have been for nine out of every ten among them, if they had had their own way to make in the world, and not been tried by a condition for which they had not the extraordinary grace requisite!

218

This, I say, seems to be what a man's consciousness, simply consulted, would tell him about the actual welfare of our Barbarians themselves. Then, as to their actual effect upon the welfare of the community, how can this be salutary, if a class which, by the very possession of wealth, power and consideration, becomes a kind of ideal or standard for the rest of the community, is tried by ease and pleasure more than it can well bear, and almost irresistibly carried away from excellence and strenuous virtue? This must certainly be what Solomon meant when he said: "As he who putteth a stone in a sling, so is he that giveth honour to a fool." For any one can perceive how this honouring of a false ideal, not of intelligence and strenuous virtue, but of wealth and station, pleasure and ease, is as a stone from a sling to kill in our great middle-class, in us who are called Philistines, the desire before spoken of, which by nature for ever carries all men towards that which is lovely; and to leave instead of it only a blind deteriorating pursuit, for ourselves also, of the false ideal. And in those among us Philistines whom this desire does not wholly abandon, yet,

219

having no excellent ideal set forth to nourish and to steady it, it meets with that natural bent for the bathos which together with this desire itself is implanted at birth in the breast of man, and is by that force twisted awry, and borne at random hither and thither, and at last flung upon those grotesque and hideous forms of popular religion which the more respectable part among us Philistines mistake for the true goal of man's desire after all that is lovely. And for the Populace this false idea is a stone which kills the desire before it can even arise; so impossible and unattainable for them do the conditions of that which is lovely appear according to this ideal to be made, so necessary to the reaching of them by the few seems the falling short of them by the many. So that, perhaps, of the actual vulgarity of our Philistines and brutality of our Populace, the Barbarians and their feudal habits of succession, enduring out of their due time and place, are involuntarily the cause in a great degree; and they hurt the welfare of the rest of the community at the same time that, as we have seen, they hurt their own.

But must not, now, the working in our minds of considerations like these, to which culture, that is, the disinterested and active use of reading, reflection, and observation, carries us, be really much more effectual to the dissolution of feudal habits and rules of succession in land than an operation like the Real Estate Intestacy Bill, and a stock notion like that of the natural right of all a man's children to an equal share in the enjoyment of his property; since we have seen that this mechanical maxim is unsound, and that, if it is unsound, the operation relying upon it cannot possibly be effective? If truth and reason have, as we believe, any natural irresistible effect on the mind of man, it must. These considerations, when culture has called them forth and given them free course in our minds, will live and work. They will work gradually, no doubt, and will not bring us ourselves to the front to sit in high place and put them into effect; but so they will be all the more beneficial. Everything teaches us how gradually nature would have all profound changes brought about; and we can even see, too, where the absolute abrupt stoppage of feudal habits has worked harm. And appealing to the sense of truth and reason, these considerations will, without doubt, touch and move all those of even the Barbarians themselves, who are (as are some of us Philistines also, and some of the Populace) beyond their fellows quick of feeling for truth and reason. For indeed this is just one of the advantages of sweetness and light over fire and strength, that sweetness and light make a feudal class quietly and gradually drop its feudal habits because it sees them at variance with truth

220

221

and reason, while fire and strength tear them passionately off it because it applauded Mr. Lowe when he called, or was supposed to call, the working-class drunken and venal.

222   But when once we have begun to recount the practical operations by which our Liberal friends work for the removal of definite evils, and in which if we do not join them they are apt to grow impatient with us, how can we pass over that very interesting operation of this kind,—the attempt to enable a man to marry his deceased wife's sister? This operation, too, like that for abating the feudal customs of succession in land, I have had the advantage of myself seeing and hearing my Liberal friends labour at. I was lucky enough to be present when Mr. Chambers, I think, brought forward in the House of Commons his bill for enabling a man to marry his deceased wife's sister, and I heard the speech which Mr. Chambers then made in support of his bill. His first point was that God's law,—the name he always gave to the Book of Leviticus,—did not really forbid a man to marry his deceased wife's sister. God's law not forbidding it, the Liberal maxim that a man's prime right and happiness is to do as he likes ought at once to come into force, and to annul any such check upon the assertion of personal liberty as the prohibition to marry one's deceased wife's sister. A

223 distinguished Liberal supporter of Mr. Chambers, in the debate which followed the introduction of the bill, produced a formula of much beauty and neatness for conveying in brief the Liberal notions on this head: "Liberty," said he, "is the law of human life." And, therefore, the moment it is ascertained that God's law, the Book of Leviticus, does not stop the way, man's law, the law of liberty, asserts its right, and makes us free to marry our deceased wife's sister.

    And this exactly falls in with what Mr. Hepworth Dixon, who may almost be called the Colenso of love and marriage,—such a revolution does he make in our ideas on these matters, just as Dr. Colenso does in our ideas on religion,—tells us of the notions and proceedings of our kinsmen in America. With that affinity of genius to the Hebrew genius which we have already noticed, and with the strong belief of our race that liberty is the law of human life, so far as a fixed, perfect, and paramount rule of conscience, the Bible, does not expressly control it, our American kinsmen go again, Mr. Hepworth Dixon tells us, to their Bible, the Mormons to the patriarchs and the Old Testament, Brother Noyes to St. Paul and the

224 New, and having never before read anything else but their Bible, they now read their Bible over again, and make all manner of great discoveries there. All these discoveries are favourable to liberty, and in this way is

satisfied that double craving so characteristic of the Philistine, and so eminently exemplified in that crowned Philistine, Henry the Eighth,—the craving for forbidden fruit and the craving for legality. Mr. Hepworth Dixon's eloquent writings give currency, over here, to these important discoveries; so that now, as regards love and marriage, we seem to be entering, with all our sails spread, upon what Mr. Hepworth Dixon, its apostle and evangelist, calls a Gothic Revival, but what one of the many newspapers that so greatly admire Mr. Hepworth Dixon's lithe and sinewy style and form their own style upon it, calls, by a yet bolder and more striking figure, "a great sexual insurrection of our Anglo-Teutonic race." For this end we have to avert our eyes from everything Hellenic and fanciful, and to keep them steadily fixed upon the two cardinal points of the Bible and liberty. And one of those practical operations in which the Liberal party engage, and in which we are summoned to join them, directs itself entirely, as we have seen, to these cardinal points, and may almost be   225
regarded, perhaps, as a kind of first instalment or public and parliamentary pledge of the great sexual insurrection of our Anglo-Teutonic race.

But here, as elsewhere, what we seek is the Philistine's perfection, the development of his best self, not mere liberty for his ordinary self. And we no more allow absolute validity to his stock maxim, *Liberty is the law of human life,* than we allow it to the opposite maxim, which is just as true, *Renouncement is the law of human life.* For we know that the only perfect freedom is, as our religion says, a service; not a service to any stock maxim, but an elevation of our best self, and a harmonising in subordination to this, and to the idea of a perfected humanity, all the multitudinous, turbulent, and blind impulses of our ordinary selves. Now, the Philistine's great defect being a defect in delicacy of perception, to cultivate in him this delicacy, to render it independent of external and mechanical rule, and a law to itself, is what seems to make most for his perfection, his true humanity. And his true humanity, and therefore his happiness, appears to lie much more, so far as the relations of love and marriage are concerned,   226
in becoming alive to the finer shades of feeling which arise within these relations, in being able to enter with tact and sympathy into the subtle instinctive propensions and repugnances of the person with whose life his own life is bound up, to make them his own, to direct and govern, in harmony with them, the arbitrary range of his personal action, and thus to enlarge his spiritual and intellectual life and liberty, than in remaining insensible to these finer shades of feeling, this delicate sympathy, in giving unchecked range, so far as he can, to his mere personal action, in

allowing no limits or government to this except such as a mechanical external law imposes, and in thus really narrowing, for the satisfaction of his ordinary self, his spiritual and intellectual life and liberty.

Still more must this be so when his fixed eternal rule, his God's law, is supplied to him from a source which is less fit, perhaps, to supply final and absolute instructions on this particular topic of love and marriage than on any other relation of human life. Bishop Wilson, who is full of examples of that fruitful Hellenising within the limits of Hebraism itself, of that renewing of the stiff and stark notions of Hebraism by turning upon them a stream of fresh thought and consciousness, which we have already noticed in St. Paul,—Bishop Wilson gives an admirable lesson to rigid Hebraisers, like Mr. Chambers, asking themselves: Does God's law (that is, the Book of Leviticus) forbid us to marry our wife's sister?—Does God's law (that is, again, the Book of Leviticus) allow us to marry our wife's sister?—when he says: "Christian duties are founded on reason, not on the sovereign authority of God commanding what he pleases; God cannot command us what is not fit to be believed or done, all his commands being founded in the necessities of our nature." And, immense as is our debt to the Hebrew race and its genius, incomparable as is its authority on certain profoundly important sides of our human nature, worthy as it is to be described as having uttered, for those sides, the voice of the deepest necessities of our nature, the statutes of the divine and eternal order of things, the law of God,—who, that is not manacled and hoodwinked by his Hebraism, can believe that, as to love and marriage, our reason and the necessities of our humanity have their true, sufficient, and divine law expressed for them by the voice of any Oriental and polygamous nation like the Hebrews? Who, I say, will believe, when he really considers the matter, that where the feminine nature, the feminine ideal, and our relations to them, are brought into question, the delicate and apprehensive genius of the Indo-European race, the race which invented the Muses, and chivalry, and the Madonna, is to find its last word on this question in the institutions of a Semitic people, whose wisest king had seven hundred wives and three hundred concubines?

If here again, therefore, we seem to minister better to the diseased spirit of our time by leading it to think about the operation our Liberal friends have in hand, than by lending a hand to this operation ourselves, let us see, before we dismiss from our view the practical operations of our Liberal friends, whether the same thing does not hold good as to their celebrated industrial and economical labours also. Their great work of this kind is, of course, their free-trade policy. This policy, as having enabled the poor

man to eat untaxed bread, and as having wonderfully augmented trade, we
are accustomed to speak of with a kind of solemnity; it is chiefly on their 229
having been our leaders in this policy that Mr. Bright founds for himself
and his friends the claim, so often asserted by him, to be considered guides
of the blind, teachers of the ignorant, benefactors slowly and laboriously
developing in the Conservative party and in the country that which Mr.
Bright is fond of calling *the growth of intelligence,*—the object, as is well
known, of all the friends of culture also, and the great end and aim of the
culture that we preach. Now, having first saluted free-trade and its doctors
with all respect, let us see whether even here, too, our Liberal friends do
not pursue their operations in a mechanical way, without reference to any
firm intelligible law of things, to human life as a whole, and human
happiness; and whether it is not more for our good, at this particular
moment at any rate, if, instead of worshipping free-trade with them
Hebraistically, as a kind of fetish, and helping them to pursue it as an end
in and for itself, we turn the free stream of our thought upon their treatment of it, and see how this is related to the intelligible law of human life,
and to national well-being and happiness. In short, suppose we Hellenise a 230
little with free-trade, as we Hellenised with the Real Estate Intestacy Bill,
and with the disestablishment of the Irish Church by the power of the
Nonconformists' antipathy to religious establishments and endowments,
and see whether what our reprovers beautifully call ministering to the
diseased spirit of our time is best done by the Hellenising method of
proceeding, or by the other.

But first let us understand how the policy of free-trade really shapes
itself for our Liberal friends, and how they practically employ it as an
instrument of national happiness and salvation. For as we said that it
seemed clearly right to prevent the Church property of Ireland from being
all taken for the benefit of the Church of a small minority, so it seems
clearly right that the poor man should eat untaxed bread, and, generally,
that restrictions and regulations which, for the supposed benefit of some
particular person or class of persons, make the price of things artificially
high here, or artificially low there, and interfere with the natural flow of
trade and commerce, should be done away with. But in the policy of our
Liberal friends free-trade means more than this, and is specially valued as 231
a stimulant to the production of wealth, as they call it, and to the increase
of the trade, business, and population of the country. We have already seen
how these things,—trade, business, and population,—are mechanically
pursued by us as ends precious in themselves, and are worshipped as what
we call fetishes; and Mr. Bright, I have already said, when he wishes to

give the working-class a true sense of what makes glory and greatness, tells it to look at the cities it has built, the railroads it has made, the manufactures it has produced. So to this idea of glory and greatness the free-trade which our Liberal friends extol so solemnly and devoutly has served,—to the increase of trade, business, and population; and for this it is prized. Therefore, the untaxing of the poor man's bread has, with this view of national happiness, been used, not so much to make the existing poor man's bread cheaper or more abundant, but rather to create more poor men to eat it; so that we cannot precisely say that we have fewer poor men than we had before free-trade, but we can say with truth that we have many more centres of industry, as they are called, and much more business, population, and manufactures. And if we are sometimes a little troubled by our multitude of poor men, yet we know the increase of manufactures and population to be such a salutary thing in itself, and our free-trade policy begets such an admirable movement, creating fresh centres of industry and fresh poor men here, while we were thinking about our poor men there, that we are quite dazzled and borne away, and more and more industrial movement is called for, and our social progress seems to become one triumphant and enjoyable course of what is sometimes called, vulgarly, outrunning the constable.

If, however, taking some other criterion of man's well-being than the cities he has built and the manufactures he has produced, we persist in thinking that our social progress would be happier if there were not so many of us so very poor, and in busying ourselves with notions of in some way or other adjusting the poor man and business one to the other, and not multiplying the one and the other mechanically and blindly, then our Liberal friends, the appointed doctors of free-trade, take us up very sharply. "Art is long," says *The Times,* "and life is short; for the most part we settle things first and understand them afterwards. Let us have as few theories as possible; what is wanted is not the light of speculation. If nothing worked well of which the theory was not perfectly understood, we should be in sad confusion. The relations of labour and capital, we are told, are not understood, yet trade and commerce, on the whole, work satisfactorily." I quote from *The Times* of only the other day. But thoughts like these, as I have often pointed out, are thoroughly British thoughts, and we have been familiar with them for years.

Or, if we want more of a philosophy of the matter than this, our free-trade friends have two axioms for us, axioms laid down by their justly esteemed doctors, which they think ought to satisfy us entirely. One is, that, other things being equal, the more population increases, the more does production increase to keep pace with it; because men by their numbers and contact call forth all manner of activities and resources in one another and in nature, which, when men are few and sparse, are never developed. The other is, that, although population always tends to equal the means of subsistence, yet people's notions of what subsistence is enlarge as civilisation advances, and take in a number of things beyond the bare necessaries of life; and thus, therefore, is supplied whatever check on population is needed. But the error of our friends is just, perhaps, that they apply axioms of this sort as if they were self-acting laws which will put themselves into operation without trouble or planning on our part, if we will only pursue free-trade, business, and population zealously and staunchly. Whereas the real truth is, that, however the case might be under other circumstances, yet in fact, as we now manage the matter, the enlarged conception of what is included in *subsistence* does not operate to prevent the bringing into the world of numbers of people who but just attain to the barest necessaries of life or who even fail to attain to them; while, again, though production may increase as population increases, yet it seems that the production may be of such a kind, and so related, or rather non-related, to population, that the population may be little the better for it. For instance, with the increase of population since Queen Elizabeth's time the production of silk-stockings has wonderfully increased, and silk-stockings have become much cheaper and procurable in much greater abundance by many more people, and tend perhaps, as population and manufactures increase, to get cheaper and cheaper and at last to become, according to Bastiat's favourite image, a common free property of the human race, like light and air. But bread and bacon have not become much cheaper with the increase of population since Queen Elizabeth's time, nor procurable in much greater abundance by many more people; neither do they seem at all to promise to become, like light and air, a common free property of the human race. And if bread and bacon have not kept pace with our population, and we have many more people in want of them now than in Queen Elizabeth's time, it seems vain to tell us that silk-stockings have kept pace with our population, or even more than kept pace with it, and that we are to get our comfort out of that. In short, it turns out that our pursuit of free-trade, as of so many other things, has been too mechanical. We fix upon some object, which in this case is the production of wealth, and the increase of manufactures, population, and commerce through free-trade, as a kind of one thing needful, or end in itself, and then we pursue it staunchly and mechanically, and say that it is our duty to pursue it staunchly and mechanically, not to see how it is related to the whole

234

235

236

intelligible law of things and to full human perfection, or to treat it as the piece of machinery, of varying value as its relations to the intelligible law of things vary, which it really is.

So it is of no use to say to *The Times,* and to our Liberal friends rejoicing in the possession of their talisman of free-trade, that about one in nineteen of our population is a pauper, and that, this being so, trade and commerce can hardly be said to prove by their satisfactory working that it matters nothing whether the relations between labour and capital are understood or not; nay, that we can hardly be said not to be in sad confusion. For here comes in our faith in the staunch mechanical pursuit of a fixed object, and covers itself with that imposing and colossal necessitarianism of *The Times* which we have before noticed. And this necessitarianism, taking for granted that an increase in trade and population is a good in itself, one of the chiefest of goods, tells us that disturbances of 237 human happiness caused by ebbs and flows in the tide of trade and business, which, on the whole, steadily mounts, are inevitable and not to be quarrelled with. This firm philosophy I seek to call to mind when I am in the East of London, whither my avocations often lead me; and, indeed, to fortify myself against the depressing sights which on these occasions assail us, I have transcribed from *The Times* one strain of this kind, full of the finest economical doctrine, and always carry it about with me. The passage is this:—

"The East End is the most commercial, the most industrial, the most fluctuating region of the metropolis. It is always the first to suffer; for it is the creature of prosperity, and falls to the ground the instant there is no wind to bear it up. The whole of that region is covered with huge docks, shipyards, manufactories, and a wilderness of small houses, all full of life and happiness in brisk times, but in dull times withered and lifeless, like the deserts we read of in the East. Now their brief spring is over. There is no one to blame for this; it is the result of Nature's simplest laws!" We must 238 all agree that it is impossible that anything can be firmer than this, or show a surer faith in the working of free-trade, as our Liberal friends understand and employ it.

But, if we still at all doubt whether the indefinite multiplication of manufactories and small houses can be such an absolute good in itself as to counter-balance the indefinite multiplication of poor people, we shall learn that this multiplication of poor people, too, is an absolute good in itself, and the result of divine and beautiful laws. This is indeed a favourite thesis with our Philistine friends, and I have already noticed the pride and gratitude with which they receive certain articles in *The Times,* dilating in thankful and solemn language on the majestic growth of our population. But I prefer to quote now, on this topic, the words of an ingenious young Scotch writer, Mr. Robert Buchanan, because he invests with so much imagination and poetry this current idea of the blessed and even divine character which the multiplying of population is supposed in itself to have. "We move to multiplicity," says Mr. Robert Buchanan. "If there is one quality which seems God's, and his exclusively, it seems that divine philoprogenitiveness, that passionate love of distribution and expansion into living forms. Every animal added seems a new ecstasy to the Maker; every life added, a new embodiment of his love. He would *swarm* the earth with beings. There are never enough. Life, life, life,—faces gleaming, hearts beating, must fill every cranny. Not a corner is suffered to remain empty. The whole earth breeds and God glories."

239

It is a little unjust, perhaps, to attribute to the Divinity exclusively this philoprogenitiveness, which the British Philistine, and the poorer class of Irish, may certainly claim to share with him; yet how inspiriting is here the whole strain of thought! and these beautiful words, too, I carry about with me in the East of London, and often read them there. They are quite in agreement with the popular language one is accustomed to hear about children and large families, which describes children as *sent*. And a line of poetry which Mr. Robert Buchanan throws in presently after the poetical prose I have quoted:—

'Tis the old story of the fig-leaf time—

this fine line, too, naturally connects itself, when one is in the East of London, with the idea of God's desire to *swarm* the earth with beings; because the swarming of the earth with beings does indeed, in the East of London, so seem to revive

240

. . . the old story of the fig-leaf time—

such a number of the people one meets there having hardly a rag to cover them; and the more the swarming goes on, the more it promises to revive this old story. And when the story is perfectly revived, the swarming quite completed, and every cranny choke-full, then, too, no doubt, the faces in the East of London will be gleaming faces, which Mr. Robert Buchanan says it is God's desire they should be, and which every one must perceive they are not at present, but, on the contrary, very miserable.

But to prevent all this philosophy and poetry from quite running away with us, and making us think with *The Times,* and our practical Liberal free-traders, and the British Philistines generally, that the increase of small houses and manufactories, or the increase of population, are absolute goods in themselves, to be mechanically pursued, and to be worshipped like fetishes,—to prevent this, we have got that notion of ours immoveably fixed, of which I have long ago spoken, the notion that culture, or the study of perfection, leads us to conceive of no perfection as being real which is not a *general* perfection, embracing all our fellow-men with whom we have to do. Such is the sympathy which binds humanity together, that we are indeed, as our religion says, members of one body, and if one member suffer, all the members suffer with it; individual perfection is impossible so long as the rest of mankind are not perfected along with us. "The *multitude* of the wise is the welfare of the world," says the wise man. And to this effect that excellent and often quoted guide of ours, Bishop Wilson, has some striking words:—"It is not," says he, "so much our neighbour's interest as our own that we love him," And again he says: "Our salvation does in some measure depend upon that of others." And the author of the *Imitation* puts the same thing admirably when he says:— *"Obscurior etiam via ad cœlum videbatur quando tam pauci regnum cœlorum quærere curabant,"*—the fewer there are who follow the way to perfection, the harder that way is to find. So all our fellow-men, in the East of London and elsewhere, we must take along with us in the progress towards perfection, if we ourselves really, as we profess, want to be perfect; and we must not let the worship of any fetish, any machinery, such as manufactures or population,—which are not, like perfection, absolute goods in themselves, though we think them so,—create for us such a multitude of miserable, sunken, and ignorant human beings, that to carry them all along with us is impossible, and perforce they must for the most part be left by us in their degradation and wretchedness. But evidently the conception of free-trade, on which our Liberal friends vaunt themselves, and in which they think they have found the secret of national prosperity,—evidently, I say, the mere unfettered pursuit of the production of wealth, and the mere mechanical multiplying, for this end, of manufactures and population, threatens to create for us, if it has not created already, those vast, miserable, unmanageable masses of sunken people,—one pauper, at the present moment, for every nineteen of us,— to the existence of which we are, as we have seen, absolutely forbidden to reconcile ourselves, in spite of all that the philosophy of *The Times* and the poetry of Mr. Robert Buchanan may say to persuade us.

243   And though Hebraism, following its best and highest instinct,—

identical, as we have seen, with that of Hellenism in its final aim, the aim of perfection,—teaches us this very clearly; and though from Hebraising counsellors,—the Bible, Bishop Wilson, the author of the *Imitation*,—I have preferred (as well I may, for from this rock of Hebraism we are all hewn!) to draw the texts which we use to bring home to our minds this teaching; yet Hebraism seems powerless, almost as powerless as our free-trading Liberal friends, to deal efficaciously with our ever-accumulating masses of pauperism, and to prevent their accumulating still more. Hebraism builds churches, indeed, for these masses, and sends missionaries among them; above all, it sets itself against the social necessitarianism of *The Times*, and refuses to accept their degradation as inevitable; but with regard to their ever-increasing accumulation, it seems to be led to the very same conclusions, though from a point of view of its own, as our free-trading Liberal friends. Hebraism, with that mechanical and misleading use of the letter of Scripture on which we have already commented, is governed by such texts as: *Be fruitful and multiply,* the edict of God's law, 244 as Mr. Chambers would say; or by the declaration of what he would call God's words in the Psalms, that the man who has a great number of children is thereby made happy. And in conjunction with such texts as these it is apt to place another text: *The poor shall never cease out of the land.* Thus Hebraism is conducted to nearly the same notion as the popular mind and as Mr. Robert Buchanan, that children are *sent,* and that the divine nature takes a delight in swarming the East End of London with paupers. Only, when they are perishing in their helplessness and wretchedness, it asserts the Christian duty of succouring them, instead of saying, like *The Times:* "Now their brief spring is over; there is nobody to blame for this; it is the result of Nature's simplest laws!" But, like *The Times*, Hebraism despairs of any help from knowledge and says that "what is wanted is not the light of speculation." I remember, only the other day, a good man, looking with me upon a multitude of children who were gathered before us in one of the most miserable regions of London,—children eaten up with disease, half-sized, half-fed, half-clothed, neglected by their parents, without health, without home, without hope,—said to me: 245 "The one thing really needful is to teach these little ones to succour one another, if only with a cup of cold water; but now, from one end of the country to the other, one hears nothing but the cry for knowledge, knowledge, knowledge!" And yet surely, so long as these children are there in these festering masses, without health, without home, without hope, and so long as their multitude is perpetually swelling, charged with misery they must still be for themselves, charged with misery they must still be for us, whether they help one another with a cup of cold water or no; and the knowledge how to prevent their accumulating is necessary, even to give their moral life and growth a fair chance!

May we not, therefore, say, that neither the true Hebraism of this good man, willing to spend and be spent for these sunken multitudes, nor what I may call the spurious Hebraism of our free-trading Liberal friends,— mechanically worshipping their fetish of the production of wealth and of the increase of manufactures and population, and looking neither to the right nor left so long as this increase goes on,—avail us much here; and that here, again, what we want is Hellenism, the letting our consciousness play freely and simply upon the facts before us, and listening to what it tells us of the intelligible law of things as concerns them? And surely what it tells us is, that a man's children are not really *sent,* any more than the pictures upon his wall, or the horses in his stable, are *sent;* and that to bring people into the world, when one cannot afford to keep them and oneself decently and not too precariously, or to bring more of them into the world than one can afford to keep thus, is, whatever *The Times* and Mr. Robert Buchanan may say, by no means an accomplishment of the divine will or a fulfilment of Nature's simplest laws, but is just as wrong, just as contrary to reason and the will of God, as for a man to have horses, or carriages, or pictures, when he cannot afford them, or to have more of them than he can afford; and that, in the one case as in the other, the larger the scale on which the violation of reason's laws is practised, and the longer it is persisted in, the greater must be the confusion and final trouble. Surely no laudations of free-trade, no meetings of bishops and clergy in the East End of London, no reading of papers and reports, can tell us anything about our social condition which it more concerns us to know than that! and not only to know, but habitually to have the knowledge present, and to act upon it as one acts upon the knowledge that water wets and fire burns! And not only the sunken populace of our great cities are concerned to know it, and the pauper twentieth of our population; we Philistines of the middle-class, too, are concerned to know it, and all who have to set themselves to make progress in perfection.

But we all know it already! some one will say; it is the simplest law of prudence. But how little reality must there be in our knowledge of it; how little can we be putting it in practice; how little is it likely to penetrate among the poor and struggling masses of our population, and to better our condition, so long as an unintelligent Hebraism of one sort keeps repeating as an absolute eternal word of God the psalm-verse which says that the man who has a great many children is happy; or an unintelligent Hebraism of another sort keeps assigning as an absolute proof of national prosperity the multiplying of manufactures and population! Surely, the one set of Hebraisers have to learn that their psalm-verse was composed at the reset- 248 tlement of Jerusalem after the Captivity, when the Jews of Jerusalem were a handful, an under-manned garrison, and every child was a blessing; and that the word of God, or the voice of the divine order of things, declares the possession of a great many children to be a blessing only when it really is so! And the other set of Hebraisers, have they not to learn that if they call their private acquaintances imprudent and unlucky, when, with no means of support for them or with precarious means, they have a large family of children, then they ought not to call the State well managed and pros- perous merely because its manufactures and its citizens multiply, if the manufactures, which bring new citizens into existence just as much as if they had actually begotten them, bring more of them into existence than they can maintain, or are too precarious to go on maintaining those whom for a while they maintained? Hellenism, surely, or the habit of fixing our mind upon the intelligible law of things, is most salutary if it makes us see that the only absolute good, the only absolute and eternal object pre- scribed to us by God's law, or the divine order of things, is the progress 249 towards perfection,—our own progress towards it and the progress of humanity. And therefore, for every individual man, and for every society of men, the possession and multiplication of children, like the possession and multiplication of horses and pictures, is to be accounted good or bad, not in itself, but with reference to this object and the progress towards it. And as no man is to be excused in having horses or pictures, if his having them hinders his own or others' progress towards perfection and makes them lead a servile and ignoble life, so is no man to be excused for having children if his having them makes him or others lead this. Plain thoughts of this kind are surely the spontaneous product of our consciousness, when it is allowed to play freely and disinterestedly upon the actual facts of our social condition, and upon our stock notions and stock habits in respect to it. Firmly grasped and simply uttered, they are more likely, one cannot but think, to better that condition, and to diminish our formidable rate of one pauper to every nineteen of us, than is the Hebraising and mechanical pursuit of free-trade by our Liberal friends.

So that, here as elsewhere, the practical operations of our Liberal 250 friends, by which they set so much store, and in which they invite us to join them and to show what Mr. Bright calls a commendable interest, do not seem to us so practical for real good as they think; and our Liberal friends seem to us themselves to need to Hellenise, as we say, a little,—

that is, to examine into the nature of real good, and to listen to what their consciousness tells them about it,—rather than to pursue with such heat and confidence their present practical operations. And it is clear that they have no just cause, so far as regards several operations of theirs which we have canvassed, to reproach us with delicate Conservative scepticism; for often by Hellenising we seem to subvert stock Conservative notions and usages more effectually than they subvert them by Hebraising. But, in truth, the free spontaneous play of consciousness with which culture tries to float our stock habits of thinking and acting, is by its very nature, as has been said, disinterested. Sometimes the result of floating them may be agreeable to this party, sometimes to that; now it may be unwelcome to our so-called Liberals, now to our so-called Conservatives; but what culture seeks is, above all, to *float* them, to prevent their being stiff and stark pieces of petrifaction any longer. It is mere Hebraising, if we stop short, and refuse to let our consciousness play freely, whenever we or our friends do not happen to like what it discovers to us. This is to make the Liberal party, or the Conservative party, our one thing needful, instead of human perfection; and we have seen what mischief arises from making an even greater thing than the Liberal or the Conservative party,—the predominance of the moral side in man,—our one thing needful. But wherever the free play of our consciousness leads us, we shall follow; believing that in this way we shall tend to make good at all points what is wanting to us, and so shall be brought nearer to our complete human perfection.

Thus we may often, perhaps, praise much that a so-called Liberal thinks himself forbidden to praise, and yet blame much that a so-called Conservative thinks himself forbidden to blame, because these are both of them partisans, and no partisan can afford to be thus disinterested. But we who are not partisans can afford it; and so, after we have seen what Nonconformists lose by being locked up in their New Road forms of religious institution, we can let ourselves see, on the other hand, how their ministers, in a time of movement of ideas like our present time, are apt to be more exempt than the ministers of a great Church establishment from that self-confidence, and sense of superiority to such a movement, which are natural to a powerful hierarchy; and which in Archdeacon Denison, for instance, seem almost carried to such a pitch that they may become, one cannot but fear, his spiritual ruin. But seeing this does not dispose us, therefore, to lock up all the nation in forms of worship of the New Road type; but it points us to the quite new ideal, of combining grand and national forms of worship with an openness and movement of mind not yet found in any hierarchy. So, again, if we see what is called ritualism making conquests in our Puritan middle-class, we may rejoice that portions of this class should have become alive to the æsthetical weakness of their position, even although they have not yet become alive to the intellectual weakness of it. In Puritanism, on the other hand, we can respect that idea of dealing sincerely with oneself, which is at once the great force of Puritanism,—Puritanism's great superiority over all products, like ritualism, of our Catholicising tendencies,—and also an idea rich in the latent seeds of intellectual promise. But we do this, without on that account hiding from ourselves that Puritanism has by Hebraising misapplied that idea, has as yet developed none or hardly one of those seeds, and that its triumph at its present stage of development would be baneful. 253

Everything, in short, confirms us in the doctrine, so unpalatable to the believers in action, that our main business at the present moment is not so much to work away at certain crude reforms of which we have already the scheme in our own mind, as to create, through the help of that culture which at the very outset we began by praising and recommending, a frame of mind out of which really fruitful reforms may with time grow. At any rate, we ourselves must put up with our friends' impatience, and with their reproaches against cultivated inaction, and must still decline to lend a hand to their practical operations, until we, for our own part at least, have grown a little clearer about the nature of real good, and have arrived nearer to a condition of mind out of which really fruitful and solid operations may spring.

In the meanwhile, since our Liberal friends keep loudly and resolutely assuring us that their actual operations at present are fruitful and solid, let us in each case keep testing these operations in the simple way we have indicated, by letting the natural stream of our consciousness flow over them freely; and if they stand this test successfully, then let us give them our commendable interest, but not else. For example. Our Liberal friends assure us, at the very top of their voices, that their present actual operation for the disestablishment of the Irish Church is fruitful and solid. But what if, on testing it, the truth appears to be, that the statesmen and reasonable people of both parties wished for much the same thing,—the fair apportionment of the church property of Ireland among the principal religious bodies there; but that, behind the statesmen and reasonable people, there was, on one side, a mass of Tory prejudice, and, on the other, a mass of Nonconformist prejudice, to which such an arrangement was unpalatable? Well, the natural way, one thinks, would have been for the statesmen and reasonable people of both sides to have united, and to have allayed and dissipated, so far as they could, the resistance of their respective extremes, 254

255   and where they could not, to have confronted it in concert. But we see that, instead of this, Liberal statesmen waited to trip up their rivals, if they proposed the arrangement which both knew to be reasonable, by means of the prejudice of their own Nonconformist extreme; and then, themselves proposing an arrangement to flatter this prejudice, made the other arrangement, which they themselves knew to be reasonable, out of the question; and drove their rivals in their turn to blow up with all their might, in the hope of baffling them, a great fire, among their own Tory extreme, of fierce prejudice and religious bigotry,—a fire which, once kindled, may always very easily spread further? If, I say, on testing the present operation of our Liberal friends for the disestablishment of the Irish Church, the truth about it appears to be very much this, then, I think,—even with a triumphant Liberal majority, and with our Liberal friends making impassioned appeals to us to take a commendable interest in their operation and them, and to rally round what Sir Henry Hoare (who may be described, perhaps, as a Barbarian converted to Philistinism, as I, on the other hand, seem to be a Philistine converted to culture) finely calls the conscientious-

256   ness of a Gladstone and the intellect of a Bright,—it is rather our duty to abstain, and, instead of lending a hand to the operation of our Liberal friends, to do what we can to abate and dissolve the mass of prejudice, Tory or Nonconformist, which makes so doubtfully begotten and equivocal an operation as the present, producible and possible.

[Conclusion]

And so we bring to an end what we had to say in praise of culture, and in evidence of its special utility for the circumstances in which we find ourselves, and the confusion which environs us. Through culture seems to lie our way, not only to perfection, but even to safety. Resolutely refusing to lend a hand to the imperfect operations of our Liberal friends, disregarding their impatience, taunts, and reproaches, firmly bent on trying to find in the intelligible law of things a firmer and sounder basis for future practice than any which we have at present, and believing this search and discovery to be, for our generation and circumstances, of yet more vital and pressing importance than practice itself, we nevertheless may do

257   more, perhaps, we poor disparaged followers of culture, to make the actual present, and the frame of society in which we live, solid and seaworthy, than all which our bustling politicians can do. For we have seen how much of our disorders and perplexities is due to the disbelief, among the classes and combinations of men, Barbarian or Philistine,

which have hitherto governed our society, in right reason, in a paramount best self; to the inevitable decay and break-up of the organisations by which, asserting and expressing in these organisations their ordinary self only, they have so long ruled us; and to their irresolution, when the society, which their conscience tells them they have made and still manage not with right reason but with their ordinary self, is rudely shaken, in offering resistance to its subverters. But for us,—who believe in right reason, in the duty and possibility of extricating and elevating our best self, in the progress of humanity towards perfection,—for us the framework of society, that theatre on which this august drama has to unroll itself, is sacred; and whoever administers it, and however we may seek to remove them from the tenure of administration, yet, while they administer, we steadily   258
and with undivided heart support them in repressing anarchy and disorder; because without order there can be no society, and without society there can be no human perfection.

With me, indeed, this rule of conduct is hereditary. I remember my father, in one of his unpublished letters written more than forty years ago, when the political and social state of the country was gloomy and troubled, and there were riots in many places, goes on, after strongly insisting on the badness and foolishness of the government, and on the harm and dangerousness of our feudal and aristocratical constitution of society, and ends thus: "As for rioting, the old Roman way of dealing with *that* is always the right one; flog the rank and file, and fling the ringleaders from the Tarpeian Rock!" And this opinion we can never forsake, however our Liberal friends may think a little rioting, and what they call popular demonstrations, useful sometimes to their own interests and to the interests of the valuable practical operations they have in hand, and however they may preach the right of an Englishman to be left to do as far as possible what he likes, and the duty of his government to indulge him and connive as much as possible and abstain from all harshness of repression.   259
And even when they artfully show us operations which are undoubtedly precious, such as the abolition of the slave-trade, and ask us if, for their sake, foolish and obstinate governments may not wholesomely be frightened by a little disturbance, the good design in view and the difficulty of overcoming opposition to it being considered,—still we say no, and that monster processions in the streets and forcible irruptions into the parks, even in professed support of this good design, ought to be unflinchingly forbidden and repressed; and that far more is lost than is gained by permitting them. Because a State in which law is authoritative and sovereign, a firm and settled course of public order, is requisite if man is to bring to

maturity anything precious and lasting now, or to found anything precious and lasting for the future.

Thus, in our eyes, the very framework and exterior order of the State, whoever may administer the State, is sacred; and culture is the most resolute enemy of anarchy, because of the great hopes and designs for the State which culture teaches us to nourish. But as, believing in right reason, and having faith in the progress of humanity towards perfection, and ever labouring for this end, we grow to have clearer sight of the ideas of right reason, and of the elements and helps of perfection, and come gradually to fill the framework of the State with them, to fashion its internal composition and all its laws and institutions conformably to them, and to make the State more and more the expression, as we say, of our best self, which is not manifold, and vulgar, and unstable, and contentious, and ever-varying, but one, and noble, and secure, and peaceful, and the same for all mankind,—with what aversion shall we not *then* regard anarchy, with what firmness shall we not check it, when there is so much that is so precious which it will endanger! So that, for the sake of the present, but far more for the sake of the future, the lovers of culture are unswervingly and with a good conscience the opposers of anarchy. And not as the Barbarians and Philistines, whose honesty and whose sense of humour make them shrink, as we have seen, from treating the State as too serious a thing, and from giving it too much power;—for indeed the only State they know of, and think they administer, is the expression of their ordinary self; and though the headstrong and violent extreme among them might gladly arm this with full authority, yet their virtuous mean is, as we have said, pricked in conscience at doing this, and so our Barbarian Secretaries of State let the Park railings be broken down, and our Philistine Alderman-Colonels let the London roughs rob and beat the bystanders. But we, beholding in the State no expression of our ordinary self, but even already, as it were, the appointed frame and prepared vessel of our best self, and, for the future, our best self's powerful, beneficent, and sacred expression and organ,—we are willing and resolved, even now, to strengthen against anarchy the trembling hands of our Barbarian Home Secretaries, and the feeble knees of our Philistine Alderman-Colonels; and to tell them, that it is not really in behalf of their own ordinary self that they are called to protect the Park railings, and to suppress the London roughs, but in behalf of the best self both of themselves and of all of us in the future.

Nevertheless, though for resisting anarchy the lovers of culture may prize and employ fire and strength, yet they must, at the same time, bear constantly in mind that it is not at this moment true, what the majority of

260

261

people tell us, that the world wants fire and strength more than sweetness 262
and light, and that things are for the most part to be settled first and
understood afterwards. We have seen how much of our present perplexities and confusion this untrue notion of the majority of people amongst us
has caused, and tends to perpetuate. Therefore the true business of the
friends of culture now is, to dissipate this false notion, to spread the belief
in right reason and in a firm intelligible law of things, and to get men to
allow their thought and consciousness to play on their stock notions and
habits disinterestedly and freely; to get men to try, in preference to
staunchly acting with imperfect knowledge, to obtain some sounder basis
of knowledge on which to act. This is what the friends and lovers of
culture have to do, however the believers in action may grow impatient
with us for saying so, and may insist on our lending a hand to their
practical operations, and showing a commendable interest in them.

To this insistence we must indeed turn a deaf ear. But neither, on the
other hand, must the friends of culture expect to take the believers in
action by storm, or to be visibly and speedily important, and to rule and
cut a figure in the world. Aristotle says, that those for whom ideas and the 263
pursuit of the intelligible law of things can have much attraction, are
principally the young, filled with generous spirit and with a passion for
perfection; but the mass of mankind, he says, follow seeming goods for
real, bestowing hardly a thought upon true sweetness and light;—"and to
their lives," he adds mournfully, "who can give another and a better
rhythm?" But, although those chiefly attracted by sweetness and light will
probably always be the young and enthusiastic, and culture must not hope
to take the mass of mankind by storm, yet we will not therefore, for our
own day and for our own people, admit and rest in the desponding sentence of Aristotle. For is not this the right crown of the long discipline of
Hebraism, and the due fruit of mankind's centuries of painful schooling in
self-conquest, and the just reward, above all, of the strenuous energy of
our own nation and kindred in dealing honestly with itself and walking
steadfastly according to the best light it knows,—that, when in the fulness
of time it has reason and beauty offered to it, and the law of things as they
really are, it should at last walk by this true light with the same staunchness
and zeal with which it formerly walked by its imperfect light; and thus 264
man's two great natural forces, Hebraism and Hellenism, should no
longer be dissociated and rival, but should be a joint force of right thinking
and strong doing to carry him on towards perfection? This is what the
lovers of culture may perhaps dare to augur for such a nation as ours.
Therefore, however great the changes to be accomplished, and however

[Conclusion]   137 dense the array of Barbarians, Philistines, and Populace, we will neither despair on the one hand, nor, on the other, threaten violent revolution and change. But we will look forward cheerfully and hopefully to "a revolution," as the Duke of Wellington said, "by due course of law;" though not exactly such laws as our Liberal friends are now, with their actual lights, fond of offering us.

But if despondency and violence are both of them forbidden to the believer in culture, yet neither, on the other hand, is public life and direct political action much permitted to him. For it is his business, as we have seen, to get the present believers in action, and lovers of political talking and doing, to make a return upon their own minds, scrutinise their stock 265 notions and habits much more, value their present talking and doing much less; in order that, by learning to think more clearly, they may come at last to act less confusedly. But how shall we pursuade our Barbarian to hold lightly to his feudal usages; how shall we pursuade our Nonconformist that his time spent in agitating for the abolition of church-rates would have been better spent in getting worthier ideas than churchmen have of God and the ordering of the world, or his time spent in battling for voluntaryism in education better spent in learning to value and found a public and national culture; how shall we persuade, finally, our Alderman-Colonel not to be content with sitting in the hall of judgment or marching at the head of his men of war, without some knowledge how to perform judgment and how to direct men of war,—how, I say, shall we persuade all these of this, if our Alderman-Colonel sees that we want to get his leading-staff and his scales of justice for our own hands; or the Nonconformist, that we want for ourselves his platform; or the Barbarian, that we want for ourselves his pre-eminency and function? Certainly they will be less slow to believe, as we want them to believe, that the intelligible law of things has in itself something desirable and precious, and that all place, function, 266 and bustle are hollow goods without it, if they see that we can content ourselves with it, and find in it our satisfaction, without making it an instrument to give us for ourselves place, function, and bustle.

And although Mr. Sidgwick says that social usefulness really means "losing oneself in a mass of disagreeable, hard, mechanical details," and though all the believers in action are fond of asserting the same thing, yet, as to lose ourselves is not what we want, but to find the intelligible law of things, this assertion too we shall not blindly accept, but shall sift and try it a little first. And if we see that because the believers in action, forgetting Goethe's maxim, "to act is easy, to think is hard," imagine there is some wonderful virtue in losing oneself in a mass of mechanical details, therefore they excuse themselves from much thought about the clear ideas which ought to govern these details, then we shall give our chief care and pains to seeking out those ideas and to setting them forth; being persuaded, that, if we have the ideas firm and clear, the mechanical details for their execution will come a great deal more simply and easily than we now suppose. And even in education, where our Liberal friends are now with   267 much zeal, bringing out their train of practical operations and inviting all men to lend them a hand; and where, since education is the road to culture, we might gladly lend them a hand with their practical operations if we could lend them one anywhere; yet, if we see that any German or Swiss or French law for education rests on very clear ideas about the citizen's claim, in this matter, upon the State, and the State's duty towards the citizen, but has its mechanical details comparatively few and simple, while an English law for the same concern is ruled by no clear idea about the citizen's claim and the State's duty, but has, in compensation, a mass of minute mechanical details about the number of members on a school-committee, and how many shall be a quorum, and how they shall be summoned, and how often they shall meet,—then we must conclude that our nation stands in more need of clear ideas on the main matter than of laboured details about the accessories of the matter, and that we do more service by trying to help it to the ideas, than by lending it a hand with the details. So while Mr. Samuel Morley and his friends talk of changing their   268 policy on education, not for the sake of modelling it on more sound ideas, but "for fear the management of education should be taken out of their hands," we shall not much care for taking the management out of their hands and getting it into ours; but rather we shall try and make them perceive, that to model education on sound ideas is of more importance than to have the management of it in one's own hands ever so fully.

At this exciting juncture, then, while so many of the lovers of new ideas, somewhat weary, as we too are, of the stock performances of our Liberal friends upon the political stage, are disposed to rush valiantly upon this public stage themselves, we cannot at all think that for a wise lover of new ideas this stage is the right one. Plenty of people there will be without us,—country gentlemen in search of a club, demagogues in search of a tub, lawyers in search of a place, industrialists in search of gentility,—who will come from the east and from the west, and will sit down at that *Thyestean banquet of clap-trap, which English public life for these many years past has been. Because, so long as those old organisations, of which we have seen the insufficiency,—those expressions of   269 our ordinary self, Barbarian or Philistine,—have force anywhere, they will have force in Parliament. There, the man whom the Barbarians send, cannot but be impelled to please the Barbarians' ordinary self, and their natural taste for the bathos; and the man whom the Philistines send, cannot but be impelled to please those of the Philistines. Parliamentary Conservatism will and must long mean this, that the Barbarians should keep their heritage; and Parliamentary Liberalism, that the Barbarians should pass away, as they will pass away, and that into their heritage the Philistines should enter. This seems, indeed, to be the true and authentic promise of which our Liberal friends and Mr. Bright believe themselves the heirs, and the goal of that great man's labours. Presently, perhaps, Mr. Odger and Mr. Bradlaugh will be there with their mission to oust both Barbarians and Philistines, and to get the heritage for the Populace. We, on the other hand, are for giving the heritage neither to the Barbarians nor to the Philistines, nor yet to the Populace; but we are for the transformation of

270   each and all of these according to the law of perfection. Through the length and breadth of our nation a sense,—vague and obscure as yet,—of weariness with the old organisations, of desire for this transformation, works and grows. In the House of Commons the old organisations must inevitably be most enduring and strongest, the transformation must inevitably be longest in showing itself; and it may truly be averred, therefore, that at the present juncture the centre of movement is not in the House of Commons. It is in the fermenting mind of the nation; and his is for the next twenty years the real influence who can address himself to this.

Pericles was perhaps the most perfect public speaker who ever lived, for he was the man who most perfectly combined thought and wisdom with feeling and eloquence. Yet Plato brings in Alcibiades declaring, that men went away from the oratory of Pericles, saying it was very fine, it was very good, and afterwards thinking no more about it; but they went away from hearing Socrates talk, he says, with the point of what he had said sticking fast in their minds, and they could not get rid of it. Socrates is poisoned and dead; but in his own breast does not every man carry about

271   with him a possible Socrates, in that power of a disinterested play of consciousness upon his stock notions and habits, of which this wise and admirable man gave all through his lifetime the great example, and which was the secret of his incomparable influence? And he who leads men to call forth and exercise in themselves this power, and who busily calls it forth and exercises it in himself, is at the present moment, perhaps, as Socrates was in his time, more in concert with the vital working of men's minds, and more effectually significant, than any House of Commons' orator, or practical operator in politics.

Every one is now boasting of what he has done to educate men's minds and to give things the course they are taking. Mr. Disraeli educates, Mr. Bright educates, Mr. Beales educates. We, indeed, pretend to educate no one, for we are still engaged in trying to clear and educate ourselves. But we are sure that the endeavour to reach, through culture, the firm intelligible law of things, we are sure that the detaching ourselves from our stock notions and habits, that a more free play of consciousness, an increased desire for sweetness and light, and all the bent which we call Hellenising,   272 is the master-impulse now of the life of our nation and of humanity,— somewhat obscurely perhaps for this moment, but decisively for the immediate future; and that those who work for this are the sovereign educators. Docile echoes of the eternal voice, pliant organs of the infinite will, they are going along with the essential movement of the world; and this is their strength, and their happy and divine fortune. For if the believers in action, who are so impatient with us and call us effeminate, had had the same fortune, they would, no doubt, have surpassed us in this sphere of vital influence by all the superiority of their genius and energy over ours. But now we go the way the world is going, while they abolish the Irish Church by the power of the Nonconformists' antipathy to establishments, or they enable a man to marry his deceased wife's sister.

The End.

A Glossary
to *Culture and Anarchy*
(1869)

As a means of cross-referencing within the text of the entries, words and phrases that have their own entries are set in boldface. An asterisk marks a phrase taken from *Culture and Anarchy*; the number of the page on which the first word of the phrase occurs in the 1869 edition stands in brackets at the end of the entry.

Abelard [Peter] (1079–1142): twelfth-century theologian, remembered for his illicit marriage to Heloïse and brutal punishment as well as for his numerous theological writings.

Alcibiades (c. 450–404 B.C.): gifted but perhaps unsound Athenian general and statesman, thought to intend the overthrow of the state. Arnold used him as a metaphor for the editor (Justin McCarthy) of the *Morning Star*.

Alhambra, the: London hall in Leicester Square, used, like **St. Martin's**, for the presentation of **recreative religion**, i.e., Sunday night lectures on science, philosophy, and other subjects.

Alvey [Richard] (d. 1584): master of the Temple, a building in London then occupied by the Knights Templars and now housing the Inns of Court.

Andrewes, Bishop [Lancelot] (1555–1626): **Anglican** divine, renowned for his preaching, influential in the establishment of a theology opposed to the strictness of **Puritanism** and **Calvinism.**

Anglican Establishment: the official **Church of England**, in its hierarchical organization and in its close relation to the State and the Monarchy.

Antoinette, Elderess: a cult religious figure discussed by William Hepworth **Dixon** in his writings on the **Mormons** and other American sects.

Archimedes (c. 287–212 B.C.): Greek mathematician, physicist, and inventor, famous for his discovery that materials of different densities displaced different volumes of water, and for his illustration of the principle of the lever.

Arminius (c. 18 B.C.–17 A.D.): German hero who defeated the Romans decisively in A.D. 9. His name was appropriated by Arnold for his admired Prussian protagonist in *Friendship's Garland* (1871).

Atheism: literally, Godlessness. Arnold's use of the term here to describe the attitude of the London *Times* toward religious questions comes under what might be called religious relativism, with a strong leaning toward public, though not necessarily private, agnosticism.

Augustine [of Hippo], **St.** (354–430): transmitter of Platonism, author of the immensely powerful *Confessions* and the *City of God,* and revered by Roman Catholics as a "Doctor of the Church."

Aurelius, Marcus (121–180): great Roman emperor, celebrated for his noble character; the *Meditations,* his Stoic classic, remains one of the great works of the Western tradition.

Balaam's ass: in Numbers (22:21–30), the beast of burden who speaks to his obstinate master to convey the will of the Lord.

Bancroft [Richard] (1544–1610): Archbishop of Canterbury, whose works were in the main directed against the **Puritans**.

Barrow [Isaac] (1630–77): **Anglican** divine, also a mathematical and classical scholar, educated at Peterhouse, Cambridge; his sermons were highly regarded, and he was also noted for resigning his Cambridge professorship in favor of his pupil, Isaac Newton.

Bastiat [Frédéric] (1801–50): French economist and advocate of free trade.

Bateson, Sir Thomas (1819–85): Conservative M.P. for Devizes 1864–85, strongly opposed to electoral reform.

***Battle of the Books**: see **Swift** [23].

Baxter [Richard] (1615–91): **Presbyterian** divine, maltreated for his lapses from **Church of England** orthodoxy.

Baxter [William Edward] (1825–90): **Liberal** M.P. and writer on foreign travel; strongly advocated the eventual disestablishment of the **Church of England.**

Bazley [Sir Thomas] (1797–1885): cotton-spinner and politician, member of Anti-Corn Law League, M.P. for Manchester 1858–80.

Beales [Edmond] (1803–81): radical advocate of electoral reform, and president of the **Reform League** (1865–69).

Beecher [Henry Ward] (1813–87): American **Congregationalist** minister and orator, brother of Harriet Beecher Stowe. A leading abolitionist, he was also sympathetic to female suffrage and influential in England as an advocate of the Union cause.

Belles-lettres: literally, literature of inherent imaginative rather than scientific or literary qualities; often used, however, to characterize trivial and merely "pretty" writing. It was in this sense that Frederic **Harrison** disparagingly applied the term to the work of Arnold and his idea of culture in his 1867 attack on what later became *Culture and Anarchy* [2].

*Be not ye called Rabbi: Matthew 23:8; this famous phrase is in Matthew part of an attack on those who observe the letter rather than the spirit of the law [45].

Bentham [Jeremy] (1748–1832): writer on law and ethics, best known for his utilitarian calculus of pleasure and pain: that "the greatest happiness of the greatest number is the foundation of morals and legislation." He exerted a great influence on James Mill, and thus on the education of Mill's son, John Stuart **Mill**; it was only through finding the utilitarian calculus heartless and empty that the young Mill was able to surmount the profound spiritual crisis of his early adulthood.

Binney [Thomas] (1798–1874): Nonconformist, i.e., **Congregationalist** divine; widely respected as far away from Britain as America and Australia.

Bolingbroke, Lord (1678–1751): statesman and political writer, later a friend of Alexander Pope and Jonathan **Swift**; his conception of monarchy as above factions was later to influence (with widely differing results) such diverse figures as George III and Benjamin **Disraeli**.

Bradlaugh [Charles] (1833–91): a social reformer, though opposed to socialism; he was a militant **atheist** who nonetheless claimed the right to occupy a seat in Parliament despite his being refused three times the right to take the oath or to affirm. First elected in 1880, finally, in 1886, he was permitted to take the oath and was seated.

*breaks down the park railings: see **Hyde Park riots**.

Bright, Jacob (1821–99): younger brother, with similar opinions, of **John Bright**.

Bright, John (1811–89): radical politician; opposed the Corn Laws and the Crimean war, supported the North in the American Civil War, and was an enthusiastic advocate of electoral reform; called by the political historian John Vincent "**Gladstone**'s bulldog."

British Banner: described by Super as "a weekly newspaper of the Evangelical **Nonconformists**, and more especially of the English Congregationalists. . . . Its intellectual caliber was low and its appeal to the families of the 'middle classes of Society' was through a curious combination of piety, scandal, and horror."

British College of Health: a large, imposing building dispensing vegetable pills devised by a certain James Morison (1770–1840) as a universal cure for human ills. For Arnold it was an example of quackery amongst the middle class.

British Constitution: unlike its written American counterpart, the British Constitution is unwritten, a congeries of history, customs, precedents, and legislation. Thus it is rather a way of life than a legal document, though it does include documents; again unlike its American counterpart, it may be changed by simple Act of Parliament, rather than by the cumbersome American process of amendment and ratification.

Broad Church: a constituent part of the **Church of England**, supported by those who downplayed positive theological definitions and interpreted **Anglican** practices and doctrine in a broad and liberal rather than narrow and conservative sense.

Browning, Oscar (1837–1923): assistant master at **Eton** (1860–75), dismissed on what the *Concise Dictionary of National Biography* calls "unsubstantiated charges of misconduct." Later became an important figure at King's College, Cambridge, where, as the story is told by E. F. Benson, he was administered a notable rebuff by Alfred **Tennyson**: responding to Browning's bluff opening words "I am Browning," the poet answered back, "No, you're not."

Buchanan, Robert (1841–1901): poet and novelist, who attacked Arnold and then (at least according to Arnold himself) suspected the victim of writing anonymously against him. Buchanan's chief claim to fame lay in attacking D. G. Rossetti, Algernon Swinburne and their associates in an article titled "The Fleshly School of Poetry."

Buckle [Henry Thomas] (1821–62): author of the Victorian popular classic *The History of Civilisation in England*; partisan of freethinking.

Burghley, Lord [William Cecil] (1520–98): lord high treasurer (1572–98) and chief minister of Queen Elizabeth; responsible for the execution of Mary Queen of Scots.

Bush, Professor: a cult religious figure discussed by William Hepworth **Dixon** in his writings on the **Mormons** and other American sects.

Butler, Deborah: a cult religious figure discussed by William Hepworth **Dixon** in his writings on the **Mormons** and other American sects.

Butler [Joseph] (1692–1752): bishop of Durham, said to have refused the see of Canterbury in 1747. Arnold admired him because he worked within the Establishment, though he was thought by some to have died a Roman Catholic.

Buxton, Charles (1823–71): **Liberal** politician and brewer.

Calvin [John] (1509–64): one of the most important figures of the Protestant **Refor-**

mation. He was living in and virtually ruling Geneva, was brilliant and intolerant, and to this day is a symbol of stern and unbending moral conduct. At his most powerful, he controlled all aspects of individual and civic life in Geneva.

Canning [George] (1770–1827): prime minister under George IV in 1827 and chancellor of the exchequer in 1827. In 1797 he wrote a skit on the poet Robert Southey for the *Anti-Jacobin*, in which a "friend of humanity" attempted to inflame a "needy knife-grinder" against the rich, and failed to excite the downtrodden man's egalitarian passions.

Canterbury, Dean of [Henry Alford] (1810–71): translated the *Odyssey* in blank verse and was the first editor of the *Contemporary Review*.

Carlyle [Thomas] (1795–1881): the great prophet-cum-social critic of the nine-teenth century in England. Deeply affected by **Goethe**, he was perhaps most influen-tial for his idea of the aristocratic hero as redeemer of society. Though his last years were spent in a kind of rhetorical crankiness, he did, in the earlier parts of *Shooting Niagara: And After?* (1867), understand (despite an insupportable overvaluation of the capacities of an aristocracy—even one of his own imagining—to lead society) many of the risks being run in a sudden expansion of the franchise.

Cartwright [Thomas] (1535–1603); English **Puritan** churchman; led the English congregation at Antwerp in the 1580s.

Cattle, Rev. W[illiam] (?): a **Wesleyan** minister in the chair at the 1867 anti-Catholic speech in Birmingham of William **Murphy**; the remarks Arnold attributes to Cattle were actually made by Murphy.

Cecils: English family of statesmen, whose eminent members have included Lord **Burghley** and Lord Salisbury (1830–1903), three times prime minister under Queen Victoria.

Chambers [Thomas] (1814–91): **Liberal** M.P. 1852–57 and 1865–85; supporter of legislation permitting a man to marry his deceased wife's sister.

Church of England: term used variously to refer to the institution of Christianity in England from its beginnings in the fourth century or earlier, or to the institution that remained as the national religious establishment after **Henry VIII**'s break with Rome.

*Church rates: taxes levied on members of all religious denominations for the support of the local **Anglican** church. Not surprisingly, these rates were highly distasteful to **Dissenters** [xix].

Clarendon [Edward, Earl of] (1609–74): barrister, significant political figure, and historian; author of *The History of the Rebellion* (1703–7). It is for him that the Clarendon Press, a distinguished imprint of Oxford University Press, is named.

Glossary

Cobbe [Frances Power] (1822–1904): philanthropist and religious writer; editor of the works of the American Unitarian Theodore Parker (d. 1860). She was also a supporter of Bishop **Colenso**, whose debunking of the literal meaning of the Bible had been attacked by Arnold as naive and mean-spirited in "The Bishop and the Philosopher [Spinoza]" (1863), one of the *Essays in Criticism, First Series* (1865).

Colenso [Bishop John William] (1814–83): **Anglican** divine and bishop of Natal in South Africa, who attempted to prove the literal falsity of the Pentateuch by finding numerous arithmetical and historical inaccuracies, inconsistencies, and contradictions.

Commercial Travellers: group of what in America would be called traveling salesmen, which founded a school in 1845 for the education of members' needy children.

Comte [Auguste] (1798–1857): French philosopher and sociologist, and the founder of Positivism. His freethinking system was based on what might be called the religion of humanity, and toward the end of his life he was supported by gifts from the philosopher John Stuart **Mill** and the historian George Grote.

Congregational Church: church organization based on the autonomy of each individual church. In its emphasis on local self-government, it represented a further extension of Protestantism from the idea of a national church, such as the **Church of England**.

Congreve [Richard] (1818–99): positivist who at Oxford converted Arnold's future antagonist Frederic **Harrison** to Comtism.

Constantine (c. 274–337): Roman emperor; established Christianity as a state religion in 324.

*****Corinthian style**: term used by Arnold to attack newspaper articles and editorials in general, and the *Daily Telegraph* and G. A. **Sala** in particular, for what he saw as their tawdry, empty, and brutal expression [x].

Corinthians, Epistle to the: 1 Corinthians, in which St. **Paul** describes the resurrection of the dead.

Cornell [Ezra] (1807–74): capitalist and founder of Cornell University in Ithaca, New York. In its founding in 1865 by an act of the New York State legislature, it was made clear that its paramount purpose was to be the teaching of matters concerning "agriculture and the mechanic arts."

corpus vile: according to *The Concise Oxford English Dictionary* (1976), a "thing worthless except as object of experiments."

Daily News: **Liberal** newspaper of large circulation, founded in 1846; in 1869, it absorbed Bright's paper, the *Morning Star*.

Glossary

Daily Telegraph: London mass circulation newspaper, founded in 1855 and edited for a short time by Charles Dickens. It soon became a **Liberal** organ and was a persistent and often caustic critic of Arnold. For his part, Arnold disliked what he saw as its philistine, juvenile, and vulgarly patriotic—not to say self-satisfied and complacent—tone.

Daniel, Book of: a description of the Babylonian Captivity, this book of the Bible was traditionally thought to have been written in the sixth century B.C., but is now appears to have been written between 168 and 165 B.C.

Dennison, Archdeacon [George Anthony] (1805–96): a combative leader of High Church **Anglicans** in their opposition to Bishop **Colenso** and the later *Essays and Reviews* (1860), the collection of liberalizing religious articles that brought charges of heresy down on their clergyman authors, including Benjamin Jowett (1817–93), later headmaster of Balliol College, Oxford, and translator of Plato.

Deontology: a work (posthumously published in 1834) by Jeremy **Bentham** treating of the "science" of duty and moral obligation.

Dickson, Col. [Lothian Sheffield] (?–?): a leader of the **Reform League** in its organization of the **Hyde Park riots** in 1866.

Diggs, Zephaniah: a wily poacher, whose children would grow up to be as unschooled as their father, shown by Arnold in *Friendship's Garland* as an example of the less attractive aspects of English rural life.

Disraeli [Benjamin] (1804–81): statesman and novelist, twice prime minister under Queen Victoria, and the chief proponent, if not the actual discoverer, of "Tory Democracy"—the notion of a continuing alliance between the Conservatives and the working classes. He seems to have been something of an admirer of Arnold, who, in a letter (February 21, 1881) to his sister, wrote of a meeting with Disraeli at Lady Airlie's: "I told him of my having mentioned to Gladstone some of the epigrammatic things in *Endymion,* and he said—'But I don't want to talk about my things, I want to talk about *you.*' He went on to say that he read me with delight, that I was doing very great good, and ended by declaring that I was the only living Englishman who had become a classic in his own lifetime. The fact is that what I have done in establishing a number of current phrases—such as Philistinism, sweetness and light, and all that—is just the sort of thing to strike him. He had told Lady Airlie before I came that he thought it a great thing to do, and when she answered that she thought it was rather a disadvantage, for people got hold of my phrases and then thought they knew all about my work, he answered—Never mind, it's a great achievement!"

Dissenters: those protestants who separated themselves in the seventeenth century and thereafter from membership in the established **Church of England** and thus from the **Anglican** Communion; the term is similar to **Nonconformists**.

Dives: as explained by Super, *dives* is the word in the Vulgate (the Latin translation of the Bible) for the rich man in Luke 16:19 who dines luxuriously while the beggar Lazarus wanted the crumbs from his table.

Dixon, [William] **Hepworth** (1821–79): editor of the *Athenaeum*, journalist, and travel writer; caused a great stir with his books on the variform religious life in America. His chief book discussing the **Mormons**, *Spiritual Wives* (Arnold seems to have gotten the title wrong), appeared in 1868.

*editor of the *Daily Telegraph*: according to *The Concise Dictionary of National Biography*, Edward Levy-Lawson (1833–1916) was editor of the *Daily Telegraph* from 1855; *Peterboro Court* (1955), the quasi-inside history of the paper by Lord Burnham, suggests that Levy-Lawson (the son of the proprietor) was editor in fact but not in name [52].

Edmonds, Judge: a cult religious figure discussed by William Hepworth **Dixon** in his writings on the **Mormons** and other American sects.

Elcho, Lord (1818–1914): opponent in the House of Commons of the extension of the franchise in 1866, and hooted by the **Hyde Park rioters**, who also damaged his house in St. James's Place.

Ephraim: younger son of Joseph and progenitor of one of the twelve tribes of Israel.

Epictetus (c. 55–c. 135): Stoic philosopher, through his posthumous publications a major influence on the Emperor **Marcus Aurelius**.

Episcopalianism: the principles of an Episcopalian, a member of a church governed by bishops; used to describe the practices of the **Church of England** and related churches throughout the world.

Epsom on the Derby day: race course in Surrey, near London, where each year is run the Derby, named after the Earl of Derby and founded in 1780.

Eton: English boy's school, of a type called public in England and private in the United States, renowned for its social panache and for the excellence (in the nineteenth century) of its classical education.

Faraday [Michael] (1791–1867): great English chemist, responsible for major discoveries in electricity, magnetism, and the behavior of gasses under pressure.

Fenian: member of the Fenian Brotherhood, a secret society established in the late 1850s in Ireland and the United States to achieve Irish independence by armed force.

Figaro: the French words, meaning roughly "Who's being fooled here," according to Super are an aside of Don Bazile (not Figaro) in Beaumarchais' *Le Barbier de Séville*, act 3.

Francis, St.: presumably (since there are several other saints Francis) St. Francis of Assisi (1181/2–1226), founder of the Franciscan Order. In the popular mind, he is best known for the story of his having once preached to the birds at Alviano.

Franklin [Benjamin] (1706–90): American Founding Father, natural scientist, diplomat, and crackerbarrel philosopher.

Frederick, Elder: a cult religious figure discussed by William Hepworth **Dixon** in his writings on the **Mormons** and other American sects.

French Academy: founded in the 1630s by Cardinal Richelieu, the Académie française has served as a symbol of hierarchical control of the French language and literary culture. Intensely conservative due to its self-selecting membership, limited to forty, it nonetheless has seemed to many, very much including Arnold, as establishing a principle of cultural order and taste. Arnold was well aware that such an academy was not possible in England, but he never tired of pointing out (as in his 1864 essay "The Literary Influence of Academies," in *Essays in Criticism: First Series*) the losses his own country suffered thereby.

Froude [James Anthony] (1818–94): English historian and editor, originally sympathetic to John Henry **Newman** but later a disciple and close friend of Thomas **Carlyle**, whose literary executor and biographer he was.

*Geneva church discipline: see **Calvin** [xxxix].

Gladstone [William Ewart] (1809–98): with **Disraeli**, the leading British political figure of the second half of the nineteenth century. At first a Conservative, he became a devout Liberal in politics, and indeed a symbol of classical liberalism in both politics and economics. He was also an equally devout **Anglican**. Nevertheless, he presided over both the increasing rhetoric of democratically responsive government and the growing secularization of the state. His relations with Arnold were cool, and marred, one suspects, by mutual accusations of humbuggery.

Goethe [Johann Wolfgang von] (1749–1832): German poet, dramatist, novelist, and scientist. Vastly more than a German, he was a great European, and to this day represents the highest achievements of post-antiquity Apollonian culture. His influence on England, first on Carlyle, and then on Arnold, was incalculable.

Gooch, Sir Daniel (1816–89): English engineer and industrialist who went from a position as locomotive superintendent of the Great Western Railway to supervising the laying of the Atlantic cable. He then saved the Great Western Railway, headquartered at Swindon, from bankruptcy.

Graham's useful education clauses: in 1843, Sir James Graham (1792–1861) introduced a bill into the House of Commons limiting the hours worked by children and requiring that schools be provided for them. Objections by **Dissenters** and Roman

Catholics forced the withdrawal of the bill because of their fear of **Church of England** control.

Greg [William Rathbone] (1809–81): social and political essayist and mill owner who wrote an article against Arnold's essay attacking Bishop Colenso.

Hammond [Edward Payson] (1831–1910): according to Super, citing Ian Gregor, an American evangelist who in 1868 led revival meetings for children in London much criticized as tasteless.

Hardy [Gathorne, Earl of Cranbrook] (1814–1906): Conservative statesman, home secretary who replaced Spencer Walpole in office after the **Hyde Park riots**.

Hare, Dr.: a cult religious figure discussed by William Hepworth **Dixon** in his writings on the **Mormons** and other American sects.

Harrison, Frederic (1831–1923): lawyer, historian, critic, and Positivist. He roundly mocked Arnold's mature conception of culture (which emerged full-blown two years later in *Culture and Anarchy*) on its first magazine appearance in 1867.

Hebrews, Epistle to the: a part of the New Testament once ascribed to St. **Paul**, it definitively proclaims the superiority of the new Christianity to Judaism, which, in the author's eyes, it has replaced.

Heine [Heinrich] (1797–1856): German lyric poet and essayist of Jewish birth. As Super points out, Arnold took from Heine such core ideas as the contrast between Hebraism and Hellenism, as he also took from him the use of the word *Philistine*.

Henry VIII (1491–1547): from 1509 king of England, Henry was in effect the founder of the **Church of England**, as distinct from the Church of Rome. He was particularly interested in the issue of **marriage with a deceased wife's sister**.

Herbert, George (1593–1633): English poet and divine, influential nearly two centuries later on Samuel Taylor Coleridge.

Herder [Johann Gottfried von] (1744–1803): German philosopher and critic who exerted strong influence on **Goethe** and the Romantics. He also influenced Arnold's ideas of culture as in some sense taking the place of religion.

Hoare, Sir Henry (?–?): **Liberal** M.P. during the 1860s, campaigned for the abolition of the purchase system (of officers' commissions) in the army.

*hole-and-corner churches: Arnold's contemptuous term for **Dissenters** and **Nonconformists**, strongly suggesting something (in the words of *The Shorter Oxford English Dictionary*) "secret, clandestine, and underhand" [xlvi].

Hooker [Richard] (c. 1554–1600): **Anglican** divine, author of *Laws of Ecclesiastical Polity* (1594 and various dates thereafter), opposed to the **Puritans** and thus to the literal construction of the Bible. As Super points out, Arnold admired Hooker because he, like Joseph **Butler** worked for change within, rather than outside, the Establishment.

Horton, Sarah: a cult religious figure discussed by William Hepworth **Dixon** in his writings on the **Mormons** and other American sects.

Humboldt [Karl Wilhelm von] (1767–1835): Prussian statesman and philologist. As Prussian minister of education he was responsible for the founding of the University of Berlin.

Huxley [Thomas Henry] (1825–95): natural scientist and spokesman for science. Though he was a personal friend of Arnold's, his essay (and earlier address) "Science and Culture" (1881), in its advocacy of scientific rather than classical education, was responsible for Arnold's answering essay "Literature and Science" (1882), included in *Discourses in America* (1885).

*****Hyde Park riots**: July 23–24, 1866. The Reform League, in its advocacy of electoral reform, organized a huge meeting to take place in London's Hyde Park; denied the use of the park by the government, the mob broke down a section of park railings and held the meeting anyway. The ineffectuality of the official response to the rioting spurred Thomas **Carlyle** and Arnold, among others, to see the danger of anarchy.

Imitation of Christ: classic of Christian devotional literature, traditionally ascribed to the German monk Thomas á Kempis (c.1380–1471).

Independent chapel: the Independents was another name, in use in Britain in the eighteenth century, for the **Congregational Church**.

*****Indo-European people**: in its contrast to "Semitic people," the use of this phrase is an example of the kind of racial analysis so popular in the nineteenth century as a means of explaining the particular characteristics of nations and peoples. In fairness to Arnold, this whole passage must be closely read for its careful balance and respectful tone [162].

*****invades a secretary of state's office**: a reference to an incident in 1867 when a group of English sympathizers of the **Fenians** penetrated the outer office of the Home Secretary to demand a pardon for several Fenians who, in the act of rescuing two prisoners in Manchester, killed a police sergeant and had thereupon been sentenced to death [60].

Irish Church: the Anglican church in Ireland, disestablished by legislation in 1869.

Jackson, Father [Thomas] (1783–1873): Wesleyan minister, preacher, edited works of John **Wesley** and his brother Charles.

Jacobinism: the most radical ideology of the French Revolution, suggesting the practice and necessity of widespread political murder. Arnold's use of the term in *Culture and Anarchy* stopped well short of the most violent aspects of the ideology.

James, St. (d. 44 A.D.): first of the Apostles to be martyred; the phrase quoted by Arnold is to be found in James 1:22.

Jeremiah (7th cent. B.C.): according to the *Oxford Dictionary of the Christian Church* (1957), "the most personal and sensitive of the O[ld] T[estament] prophets."

Joubert [Joseph] (1754–1824): French author of *pensées* (maxims or sayings) of wit, concision, elegance, and wisdom.

Journeyman Engineer: according to Gregor, the pseudonym of Thomas Wright, who wrote about the condition of the working classes from his own experience.

Lacordaire [Jean-Baptiste-Henri] (1802–61): Roman Catholic priest who became a Dominican; he was renowned for his funeral orations.

Latitudinarianism: seventeenth-century religious movement within the **Church of England** that put little weight on conformity to dogma, liturgy, and hierarchy.

Leo X (1475–1521): Giovanni de' Medici, second son of Lorenzo the Magnificent. As pope, he was easy-going and generous with money and offices, and oblivious to the larger significance of Martin **Luther**, whom he excommunicated in 1520.

Lessing [Gotthold Ephraim] (1729–81): German dramatist and man of letters; wrote the *Laokoon* (1766), to this day a central work in aesthetic theory. In his dramatic poem *Nathan the Wise* (1779) the title character was modeled sympathetically on the Jew Moses Mendelssohn, the grandfather of the composer Felix Mendelssohn.

Leviticus: third book of the Pentateuch, containing laws on sacrifice, ritual purification and holiness, and vows and tithes. Its regulation of sexual conduct has been a particular bone of contention in modernity.

*Liberals: a term for the holders in nineteenth-century England of a political position quite different from that advocated by liberals in twentieth-century America. In England its holders were in favor of the uninhibited exercise of the rights of private property, along with the absolute minimum of state interference in economic or any other aspects of life [xxviii].

Liberation Society: "the Society for Liberating Religion from State Patronage and Control," founded by Edward **Miall,** among others, in 1845.

Licensed Victualers: the Incorporated Licensed Victualers' Society, an association of what in America would be called saloon or tavern owners, which had founded a school for the education of members' needy children.

Glossary

Lincoln, Mrs. [Mary Todd]: President Abraham Lincoln's widow, who was unhappy and in financial difficulties after her husband's assassination.

Lincoln's Inn: one of four English legal societies that regulate admission to the bar.

Lowe [Robert; created Viscount Sherbrooke 1880] (1811–92): Liberal politician and Arnold's powerful adversary in education. Lowe advocated a shift from the teaching of classical languages to modern languages as well as the payment to state-supported schools for the learning of basic skills rather than the humanistic education advocated by Arnold. Lowe's speech on the teaching of languages was given in Edinburgh on November 1, 1867. Lowe is also remembered for his remark in an 1867 speech to the House of Commons: "I believe it will be absolutely necessary that you should prevail on our future masters to learn their letters." Arnold's answer to Lowe's basic educational philosophy is contained in his essay "The Twice-Revised Code" (1862).

Lucretius (c. 99–55 B.C.): Roman poet, opposed to all forms of religious belief.

Luther [Martin] (1483–1546)/**Lutheran Church**: German founder of the Protestant **Reformation** in 1517. The church named after him gained its greatest ascendancy in his native country.

*****machinery**: Arnold's dismissive term for the arrangements and procedures of society and government, which he found at best only accessories to the achievement of human perfection—a change in the state of inner consciousness and being that could only be achieved through religion and culture [li].

*****Malvina's Oscar, as recorded by the family poet Ossian**: a jocular reference to the Ossianic poems by the Scots-Gaelic poet James Macpherson (1736–96). These poems were originally ascribed to Ossian, a legendary third-century Gaelic warrior, but were in fact combinations of traditional poems with fragments of Macpherson's own invention [xiv].

*****man who gives an inflammatory lecture**: a reference to William **Murphy** [60].

*****marriage with a deceased wife's sister**: English law, following **Anglican** ordinances, prohibited a man from marrying his deceased wife's sister or the widow of his brother; the origins of this prohibition go back to the English **Reformation**, when **Henry VIII** attempted to have his marriage to Catherine of Aragon (the widow of his elder brother Arthur) declared invalid, that he might be able to marry Anne Boleyn. In the face of opposition from the pope, Henry insisted on the legality of his proposed marriage to Anne. Thus the issue became an important element in the independence of the **Church of England** from Rome, and an integral part of the **Anglican Establishment**. In Arnold's time, this issue was a symbol of the **Dissenters'** demand for control over their own religious laws, which included the right of marriage to a deceased's wife's sister. Arnold's opposition to the demanded change in the law arose less from any sympathy for the Anglican position than from his fervid support of the principle of religious, in this case Anglican, establishment [xix].

Martinus Scriblerus [*Memoirs of*]: satire attacking "false tastes in learning" written mainly by John Arbuthnot (1667–1735), a physician, friend of Jonathan **Swift**, and acquaintance of Alexander Pope. The work was included in Pope's *Works* (1741).

Melancthon [Philipp] (1497–1560): German Protestant reformer and disciple of **Luther**, though less stringent than his master.

Memorabilia: work by Xenophon (c.430–c.354 B.C.); Greek historian; it contains an account of Socrates somewhat different from Plato's.

Miall, Edward (1809–81)/Mialism: leader of the English **Dissenters**, founded the newspaper the **Nonconformist** in 1840; Arnold gave his name to Mialism, by which he meant "nonconformity," the refusal to obey the theological and socio-political requirements of membership in the regnant **Anglican Establishment**.

Michelet [Jules] (1798–1874): French historian; wrote a 24-volume *History of France* (1833–1867).

Mill [John Stuart] (1806–73)/Millism: English (modified) Utilitarian philosopher and radical social reformer. His short book *On Liberty* (1859) is the bible of civil libertarians in the English-speaking world; his *Autobiography* (1873) gives another, and more humanly interesting, side of this remarkable mind. Arnold coined the term *Millism* to describe the Utilitarian aspect of Mill's positions.

Milton [John] (1608–74): one of the greatest English poets; author of such classics as *Paradise Lost* (1658–63) and *Paradise Regained* (1674).

Mirabeau [Honoré] (1749–91): French orator, politician, and sometime revolutionary. Later, he also attempted to save the monarchy.

Montesquieu [Charles] (1689–1755): French philosopher and jurist. His major achievement was *The Spirit of the Laws* (1748), in which the **British Constitution** was held up as a model.

Morley [Samuel] (1809–86): English manufacturer, politician, and philanthropist. Though a committed **voluntaryist**, he recommended in 1867 that **Dissenters** accept state grants for their schools.

Mormons: name most often used for the Church of Jesus Christ of Latter-Day Saints, an originally American, though now worldwide, religion based upon the discovery by Joseph Smith in 1830, through revelation, of the Book of Mormon.

Morning Star (1856–69): a penny newspaper controlled by **John Bright** and his fellow radical Richard Cobden.

Murphy [William] (1823–72): described by Super as "an agent of the L
Protestant Electoral Union," Murphy was a firebrand who in 1867 gave a ser
anti-Catholic lectures in Birmingham, attacking the existence of nunneries
warning women of the supposed dangers of the confessional. After many prot
his right to speak was officially upheld.

*muscular Christianity: a conception of religion associated with Rev. Charles Kin
ley (1819–75), an **Anglican** clergyman, social reformer, and novelist. This conce
tion, to some extent stemming from the work of Arnold's father Thomas as mast
of Rugby School, combined high Christian ethical ideals with the enjoyment o
high spirits, physical exercise, and a general enthusiasm for life [32].

Nation, The: American weekly of independent liberal politics founded in 1865 by
E. L. Godkin, who served as its editor from 1865 to 1881; its editor from 1909 to
1914 was the conservative classicist and philosophical historian Paul Elmer More.
For the past half-century and more it has been a leading organ of advanced left-
wing opinion.

Newman [John Henry] (1801–90): English theologian. Prior to 1845, when he
became a Roman Catholic, he led a conservative reform group (known as the
Tractarian or **Oxford movement**) within the **Anglican Church** of great power, influence,
and intellectual and moral distinction. For Arnold, who found himself deeply
opposed to Newman's theology, Newman nonetheless represented the true spirit of
Oxford, of (in Arnold's words in *Culture and Anarchy*) "the beauty and sweetness
of that beautiful place" [35]. Newman's *Apologia Pro Vita Sua* (1864), written to
answer charges of mendacity leveled at him and his fellow Catholics by Charles
Kingsley, is a classic of intellectual biography.

Nicole [Pierre] (1625–95): French moralist and theologian.

Nonconformists: synonymous with **Dissenters**.

Nonconformist, the: newspaper edited by Edward **Miall**, whose motto, made much of
critically by Arnold, was taken from Edmund Burke's Speech on Conciliation
(1775).

*Nonconformist Union: it is unclear to which group Arnold is referring here. The
N.U. has not been identified by any of Arnold's editors [205].

Notre Dame: cathedral church of Paris and the most notable example of early French
Gothic architecture. Its cornerstone was laid in 1163, but the building was not
completed until c. 1230. In the revolution of 1789, rioters turned the Cathedral into
a "Temple of Reason," in the process destroying some of its art.

Noyes, Brother [John Humphrey] (1811–86): radical American religious reformer,
founder of the Oneida Community, a utopian communist society practicing group
marriage, eugenics, and communal childcare.

Glossary

Odger [George] (1820–77): English trade-union leader, supporter of working-class political activity and extension of the franchise.

***one primeval language**: a crackpot theory of the origin of language in Sinaitic inscriptions, much derided by Arnold [x].

Oxford, bishop of [Samuel Wilberforce] (1805–73): a son of the renowned abolitionist William Wilberforce (1759–1833) and a mediator force in the conflicts within the **Anglican Church** between Evangelicals (those laying stress on personal conversion and salvation by faith) and Tractarians (followers of **Newman**).

Oxford movement: tendency in the **Church of England** that flourished between 1833 and 1845. It attempted, under the leadership of John Keble, John Henry **Newman**, and Edward **Pusey**, to defend the Church of England as a divine institution and to safeguard its rule from control by the State. It looked longingly to earlier, pre-Reformation Christianity for examples of devotion and strict dogma. The movement is also called Tractarian, after the ninety tracts published by its leaders.

Pericles (c. 490–429 B.C.): Athenian statesman, best known today through Thucydides' recounting of his funeral oration over the fallen in the Peloponnesian War.

Phaedo: The Platonic dialogue that treats of the final hours and death of Socrates.

Polly, Elderess: a cult religious figure discussed by William Hepworth **Dixon** in his writings on the **Mormons** and other American sects.

***pouvoir sans savoir est fort dangereux**: "Power without knowledge is terribly dangerous" [218].

posse comitatus: group of men over fifteen years of age, summoned by the sheriff of a county to put down riots, and other disturbances.

Preller [Ludwig] (1809–61): according to Gregor, Arnold is referring to Preller's *Römische Mythologie* (1858).

Presbyterianism: a form of Protestant organization in which church government is in the hands of presbyters or elders, with all leaders of equal ecclesiastical rank.

***Prime Minister**: Arnold here is referring to Lord **Burghley**, a particular favorite of Queen Elizabeth I [xxxix].

Puritans: English Protestants who regarded the original English **Reformation** as being incomplete in that it retained forms, observances, and practices of Roman Catholicism and demanded "purification" from what it saw as these continuing corruptions.

Pusey, Dr. [Edward Bouverie] (1800–1882): Regius Professor of Hebrew at Oxford,

a leader of the **Oxford movement**, but unlike John Henry **Newman** never a convert to Roman Catholicism.

Quarterly Review: influential literary-cum-political magazine founded in 1809 as a **Tory** counterweight to the Whig *Edinburgh Review*.

Quietism: a kind of mysticism that emphasizes passive devotion, extinguishing of the will, and total removal from the tyranny of the senses.

*quae regio in terris nostri non plena laboris? Vergil, *Aeneid* 1.460; in Gregor's translation, "What part of the world is not full of our calamities?" [36].

*recreative religion: according to Gregor, a reference to the removal in 1868 of the legal ban on serious lectures on the Sabbath [iii].

Reeve, Henry (1813–95): formed the foreign policy of the London *Times* 1840–55, and edited the *Edinburgh Review* 1855–95.

Reformation: word loosely used to describe the changes in the Western Christian church between the fourteenth and the seventeenth centuries, which resulted in loss of unity under the aegis of the Roman Catholic Church and the pope.

Reform Bill of 1832: extension of the franchise to the middle class, accompanying a shift in representation from rural areas to the cities.

Reform League: founded in 1865 to promote the extension of the franchise; led by Edmond **Beales**. It played a major role in the **Hyde Park riots** of 1866, but with the Second Reform Act in 1867 its day had passed, and by 1869 it had disappeared.

Renan [Ernest] (1823–92): French revisionist religious historian, best known for his *Life of Jesus* (1863), which rejected the supernatural aspect of Jesus' life and presented him merely as a man.

Reville, Albert (1826–1906): French Protestant theologian of progressive views; an attack on his work by Gladstone caused a well-known argument between William **Gladstone** and T. H. **Huxley** on the Book of Genesis.

Robertson, Frederick (1816–53): **Anglican** preacher associated with a **Broad Church** theology; he was much respected for his sermons rather than his theology, and he appealed greatly to audiences of working men.

Roebuck [John Arthur] (1801–79): M.P., disciple of Jeremy **Bentham** and much praised by John Stuart **Mill**.

Rolt's Hall: according to Super, this name refers to Pratt's Hall, in Broad Street, Providence, R.I., where the third annual convention of the Spiritualists, an American religious sect, was held in 1866.

Romans, Epistle to the: the longest and most structured of the Epistles of St. **Paul**, this core document of Christianity describes the Gospel he preaches, and discusses the future of Israel and the daily requirements of Christian life.

Sainte-Beuve [Charles Augustin] (1804–69): great French literary critic, extravagantly admired by Arnold. For his part, Sainte-Beuve also praised Arnold highly.

Sala, [George Augustus] (1828–96): English journalist, foreign correspondent, and novelist; much mocked by Arnold (especially in *Friendship's Garland*) for his inflated style of writing in the *Daily Telegraph*.

Sallust (86–34 B.C.): Roman historian. The words he ascribed to Cato may be translated as "public poverty, private opulence."

Sandemanian: follower of Robert Sandeman (1718–71), a former Scottish Presbyterian; espoused the rigid doctrines of John **Calvin**, but opposed central or state control of religion.

Saturday Review: weekly of moderate opinions founded in 1855; amongst its many brilliant contributors were (as drama critics) George Bernard Shaw and Max Beerbohm.

Schleiermacher [Friedrich] (1768–1834): German theologian much interested in education and the reunion of religion, science, and philosophy. He was also an associate of Wilhelm von **Humboldt**.

Shakerism: an English religious sect, arising out of the Quakers in 1747, emphasizing communist and pacifist principles. The Shakers had their greatest success in the United States but by 1930 seemed on the verge of dying out. The shaking for which they are named comes from their physical behavior in meetings during moments of spiritual transport.

Sidgwick, Henry (1838–1900) English philosopher, much influenced by John Stuart **Mill**; harsh critic in 1867 of the opening chapter of *Culture and Anarchy* on its first appearance in the *Cornhill Magazine*.

Smith, Joe [Joseph] (1805–44): founder of the **Mormons**. In addition to the revelation to him of the Book of Mormon, he was later the recipient of a revelation concerning polygamy.

Smith, Dr. William (1813–93): editor of the *Quarterly Review* 1867–93, author of classical grammars and school editions of the classics. Though born a **Nonconformist**, he told Arnold that he agreed with Arnold's harsh criticism of them.

Socinian: one who denies the divinity of Christ. The origins of this position were in Italy in the sixteenth century, and it influenced later Unitarianism.

***Socrates is terribly at ease in Zion**: as Super points out, the origin of this phrase is in

Glossary

Amos 6:1: "Woe to them that are at ease in Zion." Arnold's use of this phrase, perhaps drawn more directly from Thomas **Carlyle**, is a powerful accusation against Socrates and Hellenism, and in effect an advocacy of Hebraism—the Old Testament emphasis on moral conduct—as against the calm sophistication of Hellenism [151].

SPCK: the Society for Promoting Christian Knowledge, founded in 1698 to promote charity schools in England and Wales, to provide bibles and religious tracts, and to conduct all manner of Christian education. It is still active today in both education and publishing.

Spurgeon's Tabernacle: The Metropolitan Tabernacle in London. Built by Charles Spurgeon (1834–92), a famed English Baptist preacher of the day, it opened in 1861 and could hold up to six thousand spectators.

Stanhope, Lord [Philip, fifth Earl of] (1805–75): historian, instrumental in creating the Historical Manuscripts Commission (1869); chairman of copyright commission (1875).

St. Martin's Hall: according to Gregor, a building in Long Acre that won the right in 1868 to present Sunday night lectures by T. H. **Huxley** on serious subjects. See also **recreative religion**.

Stuarts: Scottish noble family, fourteen of whose members occupied the Scottish throne and six also the English.

sweetness and light: see **Swift** [23].

Swift [Jonathan] (1667–1745): English satirist perhaps best known today for *Gulliver's Travels* (1726). Arnold took the phrase *sweetness and light* from Swift's *Battle of the Books* (1697), in which the conflict is between the ancients (represented by a bee) and the moderns (represented by a spider). For Swift, as for Arnold, the winner is the bee, who provides honey and wax, as the ancients provide sweetness and light.

Swinburne [Algernon] (1837–1909): English poet and aesthete, with whom Arnold seems to have had an amiable relationship. Soon after the writing of *Culture and Anarchy,* however, Arnold objected to Swinburne as both poet and man on grounds of his moral conduct, as we see in a letter from Arnold to Charles Kingsley (quoted in G. W. E. Russell's *Matthew Arnold* (1904): "If I was to think only of the Dissenters, or if I were in your position, I should press incessantly for more Hellenism; but, as it is, seeing the tendency of our *young* poetical litterateur (Swinburne), and, on the other hand, seeing much of Huxley (whom I thoroughly liked and admire, but find very disposed to be tyrannical and unjust), I lean towards Hebraism, and try to prevent the balance from on this side flying up out of sight."

Tarquins: legendary Etruscan family that ruled Rome beginning in the seventh century B.C.

*__Temple, Master of the__: Richard **Alvey** [xxxviii].

Tennyson [Alfred] (1809–92): celebrated English poet, appointed poet laureate in succession to William Wordsworth in 1850.

*__Thyesteän banquet of claptrap__: a reference to a banquet given by Atreus to celebrate his reconciliation with his brother Thyestes. Unbeknownst to Thyestes, Atreus served him with the flesh of Thyestes' own children; at this, the sun in revulsion turned back in its course. "Claptrap" is Arnold's word for the pretentious and empty rhetoric with which he found English public life to be conducted; the entire phrase refers (in *Friendship's Garland*) to the meeting of Parliament [268].

Times [of London]: most important of English newspapers, founded in 1785 and still existing today, though diminished in influence. It was the *Times*'s genius, during the century before World War II, to project to its powerful readers a position at once independent and reflective of the Government of the day. The *History of The Times,* in five volumes to date, represents the most significant, objective, and detailed account ever written of a great newspaper.

Timothy, Epistles to: St. **Paul**'s charge to his disciple regarding the combating of heresies and the organization of the church, including qualifications for the offices of presbyter and deacon.

Tories: originally a name for Irish outlaws, and later a name for those who opposed the exclusion of the Roman Catholic James, Duke of York, from the English throne. After 1689, it became a name for the party of Royalists and Cavaliers, and still later was opposed to the other great English political party, the Whigs. After 1830, the name was superseded by "Conservatives," though "Tories" is still in use as a reasonably honorific name for committed members of the Conservative party.

Tractarian movement: see **Oxford movement**.

Travers [Walter] (1548?–1635): **Puritan** divine.

*__truss manufactory on the finest site in Europe__: the placing of a truss factory and shop on Trafalgar Square, often called "the finest site in Europe" [64]. One may doubt whether Arnold himself had ever suffered from a hernia.

valley of Jehoshaphat: in Joel 3:1–14, the place of the day of the Lord's Final Judgment.

Villers: Elizabethan churchman; identified by Super as a "Calvinist divine."

Voluntaryism: the Protestant doctrine that the Church should have no spiritual relation to the State; it also opposes church establishment and the existence of State endowments for church support.

Walton, Isaac [or Izaak] (1593–1683): in his own time a famed biographer of such men as John Donne and Richard **Hooker**, known today as the author of *The Compleat Angler* (1653, 1655).

Watts, Dr. [Isaac] (1674–1748): English hymn writer, author of "Our God, our help in ages past."

Weeks, Newman: a cult religious figure discussed by William Hepworth **Dixon** in his writings on the **Mormons** and other American sects.

Wellington, Duke of [Arthur Wellesley] (1769–1852): celebrated English general and political leader, hero of the battle of Waterloo. As prime minister in 1829 he presided over Catholic Emancipation; he resigned office in 1830 over his opposition to electoral reform.

Wesley [John] (1703–91): founder of Methodism, a branch of Protestantism based on the priesthood of all believers.

Westminster Abbey: according to legend founded in the seventh century, it has been throughout its history the center of English national religious life. It houses the relics of Edward the Confessor; it is the traditional place for the coronation of the sovereign, and many of England's greatest figures from all walks of life are buried there.

Westminster, Dean of [Arthur Penrhyn Stanley] (1815–81): Broad Churchman, close friend of Arnold, student (and later biographer) of Arnold's father Thomas at Rugby School, and historian of Christianity and Judaism.

Westminster Review: founded in 1824 by Jeremy **Bentham** and James Mill, the father of John Stuart, as a platform for philosophical radicals.

White, Rev. Edward (1819–98): English minister identified by Super as a friend of Dean Stanley (see **Westminster, Dean of**) and by Wilson as a friend of Edward **Miall**.

Whitfield: perhaps a misspelling of George Whitefield (1714–70), a Methodist evangelist influenced by John **Wesley** and his brother Charles, but more inclined toward **Calvin** than they.

Whitgift, Archbishop [John] (c. 1530–1604): at the same time a supporter of the government of the church by bishops and the uniformity of ritual, and a follower in theology of John **Calvin**.

Wilson, Alderman [Samuel]: remembered today only for his refusal as colonel of militia to use force in putting down the **Hyde Park riots**, Wilson was a kinsman of J.

Dover Wilson, the Shakespearian scholar and invaluable editor of *Culture and Anarchy*.

Wilson, Bishop [Thomas] (1663–1755): his devotional writings, about which Arnold here is so complimentary, received wide circulation; they have been reprinted since the initial appearance of *Culture and Anarchy*.

Wotton, Sir Henry (1568–1639): diplomat and poet. According to Wilson, Arnold's quotation is "probably" from *The State of Christendom* (1657).

Xenophon: see **Memorabilia**.

Young [Brigham] (1801–77): American **Mormon** leader, who in 1847 led the Mormon migration west to Utah.

*****Young lions of the *Daily Telegraph***: Arnold's patronizing reference to his literary opponents on the *Daily Telegraph* and their display of jejune arrogance. One also assumes some rather more subtle reference to the British Lion, for Arnold so unsophisticated in comparison to his (the Lion's) counterpart nations on the Continent [35].

Zechariah: Old Testament prophet and author of the book of the Bible bearing his name.

Steven Marcus

Culture and
Anarchy Today

I

Culture and Anarchy is one of the chief English books of the nineteenth century. It occupies a prominent place among the canonical Victorian works of cultural criticism—both of the words that go into this characterizing descriptive term being permanently associated with Arnold's intellectual and spiritual life project. It is, moreover, an integral part of a tradition to which the principal writings of Thomas Carlyle, John Henry Newman, John Stuart Mill, and John Ruskin preeminently belong, as do, in equal measure, the works of the great Victorian novelists, and to which Walter Pater, Oscar Wilde, and William Morris, to stop at that point, were to make later, if lesser, contributions. *Belong* is probably too inactive a term for what should be properly thought of as constituting an institution of discourse that at least until recently sustained vital and cogent bearings upon a number of the most vexing and momentous problems of modern civilization.

Today, however, *Culture and Anarchy* often appears to be remembered as much for its language—its felicitous terms, phrases, and formulations—as it is for its arguments. Sweetness and Light; the best that has been thought and said in the world; Barbarians, Philistines, and Populace; Doing as One Likes; Hebraism and Hellenism, among many other terms, have entered into the permanent currency of critical diction in circulation among educated groups and academic audiences in the English-speaking world. But those handy and detachable bits of phraseology are memorable not merely by virtue of their ingenuity but also because they refer to and are a part of spirited and significant argumentative discussions that have a resonance beyond their original historical context and still retain some connections with matters of issue today.

That dense specific context can be briefly adverted to. The late 1860s in England contained among much else episodes of widespread political drama and agitation which culminated in the enactment of the Reform Bill of 1867. This new law broadened—indeed doubled—political representation in Britain: about one-third (or 2.5 million adult males) were enfranchised, and for the first time there was a large working-class presence among potential voters.[1] The expansion of the franchise was in large measure strategically located in the ugly, filthy, unhealthy, and planlessly expanding industrial regions and towns, as early industrial capitalism put its permanent mark upon British material life and its social and intellectual organizations and structures.

Arnold regarded the unprecedented historical panorama before him as a scene of both actual and increasingly possible anarchy. He perceived this anarchy as divided generally into two kinds: spiritual anarchy, which he associated largely with untrammeled middle-class economic and social forms of laissez-faire and a hyper-individualistic range of religions and intellectual actualities; and social anarchy, which he connected with what he recognized as the inevitable advent of modern democracy in a variety of manifestations. On both accounts, he was in the long run to be proved fundamentally right.

Although it would be excessive to say that Arnold foresaw an America of the end of the twentieth century as the inescapable outcome of the largest tendencies in modern society, there can be no doubt that the America of the 1860s—insofar as he understood it—was lodged very much in the forefront of his more anxious imaginings. More specifically, it was the kind of anarchy that the rising nonconformist and largely middle-class Protestant sects represented that dramatized for Arnold the spectrum of spiritual disorders and confusions that he undertook chiefly to address. Like almost all the great Victorian figures, he set himself—consciously and in the wake of such world-historical developments as the French and industrial revolutions—to confront the immense questions of how to reconcile progress or change with order and continuity.

The sets of problems entailed by such questions were compounded in their difficulty by the circumstance that the foremost ideological leanings of the imminently dominating socio-cultural stratum were strategically summed up—and called up—for him in the phrase "Doing as One Likes" in the economic, as well as some social and some intellectual, spheres of

---

1. Glyn Williams and John Ramsden, *Ruling Britannia: A Political History of Britain, 1688–1988* (London, 1990), p. 256. For a general contextual review, see Parke Honan, *Matthew Arnold: A Life* (New York, 1981), chaps. 14 and 15.

Steven Marcus

effort; while the correlative slogan *the dissidence of dissent and the Prot-estantism of the Protestant religion* captured for him allied tendencies in religion and what we would today call culture. Indeed, it is not, I believe, excessive to say that Arnold sensed or intuited in the matrix of nineteenth-century Dissenting British Protestantism a very early precursor of what nowadays goes by the temporary name of multiculturalism. I say tempor-ary because it is the most recent momentary form taken by a permanent current of thought, emotions, and general attitudes of preference in mod-ern democracies.

Arnold's sense of the way through this embroiled medium of endless difficulties is to recommend two connected remedies. The first takes a practical form and is to be actualized in an increased provision of educa-tion for both middle- and working-class children, a provision to be largely sponsored and implemented by the national state. The second, which in some sense includes the first, is the inculcation by a variety of means of the ideas, attitudes, practices, and habits of temperament and sensibility that are implicit in his master term, *culture*.

The precondition which allows for both of these recommendations to be allocated such a high spiritual priority, and indeed the presupposition for the entire array of arguments that Arnold puts forward in this book, is that revealed religion, specifically Christianity, has simply gone, van-ished, evaporated as the supreme truth of the world and hence as the ultimate authority or standard of values and spiritual ordering, and that modern societies must, in this primary sense, make do without it. Arnold says this almost at once in the Preface, when he speaks about the "divine impossibilities of religion" [vii]. This does not at all mean that religion is not extremely important to Arnold; far from it; but its importance to him is almost entirely moral and social, that is to say, generally institutional and secondary. Its binding importance is, in other words, no longer literally religious. What is to take the place of religion? For Arnold, the new, secularized, and displaced form that religion is to take is embodied in his protean conception of culture.[2] For example, he asserts that "earnest young men at schools and universities" must in the modern world con-ceive of "*salvation* as a harmonious perfection only to be won by unreser-vedly cultivating many sides in us" [xxxi] (emphasis added). The "forms of religion," he goes on (recklessly) to say, are "non-essentials" and indeed can detrimentally invade and preoccupy our minds [xxxii]. More-

---

2. It is never entirely clear how Arnold distributes the force of this assertion between its literal and metaphorical senses.

over, he presses on, it is impossible that "the forms in which the human spirit tries to express the inexpressible, or the forms by which man tries to worship, have or can have . . . for the follower of perfection, anything necessary or eternal. . . . What is alone and always sacred and binding for man is the making progress towards his total perfection; and the machinery by which he does this varies in value according as it helps him to do it" [xliv–xlv].

In other words, the "forms" that religion takes—namely, divine revelation, sovereign dogma, orthodox doctrines, inspired teachings, eternal commandments, sacred rituals, and sanctified traditions—are all secondary. The truth value of religion is, if not nugatory, then secondary, since all religions are almost altogether a circumstance of accidental or contingent historical formations. They are bits of "machinery" whose transhistorical moral, personal, and spiritual contents are separable from the concrete institutions in which they have been inessentially eventuated and are transferable to other contexts of experience. And Arnold proceeds to drive home this conclusion when he affirms at the end of the Introduction (and in the context of his profession that he is a Liberal) that he is, "above all, a *believer* in culture," and that he seeks to find grounds on which his "*faith* in culture . . . may rest securely*" (4–5) (emphasis added).

It hardly needs to be argued that this position put forth in these terms is logically unsustainable.[3] Once divine claims and supernatural sanctions are abducted from religion, once religion is naturalized, historicized, and relativized, there is no consequent way of investing any other set of beliefs that concern or prescribe norms, values, or truths of conduct and judgment—let alone ultimate truths—with anything that remotely resembles the credent certitude that the propositions and prescriptions of revealed religion carry. Arnold certainly knew this; he learned it from his great teacher, Newman. *Culture and Anarchy*, as a result, is logically built on sand. And yet this logical vulnerability and impairment are at the same time compact with its historical and intellectual relevance and life. It belongs to that inevitable process of the secularization of the spiritual which Hegel regarded as *the* essential component in the evolution of modern historical life. And by the same token it is part of a reciprocal process by which certain secular modes of experience were, at least for a significant historical interlude, partially and imperfectly resacralized.

---

3. Perhaps only an adherent of the Anglican church could have, even semi-seriously, brought it forward. As an intelligent wag once remarked, "Someone who is able to take the oath of allegiance to the Thirty Nine Articles will swear to anything."

Steven Marcus

The sacralization of culture that Arnold institutes has profound analogous bearings on the sacralization of art and the figure of the artist, along with other exceptional creative figures or geniuses, that was taking place in Europe throughout the same epoch.[4] That this sacralization could also lead in due course to the demonization of both art and the artist, and to cultural and social activities of destructive negation, subversion, and disintegration, is not to be disaffiliated from the circumstance that Arnold's culture in its Hellenistic emphases gave way, also in due course, to the lesser Hellenisms of Pater and Wilde, and then in turn to aridity, triviality, and anomic despair. The remarkable strengths of *Culture and Anarchy* have to do with the paradoxical actuality that its enabling set of argumentative presumptions are insupportable, and that its most telling passages have no warrant that extends beyond their historical and cultural contexts. These contexts are, nonetheless, expansive enough to include many of our present circumstances and perplexities.

If we move from this general frame of discourse into Arnold's more particular stipulations, we find that the term or idea of culture can for the purposes of the present discussion be conveniently regarded as divided itself—in the internal life of the text—into several principal themes or heuristic motifs.[5] In the first instance culture is understood as a complex activity:

> a pursuit of our total perfection by means of getting to know, on all
> the matters which most concern us, the best which has been thought
> and said in the world, and, through this knowledge, turning a stream
> of fresh and free thought upon our stock notions and habits, which
> we now follow staunchly but mechanically, vainly imagining that
> there is a virtue in following them staunchly which makes up for the
> mischief of following them mechanically. [viii]

On this account, culture is a development and elaboration of Arnold's notion of criticism. It is criticism that has both gone to heaven and come down to earth again and turned in the direction of practical life. (Arnold's detractors would say that it is criticism that has undergone a reification.) It

---

4. See in particular Carl Pletsch, *Young Nietzsche: Becoming a Genius* (New York, 1991).

5. I annex this diction from music to direct attention to Arnold's noted method of advancing his views by means of the repetition, recurrence, and variation of a significantly limited number of terms, phrases, and more extended verbal formulations or intellectual melodies.

is of course bookish, but its bookishness is focused upon the "stock notions and habits" by which we regulate the course of daily life and carries the intention of renovation and liberation. Moreover, such goals can "never be reached without seeing things as they really are" [lv].

Arnold is alertly aware that such a simple formulation is only a facade for infinitely receding complexities, and when he remarks that the aim of criticism is "to see the object as in itself it really is," he is, I believe, equally cognizant of the epistemological vertigo that the pursuit of such a statement's implications is bound to induce, as much as he is sensible of its apparent amusing naivete—or alternatively of its quibbling, and slightly objectionable, character. What is "fatal" [lvi], then, is not to attend to unflattering critical truths about ourselves and our group allegiances. On this ground culture bids us also to be wary of the immediate practical life that it simultaneously urges us towards, "to stand more aloof from the arena of politics at present, and rather to try and promote, with us, an inward working" [lvi]. Whatever general ends culture may eventually achieve will come about only by way of indirect means. Precisely because culture, as Arnold speaks for it, rejects machinery and politics as ends, it insists upon the priority of an "inward working" as the mediating means by which its larger aims will be brought closer to us.

That "inward operation" is "essential"; "the essential inwardness of the operation" (ix–x) can never be lost sight of. What this means, among much else, is that in the first instance culture is personal and spiritual, as is the "perfection" it studies and holds up as an ideal. That perfection is "*harmonious* . . . developing all sides of our humanity." Such a "true way of salvation" [xvi] is in this perspective of personal development Arnold's articulation of Goethe's *Bildung.* [6] Once again, this secular ideal is construed in religious terms: "What is alone and always sacred and binding for man is the making progress towards his total perfection" [xlv], although the means by which we achieve this ideal goal may vary.

Moreover, what is entailed in such statements is some idea of the human self. That self is not merely an agent of its own redemptive construction; it is also an entity capable of achieving a harmonious or integrated "totality" among competing claims [xlvi, xlviii]. Indeed, the irrepressible contrarieties among such claims, both internal and external, tend to be minimized in this construction by Arnold of what Max Weber would call

6. See especially David J. DeLaura, "Matthew Arnold and Culture: The History and the Prehistory," in *Matthew Arnold in His Time and Ours: Centenary Essays,* ed. Clinton Machann and Forrest D. Burt (Charlottesville, 1988), pp. 1–16.

Steven Marcus

an ideal type; and as a result this secularized religious personal ideal is clearly recognizable as a modernized adaptation of classical humanist goals.

The social sides of this ideal are concomitantly "general." They seek to develop "all parts" of our society [xvi], and they do so in opposition to Protestantism's tendencies towards "provinciality" and in favor of an inclusive goal of "totality." This totality is, in Arnold's conception of it, both urban (and urbane) and "national." That is to say, it seeks to locate institutional centers or concentrations of interest and to connect itself wherever it can "with the main current of national life" [xxii]. It seeks and perceives balance, moderation, and the possibilities for social sanity and peace in institutions that are historical and that think of themselves as Establishments. In such Establishments the compromises that go toward making up collective traditions are struck—and, in turn, it is within such compromise formations that the social life of culture can find ways to thrive.

Establishments, Arnold writes, "tend to give us a sense of a historical life of the human spirit" [xxxii]. They tend to lead us beyond ourselves and our immediate allegiances and interests: they help to modulate ideological intensities and animosities and weaken our dependence or insistence upon certain means as if they were ends. It is within such an idealized spiritual space that Arnold can make out the workings of culture—indeed, it is within that imagined space that *Culture and Anarchy* is written. That space has become remote enough as to be intermittently unrecognizable today. Nevertheless, it is important that we be able to reconstruct it.

Such a reconstruction begins with the perception of the tripartite general character of culture in this book: it is an activity; it is inward and personal; and it is social. These general attributes are unforgettably set out in Arnold's great summarizing Preface.[7] The balance of the book, its six famous chapters, represents expansions, recurrences, and recursive specifications in a variety of changing contexts of these diverse and inclusive themes.

II

The first two chapters, "Sweetness and Light" and "Doing as One Likes," comprise in effect a single unit of exposition. At the outset Arnold once more puts forward one of his extended, and now augmented, descriptions of culture. Culture is not merely intellectual, or a passion for intellectual

---

7. It was written last.

goods and truths, but is decidedly moral and social as well. It is not only the desire to learn and know what "reason and the will of God" [8] are— the desire that generally characterizes the predisposing act of criticism. It is equally the desire to make them "prevail" [10], to turn that knowledge to account by putting into action "the moral and social passion for doing good" [8].

In this particular sense culture is analogous to religion, since it reformulates "The kingdom of God is within you" as the effort to attain "human perfection" in and as an "internal condition," and as the "general harmonious expansion" of "our humanity proper" [12]. This humanistic affirmation is then represented in a characteristically nineteenth-century paradox. "Not a having and a resting, but a growing and a becoming, is the character of perfection as culture conceives it" [13].

Hence culture is a process and an action that never ends. Its conception of perfection is to be found in ideas of growth, progress, evolution, and change. It is becoming and seeking rather than having and possessing. Although these formulations of Arnold's were soon enough to become deadened and cliché through inveterate overuse, his strivings to defamiliarize some of the key terms of standard nineteenth-century forms of liberal discourse were, and *mutatis mutandis* still are, worthy of careful examination. Here too he was anticipated by his teacher, Newman, in whose personal motto "Growth is the only evidence of life" Arnold may have found a leading.[8]

These stipulations apply with special saliency to modern civilization because of our increasing tendency to rely on the "mechanical and external" ways of thinking and living that such modernity has itself helped to make possible. Arnold's debt here to romanticism in general and to the writings of Carlyle in particular are openly clear (and Dickens and Ruskin and others had already joined in the polemic), but his arguments have kept their force and bite. Our "mechanical and material civilization" retains in augmented measure the spiritual hegemony that it already exercised when Arnold wrote, and so the relevance of his commentary is assured and unallayed.

Materialism, material progress, mechanical ways of thinking, and reliance upon machinery all persist as permanent attributes of modern societies. The mischief such mental habits and dispositions instigate occurs

---

8. John Henry Newman, *Apologia pro Vita Sua,* ed. David J. DeLaura (New York, 1968), p. 17. Newman appropriated this saying from the evangelical clergyman Thomas Scott and remarks that for years he used it almost as a proverb.

when they are regarded—as they intractably are—as ends rather than as means toward something more valuable. Among these phenomena Arnold includes such goods as economic freedom, population, material resources and wealth, railroads, and even "religious organizations." These are not "precious ends in themselves" but means—machinery— that may serve and lead to non-material rewards of another order. But then again they may not.

In any event, material progress and prosperity cannot be taken as gauges of or guides to spiritual superiority. National greatness, Arnold declares, again following Carlyle, cannot be constituted from material wealth alone [18–19]. Indeed, culture, speaking to us ventriloquially through the medium of Matthew Arnold, asks us to consider our middle class, to "look at them attentively"—at their manners and tones of voice; at the things they read; at their pleasures and speech; at "the thoughts which make the furniture of their minds." And it asks us in addition to reach a foregone conclusion: "would any amount of wealth be worth having" if one were "to behave just like these people by having it?" Because of that conclusion, "culture begets a dissatisfaction which is of the highest possible value in stemming the common tide of men's thoughts in a wealthy and industrial community, and which saves the future, as one may hope, from being vulgarized, even if it cannot save the present" [20].

This is, one may suggest, the main line of inspired English critical thinking and sensibility as it begins in the Romantics, is applied in detail by the truly eminent Victorians, and then is continued with greater asperity though perhaps less optimism by the writers of modernism. It is a line that reaches out toward us from the past ever more faintly as the forces that it has opposed for nearly two centuries become almost obliterating in their monopoly of official public discourse. Even the radical opposition to that discourse seems nowadays to be fatally infected by it and so speaks in virtually the same shamefully uncritical terms about power and wealth, as if these necessary means were somehow magical, self-justifying, and absolute ends in themselves.

That same middle class, the Philistines, is operationally represented for Arnold by the puritanical, commercial Nonconforming sects of Dissenters from the Church of England. Their virtues of moral austerity and scruple and their achievement of great "worldly prosperity" [25] go along with a harshness of tone, constriction of responsive range, and unmitigated and narrow disputatiousness of temperament. All of these are figured for Arnold in the truculent motto of the modern Independents' newspaper, the *Nonconformist:* "The Dissidence of Dissent and the

Protestantism of the Protestant religion." This sectarian sensibility inexplicitly represents an ideal of life that is for Arnold "so unlovely, so unattractive, so incomplete, so narrow, so far removed from a true and satisfying ideal of human perfection" that it can never transform the "vice and hideousness" of modern secular society as that society is symbolically embodied in "our grand centre of life . . . London" [31]. London, "with its unutterable external hideousness and with its internal canker of *publicé egestas, privatim opulentia* . . . unequalled in the world," comes in the text to seem almost as much as an expression by analogy of the unattractive sensibility of the world of dissent as it does its antitype. Although they are in moral antagonism to one another, both are in aesthetic terms, for Arnold, almost equally repellent.

And a similar series of judgments holds true for the rising working class, the democracy of the future. For the most part, the middle-class political leaders of this class regard their constituents as in training to become "Philistines to take the place of the Philistines whom they are superseding" [41]. This diagnosis by Arnold of the coming embourgeoisement of the working class has turned out to be correct. Another alternative for the working-class future was for Arnold even less attractive. That was the way of democratic radicalism or Jacobinism, which Arnold associates with the English disciples of Auguste Comte. (Comte himself was in a political sense anything but democratic.)

What Arnold particularly resists in the democratic radicalism or Jacobinism he is regarding is "its fierceness, and its addiction to an abstract system" [42]. In other words, he is antipathetic to its aggressive and overtly ideological character. Although it is difficult to imagine any modern politics without fierceness, aggressiveness, and anger—without passion—Arnold nonetheless ironically and paradoxically insists that "culture hates hatred," revealing in this self-conscious and almost whimsical internal contradiction a sense of his own argument's limitations.

But he also insists more pointedly that culture recalls the scriptural text "Be not ye called Rabbi!" Rabbis are masters and teachers; they teach doctrines, which become dogmas; doctrines and dogmas are formed into ideologies; ideologies tend to attract adherents who are fervent believers and even fanatics, who are rigid and inflexible in their faith in rabbinical, ideological authority. But culture, "eternally passing on and seeking," satisfied with no one and with no one thinker's authority, is in the eyes of ideologists "an impertinence and an offense."

In his opposition to and distaste for radical, doctrinal politics (even so mild an incarnation of it as English democratic radicalism of the mid-nineteenth century may be said to have presented) Arnold made a step toward the invention of cultural politics, a politics that has in our time become something of a mixed blessing. In this new politics of dubious distinction, cultural attitudes and preferences of sensibility come to stand for, take the place of, and finally become the functional equivalent of outright political preferences and arguments.[9]

In partial summary, then, culture, as Arnold conceives of it, does not pursue the lines of the ideological leaders of the dominant middle class or of the leaders of that part of the working class that aspires to emulate that ethos and become members of the middle class, or that part which seeks a more radically democratic distribution of power. Culture, he affirms,

> does not try to teach down to the level of inferior classes; it does not try to win them for this or that sect of its own, with ready-made judgments and watchwords. It seeks to do away with classes; to make all live in an atmosphere of sweetness and light, and use ideas, as it uses them itself, freely, to be nourished and not bound by them.
>
> This is the *social idea;* and the men of culture are the true apostles of equality. The great men of culture are those who have had a passion for diffusing, for making prevail, for carrying from one end of society to the other, the best knowledge of their time; . . . to humanize it, to make it efficient outside the clique of the cultivated and the learned, yet still remaining the *best* knowledge and thought of the time. [48–49]

Such a passage seems almost as if it were written to affront readers today, a virtually deliberate provocation. Not only does it refer to "inferior classes" and the "best ideas" of a particular time, but it speaks in the name of values that are said to transcend class locations and have a classless end in view. Culture seeks to humanize knowledge—that is, to make it general and nonprofessional and nonexclusive—to make it available without condescension to everyone. And the means of doing so are to be found in education, not politics.

The inner logic of Arnold's exposition is that it moves from an extended series of definitions of culture to a description of the middle-class

---

9. This is related to, but should not be confused with, the older ideological situation in which cultural and aesthetic preferences are simply dictated by a party line, and works of art are judged to be good or bad as they are faithful to, or deviate from, an anterior constellation of political beliefs.

world. From there it goes on to the phenomenon of the rising democratic working classes and to a rejection of immediate political solutions, and this rejection in turn leads to the introduction of the idea of education as the means by which culture—a whole sensibility and way of life—will achieve its ends.

Arnold has here in this chapter emphasized "sweetness" (beauty, comeliness, harmoniousness, and moderation) as opposed to the prevailing materialism, machinery, Dissent, harshness, narrowness of views, wealth, and ideologies of the prevailing world of the late 1860s. Light or reason is not so strongly foregrounded, although as the chapter ends with education, it is manifest that it must come back in. It is, in addition, evident that the book as a whole will live almost as much by reason of its objectionabilities—its shortcomings and irrepressible hyperboles of formulation—as by what it gets triumphantly right and argues happily.

The main argument is resumed without interruption in chapter 2, "Doing as One Likes," which is at the same time about "light" or intelligence, thought, and reason. Arnold begins by referring to John Bright's typifying statement "that the central idea of English life and politics is the *assertion of personal liberty*" [55]. Without the habits of subordination, deference, and constraint that the older and now altogether deliquescent feudal society supported and enforced, such liberty tends to drift toward aimlessness and anarchy—spiritual, intellectual and social.[10]

As opposed to this presumably untrammeled liberty Arnold proposes the idea of "*the State*—the nation in its collective and corporate character" [55–56] as a countervailing power and representative of "right reason." The state acts in "the name of an interest wider than that of individuals" and classes [56]. Arnold is here looking intellectually to Edmund Burke (and behind him to J.-J. Rousseau) and institutionally to the France and Prussia of his own time. In these diverse sources he finds the idea of an entity that goes beyond particular individual and class advantages and chances, while around him in Britain he sees on every hand signs of intellectual, social, and political confusion and disorder.

What Arnold asserts here and elsewhere in *Culture and Anarchy* about the anarchic dangers of working-class riots and pulling down fences in Hyde Park is quite vulnerable and has been frequently and accurately

---

10. It was Lionel Trilling who first directed attention to the circumstance that Arnold in these passages was carrying on a sustained disagreement with John Stuart Mill's *On Liberty,* which had first appeared in 1859.

criticized.[11] But what he has to observe about the excesses and inconsistencies of other manifestations of English liberty have not so often recently been taken into account. For example, he remarks, "it never was any part of our creed that the great right and blessedness of an Irishman, or, indeed, of anybody on earth except an Englishman, is to do as he likes; and we can have no scruple at all about abridging, if necessary, a non-Englishman's assertion of personal liberty" [63]. Such comments extend in their application far beyond the British Isles, but Arnold gets considerable mileage out of the special English oppression of Ireland (and puts Burke to additional use in the further ironic play he makes on the idea of the "rights of Englishmen").

The purposes to which this liberty is devoted, Arnold goes on, are summed up for most of both the middle and working classes by what he sardonically and cheerfully calls

> Mrs. Gooch's Golden Rule, or the Divine Injunction "Be ye Perfect" done into British,—the sentence Sir Daniel Gooch's mother repeated to him every morning when he was a boy going to work: "*Ever remember, my dear Dan, that you should look forward to being someday manager of that concern!*" [64]

To conceive of this ambition as the ultimate goal of liberty, as an ideal of self-fulfillment, is to conceive of self-realization in an inadequate, self-seeking, and essentially class-imprisoned way.

For Arnold, the English middle and working classes alike have at this conjuncture no idea of a higher value, of a corporate and collective self that is superior to our class selves, or of a state that embodies a symbolic national community. The idea of the state functions in this context, for Arnold, as an arrangement of institutions that exists beyond or outside of class interests—a supposition that is historically both problematic and only weakly arguable. What is needed, he nonetheless goes on to argue with conviction, is "a principle of authority," that is to say, some idea or entity that can stand for right reason, for judgments of value, for judgments that take precedence over the interest-begotten prejudices of class

---

11. The most notable and sensible of these criticisms is by Raymond Williams in *Culture and Society, 1780–1950,* 2d ed. (New York: Columbia University Press, 1983).

or group—judgments that today we would call something like regulative norms.

The state stands for such a principle, in particular as it expresses itself in state-established and governed systems of education. Yet this elevation or provision of the state by Arnold as the carrier of class-neutral values brings with it such difficulties as the relation between political and cultural authority or between power and intellectual standards. Indeed one may maintain that a major part of the cultural-political agenda of the European nineteenth century, set in the aftermath of the failure of the French Revolution, was addressed and directed to certain of the unanswered questions that the Revolution's aborted character brought into tragic relief: How in a modern and rapidly changing society do we confront and deal with the unabated, inherited problem of the alienation of power from intellect, of social, political, and other institutional influence and effectiveness from right reason, intelligence, and talent?

Arnold proceeds to demonstrate, unforgettably, how the three English classes by themselves do not have accessible to them such ideas as may, in this situation, avail. None of them has adequate light, reason, intellect. This aristocracy, or Barbarians, are by their traditions and ethos immunized to ideas—they are "children of the established fact"—and unfit for a universe of change. The middle class, or Philistines, have plenty of ideas, but most of them are held, however seriously, without the perspective attained through self-criticism, and all of them are held with an "incomparable self-satisfaction" [81] that is decisively disabling.

As for the working class, or Populace, they too do not distrust themselves either; and, moreover, they are at the present moment too inchoate and unformed; they have not yet had time or opportunities for the reading and thinking that might possibly generate the kind of ideas that are required to animate the whole of society with higher collaborative purposes. It is only if we try "to rise above the idea of class to the idea of the whole community, *the State,* and to find our centre of light and authority there" that we find our proper direction, that we go beyond "our ordinary selves" [87] into some totality that is beyond us and "impersonal," in which we can be united. And this is "the very self which culture, or the study of perfection, seeks to develop in us" [89].

Apart from the circumstance that there is something circular in this argument (which is repeated intermittently throughout the text), it is difficult from the perspective of the end of the twentieth century to place much confidence in it. The catastrophic experiences of our era make Arnold's confident imputations about the trustworthiness of the national state exceptionally fragile to examination. And even in those western industrial democracies that have escaped the experience of totalitarian state governments, the experiences of state bureaucracies have been something less than bracing and encouraging and have certainly not been Arnoldian, have not been expressions of a collaborative and national "best self."

It may be rejoined that Arnold is proposing the state largely as a sponsor, regulator, and ideal supervisor of education and related activities only, and that the experiences of such nation-states as France and Germany in these circumstances tend to bear him out. That may be so, but American historical experience in this connection (and, to a lesser degree, British) is of a kind and quality to induce misgivings. Let us leave to one side the national wasteland of secondary education in America, run and administered jointly by state governmental bureaucracies of education, and bureaucratically organized bodies of teachers—a system that has been and remains practically without hope of improvement. Even if we take America's most outstanding area of educational achievement and success, its system of higher education, research, and postgraduate training—our national system of great universities—the lesson of the last half century is relatively unambiguous: namely, that state support with a minimum of indirect administrative direction from the top down has produced the happiest results. What Arnold—unlike Tocqueville, say—has left out of his account are those intermediate institutions and organizations, sometimes loosely called civil society—and universities are precisely one such institution—that act as mediators and buffers between the massive and unequal forces of state governments and the less-organized bodies of individuals and groups of citizens.

It must be said, too, in response to his major institutional hope and recommendation—that the state become the educator of the nation—that the experience of the subsequent one hundred and twenty-odd years suggests that if the state is and remains an inescapable fact, and an ever-expanding one, in all our lives, it also remains a fact that we have, most of us, learned to regard with due wariness, skepticism, and a dubiety bred of frequently disillusioning experience. An unavoidable necessity, yes; a blessing and a deliverance, unfortunately, no.

On Arnold's behalf, it may be briefly adduced that English government, the British state, especially on its educational side, was at the time he wrote so rudimentary as to be virtually nonexistent—his own experience as an inspector of schools supplies lasting credibility to what he has to say about British sinful inadequacies on this score. At the same time, however, one has to remark two great geniuses in the opposition: in 1855–

57, Dickens in *Little Dorritt* had already intuited what bureaucracies, even pre-modern ones, were capable of in the way of impersonal inhumanity; and only thirty years later, Max Weber would already make out in advance the grim outlines of our own state-bedeviled century.

However innocent and full of good intentions Arnold's prescriptions certainly were, he cannot here be entirely let off the hook of error. Even so, he must still be given due credit for facing up to the circumstance that a revolution in society was on the way. That revolution, of course, was the coming of democracy, "a revolution by due course of law" [91], he writes, adapting with his singular talent for telling and constructive misquotation an observation that the Duke of Wellington delivered during the debate on the first Reform Bill of 1832.

To this we must add that the democratic revolution in Britain was to arrive much more slowly than Arnold imagined, and that in his anxieties to defend civil order, he tended at moments to conflate the State that *is* with the State that *should be*. That is to say, his misjudgments, like his much more numerous and illuminating insights into and interpretations of social-cultural phenomena, tend to group themselves rather symmetrically in the middle. And its treading generally along an imaginary middle way is, as I have been implying, one of the sources of both the durabilities and vulnerabilities of this work.

III

These strengths are never more conspicuously in evidence than they are in Arnold's repeated anatomies of the three classes—all performed quite premeditatedly from the perspective of "culture," that is to say, all anatomized in points of intellect and style or quality of life. These descriptive analyses are friendly, critical, humorous, and severe all at the same time. And they are more or less close to the mark until Arnold gets to his representation of the *Populace soi-même,* that part of the working class which is *not* "in a fair way to be, one in spirit with the industrial middle class" [103]:

> But that vast portion, lastly, of the working class, which, raw and half-developed, has long lain half-hidden amidst its poverty and squalor, and is now issuing from its hiding-place to assert an Englishman's heaven-born privilege of doing as he likes, and is beginning to perplex us by marching where it likes, meeting where it likes, bawling what it likes, breaking what it likes,—to this vast re-

siduum we may with great propriety give the name of *Populace*.
[105]

It is difficult to exaggerate the poverty, debasement, and immiseration of condition in which that vast portion of English men, women, and children had to exist during the rapidly industrializing, urbanizing decades of the nineteenth century. Arnold worked for a living as an inspector of schools and had been exposed firsthand to repeated full views of these terrible circumstances. Yet this description reveals at the same time how remote, how distant, how far away he and other middle-class observers *had to be* in a psychological sense from such proximately close phenomena.

This self-evidently class-driven imagination of the submerged, frightening, and probably violent majority of the working class puts one in mind of the return of the repressed; the description is itself a defense as well as a symptom, and the Populace in this sense is both mob and mythology. Arnold notes—with sympathy, he says—that "the eternal spirit of the Populace" is constituted out of ignorance, passion, violence, energy, brutality, and savagery [108].

Nevertheless, in noting it in such a manner he is implying that it is also an abstraction, that this "eternal spirit" exists in the bosom of every one of us, and that the three classes themselves are pure social constructions and not in any sense natural divisions. For it is important to recognize, Arnold vigorously asserts, that "under all our class divisions, there is a common basis of human nature . . . in every one of us . . . there exists . . . the same tendencies and passions which have made our fellow-citizens of other classes what they are" [105].[12]

Because these distinctions are social constructions, there is nothing necessary or permanent about them; they can be changed. For

in every class there are born a certain number of natures with a curiosity about their best self, with a bent for seeing things as they are, for disentangling themselves from machinery. . . . Natures with this bent emerge in all classes, among the Barbarians, among the Philistines, among the Populace. And this bent always tends to take them out of their class, and to make their distinguishing characteristic not their Barbarism or their Philistinism [or their Populism] but their *humanity*. . . . Therefore, when we speak of ourselves as di-

---

12. It is in this passage that Arnold declares himself to be "properly a Philistine . . . the son of a Philistine" [106].

vided into [three classes] . . . we must be understood always to imply that within each of these classes there are a certain number of
aliens, if we may so call them,—persons who are mainly led, not
by their class spirit, but by a general *humane* spirit, by the love of
human perfection; and that this number is capable of being diminished or augmented. [109–110]

Arnold had already prepared the way for such a passage in "The Function of Criticism at the Present Time." There he wrote that the action of
criticism is "subtle and indirect"; that it embraces "the Indian virtue of
detachment" and has abandoned the "sphere of practical life"; that it
condemns itself to a "slow and obscure work"; and that "whoever sets
himself to see things as they are will find himself one of a small circle; but
it is only by this small circle resolutely doing its own work that adequate
ideas will even get to current at all" [Super 3:274]. Culture and criticism,
in other words, also represent efforts to deal with, recognize, and relatively neutralize the class-constrained nature of our minds, sensibilities,
and ideas. They represent an undertaking "to hinder the unchecked predominance of that class-life" which makes up so much of our mental life,
and which is so difficult to moderate, and perhaps intractably difficult to
get beyond. But they do so by trying to situate us in our humanity, in a
common universal that may be class-expressed or articulated but may not
be altogether class-determined and directed.

In this notable effort Arnold was preceded in his own time by the young
Marx, who also located the particularly characterizing life of modern
capitalism precisely in its violation of a common humanity. And Arnold
was to be followed in this project not merely by those who called themselves humanists—who often did not follow his lines of reasoning—
but by such a figure as Karl Mannheim. In *Ideology and Utopia*, Mannheim found in the expanding numbers and ranks of modern intellectuals
a trans- or meta-class array of figures who were held together, not wholly
by class interest, but rather by virtue of their shared education and the
values and judgments that such an education had raised up in them, and
that prompted them to emerge as a distinct and quasi-autonomous social
formation.

It is, Arnold implies, precisely the ideas and sentiments of humanity
that makes such persons *aliens* to and in their classes. They are in point of
fact alienated from their social classes by reason of their humanity, and by
virtue of their commitment to the values and ideas and ways of thinking

that culture represents. [13] And hence culture once again represents a project of transcendence—an attempt to transcend the encompassing and determining world of social class, the world in which we all perforce live and work and learn and think.

This is, to be sure, a middle-class ideal, both in origins and in its social base of operations. But it is a middle-class ideal that aims at something, some notions or structure of values, findings, beliefs, and holdings, that go beyond the middle class and its ideals of life. In this sense, Arnold's culture represents a permanent contribution to an evolving ideal of what may be thinkable if not possible for modern humanity, and is hence a permanent historical accession to that humanity. And unlike Arnold's biddings about the state, it has not been either superseded or altogether defeated by historical experience.

How, then, are we to go beyond socio-economically determined group interests, class opinions, and collective prejudices? How do we discover "a source of authority," a ground upon which we can establish some "strict standard of excellence," for without such intellectual authority and standard of judgment culture cannot proceed, has nowhere to go [111]. Arnold's answer is pragmatic, anecdotal, and experientially (if not logically) convincing. He asserts that there can be something like "a certain centre of correct information, taste and intelligence" [113], and that we can be nearer to or farther away from such an ideal in our opinions.

Arnold cites an instance that will be familiar to anyone who has had to deal with such problems. He recalls a conversation with "a company of Non-conformists, admirers of some lecturer [on literature] who had let off a great firework." An intellectual review of some standing—it was the *Saturday Review*—had said that the lecture was "all noise and false lights," but the spokesman of the group tranquilly replied that "it is true the *Saturday Review* abuses the lecture, but the *British Banner* says that the *Saturday Review* is quite wrong." Arnold goes on to comment, in one of his fine moments: "The speaker had evidently no notion that there was a scale of value for judgments on these topics, and that the judgment of the *Saturday Review* ranked high on this scale, and those of the *British Banner* low" [113–14]. Arnold finds here the same nexus of problems in religion as he has in literature—problems that today are only exacerbated and raised by orders of magnitude: "We have most of us little idea of a high

---

13. What Arnold is in effect saying, with historical perspicacity, is that class life is in itself alienated life.

standard to choose our guides by, of a great and profound spirit, which is an authority, while inferior spirits are none; it is enough to give importance to things that this or that person says them decisively, and has a large following of some strong kind when he says them" [114].

Here the argument for cultural relativism—that all institutions, ideas and cultural productions are equal—joins forces with the idea of representativeness as a criterion of importance and indeed judgment. The example to hand for Arnold is the American religion of Mormonism, very much in the news at the time, and a book discussing it along with other contemporary religious cults. This book argued that Mormonism as a *religion,* as a *doctrine,* as a set of *intellectual and theological propositions and stories* was to be taken seriously largely because two hundred thousand souls armed with twenty thousand rifles believed in it as the "new covenant."[14] Arnold comments on Hepworth Dixon, the author of this work:

> If he was summing up an account of the teaching of Plato or St. Paul, Mr. Hepworth Dixon could not be more earnestly reverential. But the question is, have [the supporters of Mormonism] . . . anything of the weight and significance for the best reason and spirit of man that Plato and St. Paul have? Evidently they, at present, have not, and a very small taste of them and their doctrines ought to have convinced Mr. Hepworth Dixon that they never could have. [116]

The problem is more pressing today than it was when Arnold wrote, although he perceived its character and substance with unsurpassed clarity. The question is, how does one make a claim for standards of excellence and judgments of differential quality in a social and cultural world that is epistemologically unmoored, socially and ethnically diverse, temperamentally relativistic and that is, moreover, driven in the main by the politics of identity, group thought, and the hegemony of representativeness? The major presuppositions of this world—especially as they obtain in contemporary American schools and universities—is that there are no plausible, convincing, or intersubjective standards to which anyone can appeal in the effort to establish judgments of quality.

The corollary of these notions is that there is no way of demonstrating, say, that Shakespeare is better than Superman (or anything else, for that matter), since such claims to discrimination, superiority, and difference

---

14. Forestalling the forty-second president of the United States, Bill Clinton, by well over a century, but still locating the arena of that covenant in an American world of quasi-factitious futures.

usually entail an effort to seize, maintain, or exert power on the part of whoever it is that is making the claim. Indeed, such notions as truth, rationality, intelligence, and distinction of intellectual merit or literary or artistic value are largely discredited as part of a system of social and cultural oppression and repression.[15] Arnold's steadfast belief is that such standards do exist, can be satisfactorily demonstrated, and can, he trusts, be transmitted, taught, and internalized. He confides that this noble mission can be achieved through education, and through an educational system sponsored and directed by the state. Although justifiable doubts about the state have already been adduced and adverted to, it has not until recently been the case that a similar congregation of dubieties have come into existence about the effectiveness and powers for good of our institutions of education.

Those dubieties are at the present moment very active, very much in evidence. And even though Arnold, with his customary skepticism, insists repeatedly that there is no one answer, no one guide, to the perplexities that claim our attention, he at the same time equally, and inconsistently, insists that "education is the road to culture" [267]. It is a belief that most people who have been in a position to read *Culture and Anarchy* have shared with him until quite recently. It is a measure of the difference between the present and the period in which Arnold lived that in the midst of intellectual Victorian England's self-proclaimed doubts, distractions, and fears, he could write a book whose tone and character are nonetheless robustly optimistic, hopeful, cheerful, good-humored, and patient with its adversaries and its adverse times.

Today we no longer have easy access to such amenities of temper. Yet to lose belief in education, to cease to hope that education is the means to light, would be to admit that the cause of light is itself lost. I do not think that we are ready yet to break the connection between our historical past and the perennially embattled present. And as long as we have not severed that connection, *Culture and Anarchy* will remain as one of the sources to which we resort with the prospect of finding strength to continue, reserves of argument, phrases and language to shore up our spirits, and courage to face the darker prospects of our later, indeed perhaps our late, modern world.

---

15. In this passage I am agreeing with and borrowing from John R. Searle, "Is There a Crisis in American Higher Education?" *Bulletin of the American Academy of Arts and Science* 46, no. 4 (January 1993): 24–27.

Gerald Graff

Arnold, Reason,
and Common Culture

The current cultural war over issues of education, cultural diversity, universalism, and particularism makes the reprinting of Matthew Arnold's *Culture and Anarchy* a timely event. Arnold was not the first but he was arguably the most eloquent to voice the concern that has become so insistent today about the erosion of a common culture. He was equally eloquent in associating that erosion with an alleged eclipse of reason and rational standards. *Culture and Anarchy* established the categories and the grammar through which we think about cultural crisis.

So pervasive has Arnold's influence been on the terms of cultural diagnosis that since its publication in 1869 *Culture and Anarchy* has virtually been rewritten every decade. Notable twentieth-century restatements include Irving Babbitt's *Literature and the American College* (1908), Julien Benda's *The Treason of the Intellectuals* (1928), José Ortega y Gassett's *The Revolt of the Masses* (1930), T. S. Eliot's *The Idea of a Christian Society* (1940) and *Notes towards the Definition of Culture* (1949), and Christopher Lasch's *The Culture of Narcissism* (1979). Since the late 1980s, rewritings of Arnold's argument seem to appear annually. Allan Bloom's *The Closing of the American Mind* (1987) was followed by Roger Kimball's *Tenured Radicals* (1990), Martin Anderson's *Impostors in the Temple* (1992), and Arthur Schlesinger Jr.'s *The Disuniting of America* (1991). For the culture-and-anarchy boom, no end seems to be in sight.

Having myself written a culture-and-anarchy book, *Literature against Itself* (1979), an attack on avant-garde literary theory that anticipated many of the arguments of recent apocalyptic polemics, I think I know from the inside what it feels like to be convinced that the destruction of reason and culture is at hand, along with the rage that accompanies the conviction. But my thinking underwent a change in the mid-1980s, nip-

Gerald Graff

ping in the bud a promising career in cultural pessimism. I like to think it had to do with an honest discovery that I had been wrong about what current literary theories are saying and thus about what their implications might be. But mostly it was that I came to the conclusion that the culture-and-anarchy argument is a dead end. If we are sincere about creating a common culture under democratic conditions, that kind of argument won't get us there.

Not that the argument does not have its truth. It would be difficult to deny that the idea of common culture is on the defensive in Western societies today. New social movements based on gender, ethnicity, and sexual orientation have challenged traditional ideals of universality and claimed the right to a say in how culture will be defined. New academic theories and practices have supported the aims of these movements by questioning the universality of traditional academic assumptions and categories. An attack on traditional forms of universality, however, is not necessarily an attack on reason. On the contrary, it may be an exercise of reason.

Though many conservatives today would contemptuously reject such a suggestion, they unwittingly lend it support when they maintain that Western culture has been a uniquely self-critical culture, often being the first to condemn the evils that can be laid at its door. The moral that conservatives usually draw from this observation is that radical criticism of the West is unjustified: since the West is the epitome of the critical spirit, the critics should kindly shut up. One could draw a different moral, however: if it is indeed part of the Western tradition to encourage the critical spirit, then there needs to be *more* criticism, not less. A commitment to open, rational discourse means risking a stern challenge even to the idea of universality, though this idea could use some definition before we go to war over it.

In fact, considerable ambivalence toward rational discourse has been manifested by both sides in today's culture war. It is true that there is a strain of recent cultural radicalism—though not all recent cultural radicalism, contrary to the picture drawn by the right—that associates reason with oppression. It is also true, however, that conservatives have had their own reservations about unchecked critical rationality, which can lead to relativism, nihilism, and the dissolution of traditional certainties. The havoc wreaked on traditional values by rationalized free-market capitalism is a continuing source of embarrassment for conservative efforts to reconcile tradition with capitalism.

Then, too, in attacks from the right on the bogey of relativism, it is not always obvious whether the bogeyman is unreason or reason itself. When the journalist George Will refers to subversives in the academy who are "fighting against the common culture that is the nation's social cement," is it Will or the subversives who stand for reason? To me it sounds as if Will wants whatever constitutes "the nation's social cement" to be immune from rational criticism.[1]

My point is that reason in the cultural history of the West has often been associated with the subversion rather than the support of ethical and social certainties. Matthew Arnold understood this very well, being better placed than we latecomers to witness the corrosive effect of modern democratic reason on preindustrial traditions that still survived in his day. There is something odd about Arnold's status as a hero of reason, just as there is something odd about the coupling of reason with common culture by Arnold and those who today echo his analysis. The coupling ignores the divisive role that reason has often played in culture, a role that Arnold vividly recognizes and profoundly fears. On close inspection Arnold's defense of reason turns out to be at best qualified and ambivalent.

It is easy to overlook this fact, since Arnold invites us to think of him as the champion of the "disinterested play of consciousness upon . . . stock notions and habits" [271]. We think of Arnold as the exponent of "Hellenic" freedom of speculation over narrowly puritanical "Hebraism," the promoter of a culture of "ideas" and "criticism" that is to keep the arts from succumbing to provincialism. Arnold's celebration of free speculative intelligence tends to divert attention, however, from the extremely limited scope Arnold actually grants to such intelligence, which is always tending to foment the kind of nonconformity, sectarianism, and controversy that Arnold detests.

It is true that Arnold is often a profound analyst and critic of urban industrial society. Any attempt to push cultural analysis, criticism, and the disinterested play of consciousness too far, though, to a point where it threatens common traditions and beliefs, is for Arnold a violation of the classical rule of balance and measure. Arnold is committed to the Hellenic free play of reason only as long as its dictates coincide with those of unreflective custom, tradition, and consensus. For Arnold no true culture can exist without a common basis of things taken for granted, a culture impervious, in other words, to the more unsettling effects of rational

---

1. George Will, "Literary Politics," *Newsweek* (April 22, 1991), p. 72. As Stephen Greenblatt wrote in a response to Will, "Poets can't fly when their feet are encased in social cement" ("Opinion," *Chronicle of Higher Education,* June 12, 1991, p. B3).

inquiry. It is this view that underlies Arnold's frequently stated idea that great art requires a settled society of implicitly shared beliefs, that the great works of the human spirit, as he puts it, "come, not from Nonconformists, but from men who either belong to Establishments or have been trained in them" [xix].

Arnold's idea of defending reason in *Culture and Anarchy* amounts to repeating catchphrases like "reason and the will of God" with such mind-numbing frequency that we overlook the fact that Arnold never precisely defines these terms—indeed, he actively opposes such definition, as we will see. For one who mercilessly ridicules opponents for substituting "machinery" for substance, the substance of Arnold's own argument is surprisingly thin. His consistent appeal is not to the rationality of his readers but to their emotional loyalty to common traditions, what Arnold calls "the main current of national life" and "the main stream of human life."

Reason for Arnold has little to do with the kind of searching philosophical reflection we associate with thinkers such as Aristotle, Aquinas, Descartes, Kant, and Hegel. This makes Arnold the appropriate patron saint of those who oppose the spread of "theory" in today's literary and cultural disciplines—not just some *kinds* of theory, but theoretical reflection as such.[2] And these critics are right to oppose theory, given its proclivity for asking uncomfortable questions and for unsettling received certainties. Not that academic theory has not generated its own pet certainties; but the only antidote to one kind of theory is another theory, however unconscious of it you may prefer to remain.

Insofar as reason implies the extension of the boundaries of consciousness as far as they can reach, Arnold is eager to curtail it. He inherits the romantic fear that increasing self-consciousness means the decline of cultural health, yet missing from his constitution is any of the romantic compulsion to stretch the limits of self-consciousness regardless of the consequences.

One main trouble with reason for Arnold is its notorious habit of concocting schemes of social renovation—a "plan of doing," in Arnold's derisive phrase [x]—and its worse habit of stirring up controversy. This becomes clear if we ask precisely what Arnold means by *anarchy* in *Culture and Anarchy*. Though Arnold at times uses the word to condemn

---

2. Joseph Epstein, for example, in "The Academic Zoo—Theory in Practice," *Hudson Review* 44, no. 1 (Spring 1991), pp. 9–30; "Matthew Arnold and the Resistance," *Commentary,* April 1982, pp. 53–60.

the movement of working-class rebellion, its wider reference is to the spirit of public controversy that had erupted in the wake of the democratic expansion of the British franchise, the advance of scientific and secularist thought, and the growth of mass journalism.

What most exasperates Arnold about liberals, religious Nonconformists, utilitarians, and scientific rationalists is their habit of taking unabashed satisfaction in the kind of controversy that makes cultured people wince. What is one to do with a mentality that cheerfully names itself after so regrettable a trait as nonconformism and makes a positive slogan of so lamentable a development as "the Dissidence of Dissent and the Protestantism of the Protestant religion"?

Arnold's most biting satire in *Culture and Anarchy* is provoked by this arrogant celebration of nonconformity: "It is not fatal to Americans to have no religious establishments and no effective centres of high culture; but it is fatal to them to be told by their flatterers, and to believe, that they are the most intelligent people in the whole world, when of intelligence, in the true and fruitful sense of the word, they even singularly, as we have seen, come short" [lvi]. The satiric impact lies in Arnold's suggestion that Americans' rejection of tradition is so shallow that they hardly know what they are rejecting. The impact is diminished, however, once we recognize that, despite his disclaimer, Arnold is saying that is *is* fatal to true culture "to have no religious establishments." For few of us would any longer agree that the lack of a national church dooms a society to culturelessness.

The passage is typically Arnoldian in making its appeal not to reason but to custom, tradition, and sentiment. By appealing to "the main current of national life," Arnold can evade the substantive questions that dissenting groups and demonstrating workers were raising, questions about what the main current of national life should be and who should have a say in determining it. But then, for Arnold it is precisely the sign of an authentic state of culture that such divisive questions do not arise.

Arnold's vaunted theory of critical disinterestedness is another instance of his loathing of controversy.[3] The disinterested critic does not need to become enmeshed in petty disputes, since it is not he who speaks

---

3. Critics of Arnold from the left often dismiss this idea of disinterestedness without facing up to the problem of how interpretations and judgments can be defended if they express only interests. For an excellent critique of the Arnoldian tradition that avoids that trap, see Chris Baldick, *The Social Mission of English Criticism: 1848–1932* (New York: Oxford University Press, 1987). My argument in this essay is heavily indebted to Baldick.

but truth that speaks through him. It is again custom and convention, not rational argument, that is invoked in Arnold's unperturbed judgment that "it would still have been better for a man, during the last eighteen hundred years, to have been a Christian and a member of one of the great Christian communions, than to have been a Jew or a Socinian; because the being in contact with the main stream of human life is of more moment for a man's total spiritual growth, and for his bringing to perfection the gifts committed to him, which is his business on earth, than any speculative opinion which he may hold or think he holds" [xlvii]. Reason for Arnold always verges threateningly on "speculative opinion," the sort of thing cultivated by Jews, Socinians, and other rootless types presumably outside the main stream of "human life." (As Frederic E. Faverty pointed out many years ago in a devastating book entitled *Matthew Arnold the Ethnologist,* Arnold subscribed to some of the more unsavory versions of the theory of national racial dispositions that many Victorians entertained. These racial theories are most fully revealed in his rarely read *Study of Celtic Literature,* though traces of them are present in the opposition between Hellenism and Hebraism of *Culture and Anarchy.*[4])

Arnold's invocations of reason inevitably obscure troublesome contradictions between reason and culture, tradition, and religion. Take the facile coupling of reason with "the will of God," which papers over the fact that over the centuries reason and God had clashed more often than they had coexisted, and indeed were clashing conspicuously at the moment Arnold wrote. Arnold does grapple with the problem of reason and faith in *Literature and Dogma,* but grappling with a problem for Arnold always means finding a way to keep rational analysis of it within bounds while using ritualistically repeated slogans to conceal contradictions.

Concealing them was necessary because Arnold was right. Critical rationality was and is a threat to the commonality of culture as Arnold envisioned it. Reason does endanger the cause of national tradition, sweetness and light, and "the will of God," insisting as it does that such terms be subjected to definition, analysis, and debate. Once we try to define pet Arnoldian catchphrases like "the best that has been thought and

---

4. Frederic E. Faverty, *Matthew Arnold the Ethnologist* (Evanston, Ill.: Northwestern University Press, 1951); for a more recent study, see David Lloyd, "Arnold, Ferguson, Schiller: Aesthetic Culture and the Politics of Aesthetics," *Cultural Critique* 1, no. 2 (Winter 1985): 137–69. Franklin Court usefully clarifies Arnold's educational application of his complicated ethnological theories in *Institutionalizing English Literature: The Culture and Politics of Literary Study, 1750–1900* (Stanford, Calif.: Stanford University Press, 1992), pp. 106–18.

said in the world" or the "best self," we find that what that best *is* is far from self-evident, which is to say, we find ourselves in precisely the kind of sectarian conflict that Arnold takes to be the essence of anarchy.

But this poses a dilemma, one that we might call the Common Culture Paradox: how can Arnold argue for a restoration of cultural commonality without stirring up more of the sort of controversy he deplores? In the kind of common culture Arnold wanted to recover—if indeed such a thing had ever existed—there would have been no need for the phrase *common culture*. For such a culture would already *unconsciously* enjoy a sense of unity, consensus, and shared purpose, thereby relieving its members of the necessity to formulate, rationalize, or theorize its commonality in principles that would be open to debate. Once the rationale of a community arises as a question for self-conscious reflection and debate, the unreflective commonality that Arnold desired has been lost. A really common culture would simply be lived, with no need for its presuppositions, foundations, and beliefs to become an issue for discussion. The word *culture* itself, with its fatal aura of anthropological self-consciousness, betrays the shattering of unself-conscious consensus by divisive modern analysis and theory.

This is not to say that the very idea of common culture is suspect. The idea of common culture that seems appropriate for societies that aspire to be democratic, however, is very different from Arnold's. A democratic idea of common culture seems to entail not an inarguable body of traditions immune to the clash of "speculative opinion," but a common *debate* over culture, a debate in which the community's identity and purposes are taken to be always up for grabs and in which it is never out of order to ask, *Whose* common culture is it? or, Whom do we mean by *we* or *our?* This democratic condition of perpetual conflict, contestation, and negotiation, however, in which there is no authority that cannot be challenged and the terms of cultural commonality are always in the making, is precisely what Arnold meant by *anarchy*.

It is not that Arnold lacked sympathy with democracy—far from it. There is no reason to doubt the sincerity of his remarks about the desirability of a classless society. But Arnold evidently could not reconcile himself to democracy as a *cultural* concept, as distinct from a political and economic one. Certainly Arnold could not accept a democratized culture if it meant seeing controversy as a central and constitutive feature of culture, as the cultural norm and not the exception. For Arnold a true common culture is one in which there is no reason for fundamental controversy about cultural "values" to arise.

Gerald Graff

Unlike John Stuart Mill, Arnold had no faith that a society could flourish once its fundamental values were thrown open to democratic controversy. For him it is a case of all or nothing—either the ground values of culture transcend controversy and are unconsciously shared or there is no culture in the higher normative sense. Arnold seems to have been unable to imagine a vital culture whose citizens simply agree to disagree about religion, art, philosophy, morality, and politics.

To say all this is only to remind ourselves that Arnold belonged to a romantic and modernist tradition that has persistently lamented the destruction of traditional "organic" societies by the Enlightenment and modernity. In understanding cultural commonality as a set of loyalties that must be already given and inarguable, Arnold forms a bridge between romantic predecessors like Carlyle, Wordsworth, and Chateaubriand and subsequent modernists like Friedrich Nietzsche, T. S. Eliot, F. R. Leavis, D. H. Lawrence, and W. B. Yeats. For writers in this tradition (which Raymond Williams charted comprehensively in *Culture and Society: 1780–1950*), the condition of modernity is one of profound sickness, the cause of which lies in the crisis of belief provoked by Enlightenment science, individualism, and liberal democracy. No longer nourished by a tradition of shared beliefs, individuals are thrown back on their private resources and become neurotically self-conscious and susceptible to the shallow secular cult of freedom, Arnold's "doing as one likes." We become truly free only when we stop seeking freedom or trying to rationalize or legislate it.

Arnold would have agreed with Lawrence that "men are freest when they are most unconscious of freedom." Lawrence succinctly expressed this critique of modern pseudo-freedom: "Men are free when they are in a living homeland, not when they are straying and breaking away. Men are free when they are obeying some deep, inward voice of religious belief. Obeying from within. Men are free when they belong to a living, organic, *believing* community, active in fulfilling some unfulfilled, perhaps unrealized purpose."[5] If cultural consensus is health, then the telltale symptom of a sick culture is the appearance of endless bickering about the values and goals of the community, a sign that organic unity has given way to the spirit of polemics, politics, and theory.

T. S. Eliot scolded both Lawrence and Arnold for thinking that secular culture could replace the Christian church as the binding force of the

---

5. D. H. Lawrence, *Studies in Classic American Literature* (1923; New York: Viking Books, 1961), p. 6.

community. But Eliot's church was only another name for Lawrence's "living, organic, believing community," a community that has no need to define its beliefs because everyone takes the same ones for granted. The waning of shared systems of belief (or a shared cultural "myth") is an underlying condition of most modernist literature and criticism. Post–World War II critics called it "the problem of belief," debating vigorously the extent to which poets could or should express beliefs in their work.

Like Arnold, who chastised critics for taking the "philosophy" in Wordsworth's poetry as an important element of the poems, Eliot thought that poets should avoid trying to rationalize their beliefs. Eliot's critics often mistook his doctrine for a theory of art-for-art's-sake, but Eliot's point was not that poets should believe nothing but that they should not be consciously *aware* of their beliefs. In a well-ordered society—Eliot's model was the medieval Europe of Dante—a common belief system would be already established, thereby relieving poets and everyone else of the need to think for themselves. It is when such belief systems disintegrate, leaving us to fabricate our beliefs on our own, that literary culture according to Eliot becomes overrun by eccentric visionaries like Yeats, Lawrence, and Blake ("I must Create a System or be enslaved by another Man's"), and politics is overrun by charlatan reformers and social engineers.

For the Arnold-Eliot-Lawrence tradition, then, critical rationality is identified with the disintegration of common culture, not its defense. The underlying philosophical premise—curiously derived from the hated Enlightenment—is that reason is a purely instrumental faculty incapable of making determinations of values. Reason is presumably adept at answering questions about how things behave, but impotent when it comes to deciding how things should be or what their essential nature is. Reason can provide a calculus of the best means of arriving at a given end, but it is powerless to determine the end itself—it can tell you the most efficient way to produce more rivets, but it can't tell you if producing more rivets is a good or bad thing. Reason, then, is instrumentally potent but ethically bankrupt, and therefore has to be supplemented from some nonrational source like religion, tradition, emotion, or poetic imagination.

Arnold could easily have derived such premises from his reading of Wordsworth, Mill, and Carlyle. In his lengthy autobiographical poem, *The Prelude,* Wordsworth dramatized the nihilism into which he had been plunged by his encounter with the French Revolution, whose thinkers caused him to yield up "moral questions in despair." Mill in his *Autobiography* described an early mental crisis induced by the rigorous educa-

Gerald Graff

tion in logic imposed by his father, the utilitarian philosopher James Mill. The crisis lifted only when the young John Stuart Mill experienced an emotional catharsis through reading Wordsworth. Carlyle's protagonist in *Sartor Resartus* has a similar bout with eighteenth-century mechanistic philosophy, which plunges him into the nihilistic depression he calls the "Everlasting No."

The starkest version of this modern dichotomy of fact and value appears in early twentieth-century logical positivism, which divides the world of language into sentences that presumably refer to verifiable or falsifiable states of affairs in the objective world ("the cat is on the mat") and sentences that contain value judgments ("God's in his heaven, All's right with the world"). The second class of statements have the ostensible form of actual statements but are empirically untestable and therefore meaningless. The doctrine eventuates in the law that it is logically impossible to derive an "ought" from an "is." It follows that there is no *rationally* defensible way to move from an "is" statement like, "Hydrogen weapons have the capacity to destroy the world," to an "ought" conclusion like, "Hydrogen weapons ought to be controlled." Logical positivists allowed that there were various procedures for justifying statements like, "Hydrogen weapons ought to be controlled," but they argued that, strictly speaking, such statements have no rational basis.[6]

Arnold's most moving expression of his fear of the unchecked modern intellect is the long classical poem *Empedocles on Etna*, which he declined to reprint when he collected his poems in 1853. Driven to despair by a commitment to strict reason, Arnold's philosopher-protagonist Empedocles ends up hurling himself into the smoldering mouth of Mount Etna. Explaining in his preface to the 1853 edition why he is suppressing the poem, Arnold clearly associates Empedocles' despair with the modern predicament of divisive rationality. For Empedocles, "the calm, the cheerfulness, the disinterested objectivity [of Greek culture at its height] have disappeared: the dialogue of the mind with itself has commenced; modern problems have presented themselves; we hear already the doubts, we witness the discouragement, of Hamlet and of Faust." It is Arnold's most explicit repudiation of modern self-consciousness, "the dialogue of the mind with itself."

---

6. For representative expressions of the logical positivist argument, see *Logical Positivism,* ed. A. J. Ayer (New York: Free Press, 1959), and Ayer's *Language, Truth, and Logic* (1936; New York: Dover, 1952). Positivists ran into trouble when critics pointed out that the so-called verifiability criterion of meaning was itself unverifiable and thus by its own lights nonsense.

The problems posed by Arnold's distrust of reason and analysis become clearest, however, at the moments when Arnold treats the question of how to tell the difference between true and spurious forms of culture. Arnold most directly confronts this question, obviously a crucial one for his defense of culture, in "The Study of Poetry," an essay that would be invoked after Arnold's death to justify making the study of English literature a school and college subject and that would also provide the blueprint for the first academic English literature canon. It is in this essay that Arnold defines the nature of poetic greatness by adducing his famous poetic "touchstones."

What is great poetry? asks Arnold. It is poetry that offers a profound "criticism of life" that has the note of "high seriousness." And what precisely do these phrases mean? Arnold tells us not to ask: "Critics give themselves great labor to draw out what in the abstract constitutes the characters of a high quality of poetry. It is much better simply to have recourse to concrete examples:—to take specimens of poetry of the high, the very highest quality, and to say: The characters of a high quality of poetry are what is expressed *there*. They are far better recognized by being felt in the verse of the master, than by being perused in the prose of the critic" [Super 9:170–71]. In other words, we cannot define poetic greatness "in the abstract," but we can at least point to it. Hence Arnold's touchstones. Here, for example, is the essence of greatness in Dante and Shakespeare:

> In la sua volontade è nostra pace. (In His will is our peace.)

> If thou didst ever hold me in thy heart,
> Absent thee from felicity awhile,
> And in this harsh world draw thy breath in pain
> To tell my story . . . [Super 9:169–70]

Arnold senses something inadequate about the touchstone solution, however, for he adds: "Nevertheless if we are urgently pressed to give some critical account" of the "characters" of poetic greatness, "we may safely, perhaps, venture on laying down, not indeed how and why the characters arise, but where and in what they arise."

But instead of the promised "critical account," Arnold evades the question and falls back again on another dismissal of reasoned definition. The characters of true poetry, Arnold says, "are in the matter and substance of the poetry, and they are in its manner and style. Both of these, the substance and matter on the one hand, the style and manner on the other, have a mark, an accent, of high beauty, worth, and power. But if we are asked to define this mark and accent in the abstract, our answer must be: No, for we should thereby be darkening the question, not clearing it" [Super 9:170–71].[7] Arnold ends up concluding that it is not a problem after all that poetic value cannot be defined, for such definitions are superfluous to true connoisseurs, who just know it when they see it. "If we are thoroughly penetrated" by the power of the specimens of great poetry he has quoted, says Arnold, "we shall find that we have acquired a sense enabling us, whatever poetry shall be laid before us, to feel the degree in which a high poetical quality is wanting there" [310].

It is a significant moment: Arnold hovers on the brink of theorizing about poetry only to draw back—whether from inability or apprehension is hard to say. Yet here again a version of the Common Culture Paradox rears its head. On the one hand, the pedagogical context of his essay, the need to acculturate a newly enfranchised audience that presumably does not yet know in its bones what culture is, demands that Arnold spell out the criteria of poetic value as explicitly as he can. On the other hand, it is difficult as well as risky to spell out these criteria "in the abstract," for they have become more debatable than they had been, and formulating them abstractly figures to make them a target for still further debate.

Arnold seems instinctively to foresee the way efforts to define litera-ture theoretically would lead to the proliferation of contending literary theories of the twentieth century, where the very multiplicity of attempts to resolve sectarian disagreements over the definition of literature ends up only intensifying those disagreements. Yet for Arnold to refrain from attempting a definition of poetry would be to default on his responsibility to his readers. If Arnold's readers could have recognized good poetry by seeing it exemplified in Arnold's touchstone passages, Arnold would not have needed to write the essay in the first place.

Arnold's double bind has been inherited by twentieth-century demo-cratic pedagogy. Like that pedagogy, Arnold's essay had been called forth by a breakdown of cultural consensus, a loss of common understandings that had been taken for granted among a social elite, though to a very uneven degree, judging from Arnold's remarks on the "Barbarian" quality of the British aristocracy in *Culture and Anarchy*. This breakdown of

---

7. Michael Fischer points out these difficulties in the argument of "The Study of Poetry" in *Does Deconstruction Make Any Difference? Post-Structuralism and the Defense of Poetry in Modernist Criticism* (Bloomington, Ind.: Indiana University Press, 1985), pp. 7–9.

consensus had resulted from the democratic expansion of cultural partici-
pation. The question as Arnold saw it now was, How are people not bred
to the old elite to be helped to develop elite tastes? Touchstones from
Dante and Shakespeare are unlikely to help anyone develop those tastes
who does not already have them, and anyone who already has them does
not need touchstones.

Arnold's coy refusal to reduce his poetic standards to explicit principles finally works against his desire to perpetuate those standards. Reading Arnold's essay at a century's distance, most of us would be hard
pressed to guess precisely what it was that Arnold valued in his dozen or so
touchstone passages, passages that he himself concedes do not resemble
one another in any obvious way. In our uncertainty about what Arnold
may have meant we reexperience the uncertainty of generations of students who have sat through English literature survey courses modeled on
"The Study of Poetry" (often based on anthologies like the one it originally introduced). These students are supposed to appreciate a mysterious
poetic quality that is never quite explained and evidently can be felt only
by those who already know what it is.

It is not surprising that these same problems reappear in the work of
those who follow an Arnoldian line of argument in the present cultural
war. When Arthur Schlesinger, Jr., in *The Disuniting of America* attacks
the "divisiveness" of multiculturalism, he echoes Arnold's criticism of
liberal nonconformists. It is ironic that the unified traditional America that
Schlesinger contrasts with the "disunited" America of today was for Arnold the very model of barbarous fragmentation.

Like Arnold, however, Schlesinger writes as if the only imaginable
alternative to a common cultural identity is anarchy:

> [The American republic] embodies ideals that transcend ethnic, reli-
> gious, and political lines. It is an experiment, reasonably successful
> for a while, in creating a common identity for people of diverse
> races, religions, languages, cultures. But the experiment can con-
> tinue to succeed only so long as Americans continue to believe in
> the goal. If the republic now turns away from Washington's old goal
> of "one people," what is its future?—disintegration of the national
> community, apartheid, Balkanization, tribalization?[8]

---

8. Arthur Schlesinger, Jr., *The Disuniting of America: Reflections on a Multicultural
Society* (New York: Norton, 1991), p. 118.

Schlesinger's answer to his own question is clearly that the American republic can only disintegrate unless Americans continue to believe in the goal of "a common identity." What Schlesinger would consider an acceptable degree of common identity is not clear, but it is hardly obvious on the face of it why the United States cannot flourish economically and culturally with a very minimal degree of cultural identity.

What seems important is not that Americans find "a common identity," whatever that may mean, but that they learn to differ fundamentally with one another without always being on the brink of violence. For this reason, it would be more fruitful to shelve the present hand-wringing about common culture and begin talking about how to create a *common debate* about culture. We can hardly conceive such an alternative, however, as long as, like Arnold and Schlesinger, we equate debate and conflict with disintegration.[9]

Also like Arnold (though more crudely), Schlesinger engages in evasive talk about "our" values, as if what those values are and ought to be (and whether we need a unified *we*) were not what is in dispute:

> We don't have to believe that our values are absolutely better than
> the next fellow's, but we have no doubt that they are better *for us*,
> reared as we are—and are worth living and dying for. For our
> values are not matters of whim and happenstance. History has given
> them to us. They are anchored in our national experience, in our
> great national documents, in our national heroes, in our folkways,
> traditions, and standards. People with a different history will have
> differing values. But we believe that our own are better for us.[10]

This appeal to "our" values is not only thoroughly relativistic—our values may not be better than anybody else's but we have to embrace them because they are ours—but also clearly incoherent. Since many of the people described by Schlesinger as having "a different history" from "ours" are today themselves Americans, Schlesinger's American *we* with "our" distinctive traditions turns out to be inhabited by the alienness it supposedly contrasts with. So who is *we* after all?

The same question-begging logic turns up in a different context in Robert Alter's recent book, *The Pleasures of Reading in an Ideological*

———
9. I have developed this argument further in *Beyond the Culture Wars: How Teaching the Conflicts Can Revitalize American Education* (New York: Norton, 1992).
10. Schlesinger, *Disuniting of America*, p. 137.

Age. Alter deplores "the division of the academic study of literature, especially in the United States, into competing sectarian groups," as if such a disparagement did not align Alter himself with a sectarian group. "The new academic sectarianism" in literary critical approaches, according to Alter, "offers to the initiate a reassuring sense of certainty as well as a sense of superiority in relation to the unredeemed masses," enabling them "to achieve a certain calming elevation over the madding crowd by following one master" and "adopting one 'advanced' methodology."[11] It is Alter, however, as much as any camp follower of academic theory, who here pretends to speak from a position of "calming elevation over the madding crowd," though his viewpoint is no less sectarian than theirs. This is not to say there is no such thing as a nonsectarian position, but only that those who boast of occupying one rarely do.

A last example of neo-Arnoldian argument is David Bromwich's *Politics by Other Means: Higher Education and Group Thinking,* though Bromwich's immediate model is not Arnold but Edmund Burke. Deploring the fracturing of American society into a "culture of advocacy groups," Bromwich invokes Burke to argue that the ground of social morality lies in "a background of reasons already given and choices already made," a "wisdom without reflection."[12] Bromwich says nothing about how, short of restoring monarchy, such a background of reasons already given and choices already made could be reinstated, and since his self-declared allegiances are liberal it is clear that monarchy is not what he has in mind. Like Arnold, Bromwich is in the awkward position of having to *argue* for something that, by his own logic, must be already there prior to argument. If "wisdom without reflection" is what you want, the last thing you should do is write books reflecting on it in public.

The ultimate liability of all these defenses of common culture is that they do nothing to help create a common culture. Calling other people "sectarian" or "divisive" and blaming them for joining "advocacy groups" is not only hypocritical—for such name-calling is itself sectarian, divisive, and the gesture of an advocacy group—it is an ineffective way to persuade your opponents that they might after all share some common ground with you. What such gestures are really good for is to rally those who already belong to your advocacy group against those in the advocacy

---

11. Robert Alter, *The Pleasures of Reading in an Ideological Age* (New York: Simon and Schuster, 1989), pp. 14–15.

12. David Bromwich, *Politics by Other Means: Higher Education and Group Thinking* (New Haven: Yale University Press, 1992), pp. 133, 141.

groups you dislike, thus helping to make your own advocacy group more powerful.

Arnold did not succeed in quelling the contentiousness of the modern spirit by calling it "anarchy." He did, however, put a powerful rhetorical weapon in the hands of everyone since he wrote who cannot imagine a common culture without a common background of beliefs.

Maurice Cowling

One-and-a-Half Cheers
for Matthew Arnold

In 1984 William Bennett, then chairman of the National Endowment for the Humanities and later President Ronald Reagan's Secretary of Education, published a pamphlet which implied that Matthew Arnold could be put to conservative use in American public discussion.[1] What Bennett meant by this was not anything directly political, but that American universities were not doing enough to transmit "the accumulated wisdom of our civilisation" and should do more by creating syllabuses out of texts which embodied what Arnold had called a "disinterested endeavour to learn and propagate the best that is known and thought in the world" [Super 3:283].

As an antidote to gay, Green, or lesbian syllabuses, as a conservative utterance against the defects of tenured radicalism in American universities, and as a proleptic warning against the absurdities of Clintonianism, this may, for all an outsider can tell, have something to be said for it. But it is necessary to raise a difficulty. For the "disinterested endeavour to learn and to propagate the best that has been known and thought in the world" degenerates very easily, on both sides of the Atlantic, into consecrating thinkers who are assumed to be above criticism because of their status as authors of great texts. Bennett did not include any of Arnold's writings among *his* list of great texts. The argument of this essay is that from some points of view he was wise not to do so.

Arnoldian culture proposed a total reconstruction which would strengthen modern societies by rescuing them from narrowness, dogmatism, and intellectual anarchy, and help them find ways of filling the void left by the erosion of aristocratic authority. It also included a doctrine about the reconstruction of religion which was an essential aspect of the

---

1. William J. Bennett, *To Reclaim a Legacy: A Report on the Humanities in Higher Education* (Washington, D.C.: National Endowment for the Humanities, 1984).

Maurice Cowling

total reconstruction, and raises the question whether Arnold's religion was consistent with a conservative view of politics, morals, and culture.

In the United States there is a critical literature which takes seriously H. F. Lowry's intuition that Arnold would eventually be seen to have been a great Christian thinker. This is an interesting literature. But its assumptions are questionable. Authorial intention is an important aspect of the work of any major thinker, and Arnold's *intention* can certainly be represented as being Christian. But the sap which seeps out of an author is as important as the intention, and the sap which seeps out of Arnold is a sap which sucks out of Christianity almost everything that has been distinctive about it.

Intellectually Arnold was rooted in Newman's Oxford. *Culture and Anarchy* was an episode in the transition from Newman's attempt to preserve Oxford values in an unfriendly world to Walter Pater's attempt to preserve Oxford values in an unfriendly world. But it was also a criticism of the narrowness of the "hole-and-corner" Protestantism which Arnold had observed in nearly twenty years as an Inspector of Schools, and of the prospect of universal suffrage and working-class hegemony which had many thinkers searching urgently for antidotes—usually educational antidotes—both before and after the expansion of the electorate that was effected by the Reform Act of 1867.

Assessment of Arnold's significance for modern societies is not, therefore, a simple matter of applying his opinions to present-day conditions. On the contrary, a double action is needed. It is necessary to ask first whether his message *can* be translated out of his circumstances, and then, if it can, whether his religious opinions can be detached from his political, moral, and cultural opinions. The answer to the first question is that the connection between his circumstances and his message was so intimate and complicated that translation cannot be effected. The answer to the second is that his religious opinions cannot properly be detached and that, indeed, in Arnold's mind culture, politics, and morals were inseparable from religion once he had turned his attention to the "crisis" which England was undergoing in the early 1860s.

By the early 1860s Arnold was comparing the crisis by which England was confronted with the crisis created by the Revolution of 1789, when the whole of France had been "penetrated with an enthusiasm for pure reason" (*The Function of Criticism at the Present Time* [Super 3:264–65]). Arnold had reservations about the French Revolution. But his writings were an apology for it in face of the resistance which had been led by Pitt and the

English aristocracy, the negativity which military resistance had imposed on English politics since, and the impossibility that "aristocratic ideas" should stand up to the intellectual advances which the Revolution had made even in defeat since 1815. Not only had aristocracies an "incapacity . . . for ideas" which made them incapable of succeeding in "modern epochs" but "the old political parties which [had] governed England since the revolution" were in process of dissolution (in fact they were not) and the "growing power" (a truer insight) was the "instinct pushing the masses towards expansion and fuller life" ("Democracy" [Super 2:11]).

Though Arnold's sympathies in the 1860s were liberal, he did not identify himself with a political party and made a point of writing with the independence of an intellectual. *Intellectual* was not a word that he used; nor would he have thought of himself as a bourgeois intellectual. Neither were his values bourgeois values, since they were literary, official, or paraclerical values. But he assumed bourgeois predominance just as he assumed that working-class power was going to increase, and that it was the duty of *superior people*—again to use a phrase he did not use—to establish that right mentalities would survive the arrival of working-class power.

Bourgeois predominance, on this account, was protestant nonconformist, had emerged with the industrial revolution, and had both benefited from political economy and had its preexisting alienation from the State confirmed by political economy. "Alienation from the State" was a hangover from Anglican persecution in the seventeenth century, just as "Philistinism" was a continuation of the insensitivity to ideas with which the bourgeoisie had imitated the aristocracy. But since aristocracies attracted deference where bourgeoisies did not, and since "ideas," improbably, were said to be "the life of the multitude," it followed that the bourgeoisie would find it difficult to attract deference, create cohesion, or resolve the crisis until it did something about its ideas.

Arnold ridiculed bourgeois complacency, the bourgeois belief in the sanctity of private property, and the bourgeois assumption that the poor could be educated compulsorily without the rich suffering compulsion too. He made fun of bourgeois radicalism, "British masculinity," and bourgeois self-congratulation about British progress; for whereas "the civil organisation . . . of France, Germany, Italy, Switzerland and Holland" had been "framed with . . . design to meet the wants of modern society," the British state resembled Austria and Rome in ignorance of "the right of mind and reason to rule human affairs" ("General Conclusion Continued" [Super 4:304–5]).

The comparison with Austria and Rome—the bêtes noires of the liberal mind—was meant to be offensive. But it was also meant to be serious, to make the point that the English mind was out of step with the most modern minds in Europe, and to suggest that bourgeois-led solidarity would turn out to be an illusion unless the English got into step with these modern minds. This was true, Arnold argued, not only of politics, where the power of the state had to be increased, but also of culture as a contribution to political and religious renovation.

Arnold was the prophet of culture because he wanted culture to put a spoke in the wheel of bourgeois Philistinism and nonconformity by bringing the standards of the historic Anglican establishment to bear on them. This did not mean, however, that he identified culture with the existing Church of England.

In *Culture and Anarchy* the remolding of theology was less extensive than it was to be in Arnold's later writings; it was Newman who symbolized culture's resistance to middle-class liberalism, Newman who was the bearer of "beauty and sweetness" and the subverter of liberal complacency. But even in *Culture and Anarchy* it was obvious that "the religion of culture" had no time for the dogmatic aspects of Newman's religion, and that the attempt to make culture prevail would involve the religious world in abandoning the "mechanical use of St Paul's writings" [179].

What Arnold called for in *Culture and Anarchy* was "a free and fresh stream of thought" [xv] to "develop all sides of our humanity" in "all parts of our society" [xvi] so as to ensure that Hebraism would be supplemented by Hellenism, and the Philistine "doing" it associated with a "mechanical and material" civilization [15] by the "sweetness and light" which it associated with pursuit of general "perfection" [xvii].

Culture and Anarchy was directed at the "mutilated" humanity [xvi] which was produced by provincial nonconformity and the "self-assertion" [xxiv] which its struggle against persecution had imposed on the nonconformist character. But though Arnold agreed that universities ought to be opened to nonconformists [xxv], he opposed the disestablishment of the Church of England in the hope, ultimately, that Anglican "knowing" would act as an antidote to Hebraic "doing" [lix]. He wished to soften up Hebraic doing by suffusing it with culture and by developing an inner humanity to control its "animality" [24]. He also wished to soften up orthodoxy, not by subjecting it to Broad Church latitudinarianism, but by reinterpreting it so as to recall religion to the principle that culture was "alone . . . sacred and binding" [xlv].

About this three things need to be noticed. The sacredness of culture, though designed to subvert both the Puritan sense of sin and Renaissance intellectuality, was aimed at the first more than the second; the questioning of the assumption that all classes should do what they liked was accompanied by the belief that they should do as their best selves told them to [257]; and what was required was not only the development of a best self, as against the inferior selves held up for admiration by the aristocracy and the middle and working classes, but also the establishment of an "authoritative" law based on an increased use of state power, which was itself sacred [259].

Culture and Anarchy was the work of a subtle, mocking, and superior intelligence which was addressing the nation in order to have an effect on relations between the classes. The difficulty in translating this into modern terms is that its contribution to the religious politics of the 1860s cannot be translated into the religious politics of the 1990s, which include a strong strand of indifference to religion and do not assume, as Arnold assumed, the desirability of a positive Christian doctrine.

In the 1860s Arnold had begun to make a general statement about the religious duties of "the few" towards "the many." He exposed the inadequacy of John Colenso, *Essays and Reviews,* and other ill-considered latitudinarianisms which, instead of aiming at edification as the work of clergymen should, were upsetting the popular faith by intellectual questionings which were not good enough to instruct the instructed (*Bishop: The Philosopher* [Super 3:43–44]). It cannot be said that Arnold respected English popular religion; "perhaps in no country in the world," he wrote in 1863, "is so much nonsense so firmly believed" (*Dr. Stanley's Lectures on the Irish Church* [Super 3:79]). But he was as contemptuous of the "modern thinking" which was being proposed as its replacement, and objected to the doubts of the intelligentsia being broadcast to the "multitude" until abandonment of the doctrine of biblical inspiration had been examined intellectually and a search conducted for something else for churches to base their beliefs on.

In other words, Arnold was both rejecting theological liberalism and taking its primary assumptions seriously. He was also saying that the masses had not accepted them, and that the necessary reconstruction should be conducted initially on a closed circuit where the intelligentsia, instead of talking to its servants, talked to itself. This circuit was a "laboratory" of the mind where ideas were fashioned for use in the world, but where transference to the world involved a complicated process. It was *possible* to make "new intellectual ideas" harmonize with the religious life, but it was extremely difficult, and would need "great religious reformers" if it was to be done properly. Since none was in sight, the true religious teacher was he who, "not yet reconciling all things, at least esteem[ed] things . . . in their due order" and "shutting his mind against no ideas brought by the spirit of the age, set these ideas . . . in their right prominence . . . in the religious life" (*Dr. Stanley's Lectures* [Super 3:69–70]).

Arnold pinpointed the Bible as the problem. But he was tentative and uncertain; he knew what to say about the merits and limitations of Spinoza's view of the Bible but was not yet ready to tackle the main problem. It was not until *St. Paul and Protestantism* that he replaced the social by a theological critique of nonconformity, and began to show how he supposed that the Church of England could become as credible and intelligible as Catholicism had been in the hands of St. Francis.

St. Paul and Protestantism argued that Protestant nonconformity had been theologically aggressive and had come to exist for the sake of special doctrines, whereas the Church of England had shared the belief which the medieval church was supposed to have shared—that dogmatic definition was a matter of expediency which in no way touched "the essence of Christianity" (*Puritanism and the Church of England* [Super 6:105]). In it Arnold stated that reunion with Rome might be approached in the long term via the churches of France and Germany, but added that reunion was not "the business which the England of this generation" was "set to do," and that all *it* could do was "to bring about . . . the union of Protestants" by convincing nonconformists that "Scriptural Protestantism" was not "the gospel . . . of Christ" (*Puritanism* [Super 6:107]).

By "Scriptural Protestantism" Arnold meant election, justification, and predestination, and the Calvinistic and Wesleyan emphasis on "what God gives and works for us, not on what we bring or do for ourselves" (*St. Paul* [Super 6:17]). What he aimed to show was that St. Paul had not believed any of this and that to read him "with critical tact" would prove that the real Paul was incompatible with the Paul whom Luther and Calvin had "shut up" in a scholastic, scientific or pseudo-scientific theology [Super 6:20, 28].

Arnold's ostensible aim in theological translation was to soften up Protestant nonconformity. But he also wanted the Church of England to acquire the modern religion which, after being hinted at in *Culture and Anarchy* and implied in *St. Paul and Protestantism,* was laid out and explained in *Literature and Dogma* and *God and the Bible.*

By the time *Literature and Dogma* was published, the caution of the 1860s had disappeared. Where previously it had been dangerous to upset popular superstition unless there was something popular to replace it with, now there had been the inevitable revolution created by the high-quality secular literature of the late 1860s. What was required was *total* reconstruction, with the whole Bible replacing the Pauline epistles as the text for elucidation, with Christ's replacing St. Paul's as the teaching for reinterpretation, and with the Bible being treated comprehensively at last as "literature."

In treating the Bible as literature, Arnold was not diminishing its importance. On the contrary, since the Bible's "divine" significance had been questioned, it had to be given some other significance, by being treated as the Jews' contextualizable contribution to "culture," by attributing a meaning to "God" which annexed God to human experience, and by disparaging all other religions by comparison with the religion of the golden age when the Jews had thought naturally and without the contortions produced by subsequent, and especially by theological, development. This did not mean that the religion of the earlier books of the Old Testament was final. What it did mean was that Christ had used it to enable men to discern, through the "three-fourths of life" which regulated the impulses, both the "not ourselves which made for righteousness" and the difficulty of knowing what the "not ourselves" was like; and that, in showing the way back to that joy in pursuing righteousness which the Jews had lost by subjecting themselves to mechanical externality and a commanding God, Christ had introduced the humbleness, repentance, and sweet reasonableness which were his distinctive contribution to religion.

This was the "secret" of Jesus, and that was all it was. It had been revealed less than halfway through *Literature and Dogma* [Super 6:298], and the rest of that work, as well as *God and the Bible,* either reinforced it with biblical evidence or defended it against the criticism it attracted, both for attenuating belief and for failing to attenuate belief sufficiently. In conceiving of people as having two selves, of their need to die to the lower one, and of dying involving the annulment of sensuality, Christ was presented not only as a Carlylean moralist, without the lapsed Calvinistic harshness of Carlyle's conception of Nature, but also as pointing a gun down the ages at the "fairy tales" to which both high and low Christianity had become committed in the course of Christian history [Super 6:232].

This statement was not intended to be speculative any more than it was intended to be dogmatic. Its truth was supposed to lie in the fact that it worked, that, for nations as well as for individuals, there could be no escape from judgment by the "Eternal that loveth righteousness" [Super 6:386], and that not only would the wicked eventually be no more and the ungodly be clean gone, but also that whoever was shipwrecked would be "shipwrecked on conduct" [Super 6:396].

In Arnold's religion, as in Marx's, Mill's, or Carlyle's religions, the point was the future. It was the "immense" possibility for development [Super 6:396] once Jesus's "secret" had been disclosed that was to create a Christianity in which all men would read the Bible as Arnold read it, in which all men would treat it as a call to righteousness, and in which all men would annul their sensuality by reference to it. Arnold did not expect an easy ride either for righteousness or for the Bible as literature. But it is important to notice that he had in mind a ride on the back of the Church of England.

In *Culture and Anarchy* and *St. Paul and Protestantism* there had been defenses both of the Church of England as the Church established by the State, and of Church Establishments generally against nonconformist narrowness, on the ground that the human spirit's approaches to totality had been made chiefly by those who either belonged to establishments or had been trained in establishments. The meaning was obscure but it is certainly the case that Arnold had a High Church mind which, in *Last Essays on Church and Religion,* provided a High Church and highly political justification of his decision to rearrange Christianity from above.

In *Last Essays on Church and Religion* Arnold did three things. He explained that he was not an enemy of the Church of England. He defined the Church of England as "a great national society for the promotion of . . . *goodness*" [Super 8:65]. And he insisted that the Anglican clergy would be missing a historic opportunity if they failed to act on this assumption, since the nation would turn out to be their natural ally provided they could bring themselves to abandon not only dogma but also the social and political conservatism which went with regard for rank, property, and class interest.

One of Arnold's original aims in demythologizing the Bible had been to meet the demands of working-class skepticism. But now he was saying that it was necessary to rearrange the Church's political teaching as well, and that even an undogmatic Christianity would not save the Church of England unless it responded to working-class aspirations by changing things for the better on this side of the grave and establishing not only "righteousness" but also "felicity" and "endless self-sacrifice all round" [Super 8:77, 72]. This was "the ideal of Jesus" [Super 8:77], and not only was there no incompatibility between it, God's earthly kingdom, and working-class improvement, but the Anglican tradition, with its lack of awe in face of class, property, and station, supplied positive testimony to their compatibility.

This was what was seeping out of Arnold by the mid-1870s—the idea that a comprehensive Establishment could not only embrace Anglicans and Protestant nonconformists but could also bring the working classes within the pale of the religious constitution by providing a class as well as a personal interest in pursuing righteousness through the regulation of conduct. The question we have to ask is, How was this related to culture?

In answering this question, we need to bear three things in mind. First, according to Arnold, that one of culture's important roles was to translate theology. Arnold's introduction to selections from the English poets, as well as his versions of the Book of Isaiah, were intended as contributions to popular religion, and it was in this sense that *Last Essays on Church and Religion* announced his intention of spending the rest of his life on "literature, more strictly so-called . . . where work of the most important kind ha[d] now to be done, though indirectly, for religion" [Super 8:148]. Second, that "hole-and-corner churches" [xlvi] were damaging Christianity by isolating it from "the main current of human life" [xlvi] and needed a modern replication of the Emperor Constantine's success in bringing Christianity out of its ghetto. Finally, that "men ha[d] got into such a habit of giving to the language of religion a special application" that they could only be reached "through all the voices of human experience . . . art, science, poetry, philosophy, and history as well as religion" [12].

This was a perceptive statement of a historic difficulty. But Arnold also gave another reason for wanting to restore what Constantine had established—that culture requires totality of development. Yet this totality was not necessarily Christian, not only because culture was a living thing where orthodox, historic, dogmatic, theological Christianity for him was a dead thing, but also because, at the heart of orthodox, historic, dogmatic, theological Christianity he saw not the challenges and opportunities which were seen by Newman, Manning, Gladstone, and Salisbury (the great proponent of resurgent orthodoxy), but an anachronism which, though it was to be treated as poetry and preserved in the form of Catholic worship (where Carlyle treated it as "rotten woodwork" which had to be burnt out), was an anachronism just the same.

The "Eternal that loveth righteousness" can just about be understood to be ministering to a conservative moral posture so long as it is recognized to have been a way of disciplining working-class power and contributing to a post-Christian religion whose scriptures would consist of the books, including the Bible, which embodied "the best that had been known and thought in the world." But Newman surely said what needs to be said when he predicted, while still an Anglican and the only Arnold that anyone had heard of was Matthew's father, Thomas, the famous headmaster of Rugby school, that the time would come in the not very distant future when "literature (or science) would be judged capable of educating the masses," when "private judgment of the Bible" would make "sincerity" the "sole test of thought and conduct," and when eventually the Bible and the church would give way to a religion of beauty, philosophy, and imagination. That describes the earlier versions of Pater's religion more exactly than it describes Arnold's religion. But if the necessary Carlylean adjustments are made, it will be obvious what is meant.

As a religious thinker, Arnold has an attractive sadness and resignation towards inevitabilities to which, he implied, he might not have yielded if the choices had been his. But there was an unattractive aspect to this as well—a fatalism which made a strategy out of testing the wind and blowing with it, and a bland, accommodating, acquiescent Anglican grandeur which, while regretting the inevitability and lamenting the loss, was perfectly willing to accommodate away its own grandmother.

Arnold sometimes claimed that, if he had been born in the seventeenth century, he would have been ordained. But he was not born in the seventeenth century. He was not ordained. His most prominent objections to Whiggism, rationalism, and enlightenment were the objections which W. E. H. Lecky had made to the Stoics—that they had been unable to address the multitude—and his regard for the papacy was connected with the fact that, though aristocratic in carriage, the papacy, as Newman had said, was able to address the multitude. But what did Arnold want said to the multitude when they were addressed? What he wanted said was what Carlyle and J. A. Froude wanted said, but what Newman, Manning, Gladstone, and Salisbury did not want said—that theology should go away, that the pursuit of righteousness should be established in its place, and that culture should become the instrument of its establishment.

In England, Arnoldianism has been effective chiefly in providing an ideology for the university-educated or intellectually-aspiring classes, and in justifying virtuous, high-minded, attitudes to morals, politics and culture. But it has not been so effective at providing social solidarity, at linking low thought to high thought, or at developing that populist, philistine, materialist conservatism which has been the unexpected outcome of the newspaper revolution of the 1880s. Arnoldian culture, indeed, so far from assisting at this, has had the effect, no less than Mill's Liberalism, of dividing the educated classes from the uneducated, and of creating an anti-populist, highminded "correctness" which carries many unconservative assumptions with it.

Arnold is doubtless attractive to American conservatives by reason of his wish to attribute authority to the western cultural tradition, as he understood it. But is not his high-mindedness as objectionable as Mill's? Is it not a facet of his wish to erode historic Christianity? Ought not conservatives, whether Christian or Jewish, to be wary of this use of culture?

In practice English-speaking societies (apart from Eire) are pluralist in religion and likely to remain so for many generations to come. Arnold was not a pluralist in the modern sense; what he wanted was an established religion which could be made compatible with the modern world by incorporating "the best that had been known and thought in the world." But the difficulty is that the "best," even more than it did in the 1860s, tends now to reject not only historic, dogmatic, orthodox Christianity but also formal religion as such and the mentalities which go with it.

It would be absurd to criticize Arnold for anticipating the religious condition of the modern world. It would be equally absurd to congratulate him. Not three cheers, but at most one-and-a-half, are what is appropriate for a thinker who, if he *is* to be used to provide authoritative guidance for the secular societies of the 1990s, needs to be used with the very greatest caution.

Samuel Lipman

Why Should We Read
Culture and Anarchy?

This essay is written by way of both conclusion and introduction, though it
may well be said that I am using each of these words in a curious way. It is
a conclusion in the sense that I have attempted to summarize Arnold's
views in his time, a time different, like all times past, from our own; it is an
introduction in that I have attempted to go on from Arnold's time to ours,
that we might apply his wisdom to our problems. My initial question,
then, is but a restatement of what I have just written: Why, a century and a
quarter after its initial appearance, should we read *Culture and Anarchy?*
My answer is simple. Because we need culture, and we have anarchy.

This answer may be simple, but it is not popular. For those who make
academic—I almost said cultivated—opinion in this country, the answer
to my question is that there is no point in reading *Culture and Anarchy* at
all, for we are immensely cultured, and the one thing we lack is freedom.
The chief sign of our culture is the world-conquering success of our
popular media and its stars; the evidence of our lack of freedom is the
noisy campaign about family values and decency waged by a small conservative intellectual class in league (so the story goes) with noisy right-
wing, usually religious, yahoos.

Perhaps the best way to begin to find out which answer makes more
sense would be to search out what Arnold himself meant by these two
pregnant words, *culture* and *anarchy,* and then apply what Arnold wrote to
our lives today. So let us begin with anarchy. For Arnold, anarchy took
two forms, the social—the untrammeled behavior of disparate groups—
and the individual—the individual conscience as the ultimate arbiter of
every decision, political, economic, social, or personal. Both kinds of
anarchy stemmed from the same cause: the right of each Englishman to
make up his mind for himself, or, put another way, the right of each
Englishman to do as he likes.

Who were these people who claimed such complete personal freedoms, and how did they use them? They were the people and groups (and their descendants) who had separated themselves from the original founding of the Anglican Establishment under Henry VIII in the sixteenth century. For them, the pope in London (in the guise of the reigning sovereign) was no better than the Pope in Rome. For many Englishmen, the Reformation in England—what one might call the post-Reformation—was not just a battle for dynastic power, national self-assertion, and freedom from foreign overlords. It was a battle for how each man should live in relation to God, a battle to be decided anew each instant of each day. Beginning with Martin Luther and the Protestant Reformation, and continuing in England with a national establishment of religion, Arnold saw in the Puritans and the Unitarians, the Dissenters and the Nonconformists, the Methodists and the Wesleyans, and all the myriad of smaller sects, an increasingly embittered hegemony of personal moral decisions based on individual reading of the Bible. It was this emphasis on the strictness of the individual conscience, on right as determined by the individual, that Arnold, following Heinrich Heine (not uncritically, for Heine on occasion expressed contempt for his fellow Jews), called "Hebraism."

What is the original content of this Hebraism for Arnold? For him, Hebraism is concerned with the triumph of obedience over sin. The sin is man's animality, his being driven by the instincts of lust and flesh, by the instincts to cheat his neighbor and lie to God. Obedience is the observance of an external code, contained first in the Old Testament of the Jews and then in the New Testament of the Christians, a code that regulates every human moral action in the light of God's law. For Arnold, the then-contemporary manifestation of Hebraism was Calvinism, the total concentration on morality and conduct at the expense of all the other attributes of humanity.

So far as moral conduct—the relation between men, and between men and the Almighty—was concerned, it must on no account be thought that Arnold was an opponent of Hebraism. On the contrary: Arnold went to great lengths to place in Hebraism and the ancient Jews the source of righteousness. In *Culture and Anarchy* he quoted the phrase from *Ecclesiasticus* 37:25 "the days of Israel are innumerable" [lviii], and in the later *Literature and Dogma* (1873) he writes, "To the Bible men will return; and why? Because they cannot do without it. Because happiness is our being's end and aim, and happiness belongs to righteousness, and righteousness is revealed in the Bible" [Super 6:380].

But Arnold went beyond the Hebraism of moral conduct based on the Bible to find another Hebraism, one in which that which was appropriate to moral conduct had been transformed into a principle of individual irresponsibility. To Arnold, the connection between Hebraism and anarchy lay in man's tendency, once he had satisfied his conscience by conquering his animality and his indulgence of sensual pleasures, to pursue other, not always constructive, parts of life: religious disputation and conflict, the cultivation of trade and industry to the exclusion of the life of the mind, the loss of responsibility to a common society, the giving up of thought and reflection. It was in this principle, not of personal righteousness but of irresponsible self-determination, that Arnold found the cause of many of the ills affecting English society in the 1860s. Because of the clamorous rise of political democracy, there were the Hyde Park riots of 1866 over the extension of the franchise, which the government seemed unable to control; because of the hatred of popery, there were the anti-Catholic agitations in Birmingham, in which Protestant speakers attempted to incite violence against Roman Catholics; there was the refusal of Nonconformists, out of abhorrence of any national establishment of religion, to agree to an equitable redistribution of Irish church property to reflect the overwhelming Roman Catholic majority in Ireland; for the same reason, there was the impossibility of agreement on the responsibility of the state for mass education; owing to the evangelical reliance on the biblical injunction "Be fruitful, and multiply" [Genesis 1:28], there were the chaotic and miserable conditions in East London caused by the high birth rates of the poor. Thus he wrote in *Culture and Anarchy:* "We have found that at the bottom of our present unsettled state, so full of the seeds of trouble, lies the notion of its being the prime right and happiness, for each of us, to affirm himself, and his ordinary self; to be doing, and to be doing freely and as he likes. We have found at the bottom of it the disbelief in right reason as a lawful authority" [166–67].

Not surprisingly, Arnold wonders how such fine people as the English should think so little of "right reason, [and have] such an exaggerated value for their own doings, however crude." His answer is that their adherence to individually determined conscience, arising out of their Hebraism, has overpowered what he describes as "the group of instincts and powers which we call intellectual" [167–68].

And so Arnold (again following Heine) brings us to the other half of his philosophical constellation, "Hellenism." Here one finds in his thought the combination of the two great influences of his paternal education, fastened as it was on the Bible and the Greek and Latin classics. Whereas, for Arnold, Hebraism is "strictness of conscience," Hellenism is "spontaneity of consciousness" [168]. The aims of Hebraism and Hellenism are the same: "that we might be partakers of the divine nature" [144; 2 Peter 1:4]. But these two ways to transcendence achieve their single goal by quite different means. Hebraism pursues "conduct and obedience" [145] in order to find God; Hellenism attempts "to see things as they really are" [147] in order to find the reality that God has made. Hebraism fastens upon the biblical projection of what Arnold called "the universal order"; Hellenism strives for "an unclouded clearness of mind, an unimpeded play of thought."

If Hebraism, in its debased form, is anarchy, Hellenism, in its highest form, is culture. It must be made clear at the outset that Arnold's use of *culture* has nothing to do with our twentieth-century anthropological omnium-gatherum definition, whereby the word simply serves to describe how people behave. Now there are economic cultures, political cultures, sexual cultures, taste cultures, ethnic cultures, entertainment cultures, religious cultures—cultures, in fact, for every category that ideology in league with statistics can dream up. In this new meaning of culture there are no norms, no ideas of good and bad, better and worse, high and low; where art and learning fear to tread, the social sciences have stepped in to fill the vacuum.

By contrast, Arnold's idea of culture is nothing if not elevated. Culture is "the study of perfection" [8]. He quotes Montesquieu as providing a motto for culture: "To render an intelligent being yet more intelligent!" [7]. To make clear that culture is not to be separated from religion—from Hebraism, if you will—he cites the goal, enshrined in the maxim of one of his favorite seventeenth-century religious figures, Bishop Wilson: "To make reason and the will of God prevail!" [8].

Early on in *Culture and Anarchy* Arnold suggests a quick test of the cultured person: "More and more he who examines himself will find the difference it makes to him, at the end of any given day, whether or no he has pursued his avocations throughout it without reading at all; and whether or no, having read something, he has read the newspapers only" [ix]. But Arnold, an elitist but not a snob, quickly takes back something of his slur on newspapers: "This, however, is a matter for each man's private conscience and experience. If a man without books or reading, or reading nothing but his letters and the newspapers, gets nevertheless a fresh and free play of the best thoughts upon his stock notions and habits, he has got culture" [ix]. Arnold's point is therefore what he calls the "inward operation": thought and reflection, not compulsive doing and action.

Culture does not focus exclusively on the past, though it includes the classics of antiquity and the Middle Ages, as well as the great works of the German and French Enlightenment. Because of culture's cherishing of the past in all its richness, it engenders the flexibility to think about and even accept new ideas. Culture goes beyond religion by emphasizing the harmonious expansion of all sides, moral and intellectual, of a person's nature. For Arnold, culture is to be found inside our own minds and thoughts; for him, wealth, democracy, equality, institutions, are all *machinery,* external elements of life more—or less—necessary to the perfection of our nature. Culture attempts "to do away with classes" [49]; it does not reach down to the lower orders, and it does not try to propagandize them. Instead, Arnold's idea of culture, like the literary criticism he proposed, is concerned to propagate to all the best that human civilization has created in the several thousand years since Jerusalem, Athens, and Rome. "[T]he men of culture," in Arnold's memorable phrase, "are the true apostles of equality" [49].

If, for Arnold, the character of Hebraism is stern insistence on righteousness, the function of culture is to provide what he called, following Jonathan Swift's metaphor of the bee's honey and wax in *The Battle of the Books,* "sweetness and light" [23]. This phrase has over the years come to have a certain effete quality, but it must not be thought that Arnold, for all his gentleness and geniality, lacked a firm core of moral and political will. In *The Function of Criticism at the Present Time* he approvingly cited his favorite, Joseph Joubert: "Force and right are the governors of this world; force till right is ready" [Super 3:265]. And the same attitude is underscored in the first edition of *Culture and Anarchy* by the proud quoting of his father's injunction to fling the ringleaders of riots from the Tarpeian Rock [258].

The toughness at Arnold's center was amply demonstrated in his class analysis of society. For him, society could be divided into three constituents: Barbarians, Philistines, and Populace; indeed, he devoted a chapter in *Culture and Anarchy* to just that analysis (and, in the second and third editions, with just that title). By Barbarians, Arnold meant the aristocracy and the upper classes, with their past of buccaneering individualism, their liking for field sports, their good looks and fine manners, their chivalry, their high spirits, and their physical courage. With all these virtues, bred of a past when the aristocratic function in society was vital, Arnold finds a lack of "light" and "soul" [102]—in other words, of mind and thought. For Arnold, the Philistines are the middle class, "particularly stiff-necked and perverse in the resistance to light and its children . . . who not only do not pursue sweetness and light, but who even prefer to them that sort of machinery of business, chapels, tea-meetings, and addresses from Mr.

Murphy and the Rev. W. Cattle [referring to the anti-Catholic agitations in Birmingham], which makes up [a] dismal and illiberal life" [99]. The Populace is the working class, some part of which we today would call upwardly mobile and which dreams of becoming middle-class, thus joining the Philistines. The more important part of the working class, however, "raw and half-developed, has long lain half-hidden amidst its poverty and squalor, and is now issuing forth from its hiding-place to assert an Englishman's heaven-born privilege of doing as he likes, and is beginning to perplex us by marching where it likes, meeting where it likes, bawling what it likes, [and] breaking what it likes" [104–5]. Arnold's overall verdict about English society (contained not in *Culture and Anarchy* but in the 1882 essay "A Word about America") is harsh: "The social system of [my] own country is so far from being perfect, that it presents us with the spectacle of an upper class materialised, a middle class vulgarised, [and] a lower class brutalised" [Super 10:4].

Arnold is very far from giving to the representatives of culture any paramount place in the running of politics and society. Not only is the cultured individual to abjure "despondency and violence"; "neither, on the other hand, is public life and direct political action much permitted to him. For it is his business . . . to get the present believers in action, and lovers of political talking and doing, to make a return upon their own minds, scrutinise their stock notions and habits much more, value their present talking and doing much less; in order that, by learning to think more clearly, they may come at last to act less confusedly" [264–65].

For all Arnold's inveighing against "machinery," for all his emphasis upon a direction of life away from doing and action to thought and reflection, there runs through *Culture and Anarchy* a kind of hymn to the State. Arnold's worship of the State echoes the famous passage (itself based on Cicero) in Edmund Burke's *Reflections on the Revolution in France:* "They [by which Burke means both those who form their opinions by learning and reflection and those who take their opinions on trust] conceive that He who gave our nature to be perfected by our virtue, willed also the necessary means of its perfection—He willed therefore the state—He willed its connexion with the source and original archetype of all perfection."[1] To Arnold, "the very framework and exterior order of the State, whoever may administer the State, is sacred; and culture is the most resolute enemy of anarchy, because of the great hopes and designs for the

---

1. *The Writings and Speeches of Edmund Burke,* ed. L. G. Mitchell (Oxford: Oxford University Press, 1989), 8:148.

Samuel Lipman

State which culture teaches us to nourish" [259]. The purpose of Arnold's culture, then, is to act upon the State, to make the State the means of realizing the true fulfillment of culture: the perfection of our best self. By our "everyday selves . . . we are separate, personal, at war; we are only safe from one another's tyranny when no one has any power; and this safety, in its turn, cannot save us from anarchy" [88]. We are to find "our centre of light and authority . . . [in] the idea of *the State,* as a working power. . . . We want an authority, and we find nothing but jealous classes, checks, and a dead-lock; culture suggests the idea of *the State.* We find no basis for a firm State-power in our ordinary selves; culture suggests one to us in our *best self"* [87, 89].

Enough, then, of Arnold set in nineteenth-century Victorian England. What of Arnold in America at the end of the twentieth century? What is the state of anarchy in our time and in our place? Let us start with religion, in Arnold's time the center of Victorian life, and once of American life as well. Here we find militant divisions on all sides, between believers and nonbelievers, between fundamentalists and liberals even within the same denominations, and of course between the proponents and opponents of abortion and a surprisingly closely related issue, school prayer. In Arnold's day the great splits in opinion, the great causes for individual decision, were matters of faith and dogma; now the issues demanding individual decision are the still more anarchically divisive issues of morals and conduct.

Let us move on from religion to an issue that in Arnold's day belonged to religion but hardly does so today: sex. Whereas abortion alone among sexual matters remains, at least for its opponents, a deeply religious issue, questions of sexual orientation and behavior now so far transcend religion as seemingly to have lost any religious dimension at all. In Arnold's time, marriage and the family—strict monogamy and children legitimized only in wedlock—were publicly accepted without dispute; departures from this strictly enforced norm were universally seen as a sign of sin and social decay or the tragic result of poverty. Now, in our time, marriage is seen as a matter of convenience, as is divorce; adultery—even among the politically conservative—is often seen more as beneficial to the personality than as harmful to the family. At the time of the first publication of *Culture and Anarchy,* homosexuality was illegal, and widely reprobated; only the sophisticated admitted its existence, and none of them openly dared to challenge the societal norms. Now a majority of Americans accepts homosexuality as a "valid life-style," and a smaller number, but still sizable and growing, endorses the idea of the legal recognition of homo-sexual marriage.

The family itself—married parents, children, grandparents, grand-children, and relatives, living in reasonably close proximity—is no longer seen as central to a stable, orderly life. Intrafamilial conflict, linked to generational hostility, so far from being something to be avoided at all costs, is recommended as liberating and as a means of achieving maturity. In ever-widening areas, children are urged to make up their own minds on the most important moral and social issues; parents are urged to get out of their children's lives as quickly as possible. Professional day-care is rec-ommended as a superior form of child-rearing. Freedom from children is taken to be just as important as freedom from parents. The idea of children taking care of their parents, as parents used to take care of their children, is seen as not just old-fashioned but also tyrannical; the retirement village and eventually the nursing home turn out to be no more than the adult version of child day-care.

This destruction of hundreds and even thousands of years of traditional ordered behavior, this anarchy by social pressure, as I have just written of it, affects more or less equally our three classes: upper, middle, and lower (or working). But now in America we have an underclass, millions of people without work, hope, education, and stable rules of behavior. Here is anarchy as anomie: drug taking and drug selling, robbery, assault, rioting, looting, and murder as ways of life; here are children, orphans in all but name, who don't know their fathers and hardly see their mothers; here are all the facts of life, all the tender emotions we can observe even in domestic animals, reduced to the most sordid and cruel trivialities.

Harrowingly, what links all these anarchies—rich and poor, white and black, young and old—is a triumphant popular culture that glorifies, and profits from, the depiction of bestial acts. The children of the affluent are provided by their parents with all the paraphernalia that brutal and sadistic entertainment can devise; the children of the poor—*vide* the propaganda for rap culture—are told that the representation of lust and murder is "their" culture, one that they should take pride in as it is made available, at colossal profits, for everyone of whatever economic and social con-dition.

And what of education, the American dream in the nineteenth century of Horace Mann and the Common School, of the making of a single American nation out of disparate peoples through universal education? And what of the countervailing dream, equally American but quite differ-ent, of the right of parents to educate their children in their own religious

Samuel Lipman

and ethnic traditions? In the Common School, order, the opposite of anarchy, was to be provided by a uniform education transmitting shared values; in its opposite, parochial education, order was to be provided by the transmission of the values of the parents. Now, under the spell of our new anarchy, neither solution to the provision of social order is possible. Uniform education is seen as stifling the natural physiological and psychological urges of the children, and as projecting an image of a united America that does not exist, and indeed never existed in reality. Parochial education, by training the children to replicate the lives of the parents, in its emphasis on fulfilling the wishes of the parents, is seen as rejecting familiarity with, and therefore sympathy for, other, and more ideologically favored, groups in society.

So much, then, for the anarchy we have. What about the culture we need? We can, I think, reject out of hand what might be called the Susan Sontag approach to culture, the one delineated so forcefully in the essay "Our Culture and the New Sensibility," of which a shortened version appeared in the 1960s in (of all places) the magazine *Mademoiselle*. Here Sontag, at the height of her career as the high priestess of Camp, attacks Arnold's critical emphasis on literature and rejects those who represent that emphasis today (I am quoting from her 1966 collection, *Against Interpretation*): "Simply ignorant of the vital and enthralling (so-called 'avant-garde') developments in the other arts, and blinded by their personal investments in the perpetuation of the older notion of culture, they continue to cling to literature as the model for creative statement. What gives literature its preeminence is its heavy burden of 'content,' both reportage and moral judgment" [298].

The attack on the Arnoldian definition of culture comes now not from the trends of the art-literary world, important as these were in eroding the foundations of high culture, but from a much more broadly based, even populist quarter. In 1860, Ralph Waldo Emerson began his essay on "Culture" with the confident phrase: "The word of ambition at the present day is Culture." But as a word and as an idea, "Culture" has now been transformed into "multiculturalism." What, then, is multiculturalism? I am afraid that the word can be defined only as process, not as content. Multiculturalism is the enforced study of the behavioral practices of others, sometimes as authentic behavior in itself, and oftentimes as artificially constructed products of supposed art and learning. It would be nonsense to assume that multiculturalism means the study of Confucius, or Japanese Buddhism, or Egyptology, or Old Testament Hebrew. For the "culture" in "multiculturalism" does not mean the high culture of Arnold, the "best that is known and thought in the world."[2] In any case, whatever its geographical origin, "best" is now damned as elitist, as are also "known" and "thought." The notion of a common body of civilization, based, as reality tells us it must be, on the West but including the great achievements of all times and peoples, is now rejected in favor of the notion of "civilizations"—which in fact is just our old friend, the anthropological definition of culture, in the newest, politically most correct clothing.

And at the head of our spreading anarchy stands our proud destruction of any idea of elites, whether intellectual, academic, artistic, legal, or political. Thus far only the natural sciences have managed to maintain their right to govern their fields; yet even science—especially medicine, perhaps our greatest glory—increasingly seems unable to justify its moral ascendancy. Of the very notion of political leadership, of political authority legitimately exercised for the good of the community, nothing remains but the sour smell of financial corruption, personal scandal, and the rankest, and increasingly demagogic, opportunism.

In the 1860s Arnold counterposed to the anarchy he saw around him the idea of culture. Enough has been said of our anarchy to make clear just how little culture we have with which to oppose it. The little we do have is located in what remains of our once great institutions of learning, of art, and of publishing. Doubtless these institutions still exist: our universities and colleges, fat with faculty, administrators, and endowments; our museums, engorged with almost all the art of the past—for each day, because of our tax laws, less of such art is allowed to remain in private hands; still more museums garnering spurious legitimacy for the latest products of an art world dedicated to the products of social dissolution; our musical groups flogging the great names of the past to an ever more unsophisticated and indeed disrespectful audience, while it has been decades now since enduring new music has found its way into the established repertory; our commercial publishers, sordidly dedicated to catching the latest—and shortest-lived—trends; our newspapers and periodicals frantically searching for readers affluent enough, and young enough, to attract advertisers.

---

2. This quotation is taken from "The Function of Criticism at the Present Time" [Super 3:270]; in adding this passage to the second and third editions of *Culture and Anarchy* (it had not been present in the first edition), Arnold substituted "has been" for "is": "culture . . . seeks . . . to make the best that has been thought and known in the world current everywhere" [Super 4:113].

Indeed, the culture we have to offer up against our anarchy is itself anarchy. My own best example of this phenomenon is a billboard advertisement for Reebok ski boots showing a downhill skier in full flight; the caption reads, "Life is short—play hard!"

But whether we are talking about our schools, our museums, our concert halls, our publishers, or our consumption-oriented rat race, we know instantly that true education—what Arnold called the study of perfection—is nowhere to be found. Our elementary and secondary schools are able to find time only for the inculcation of "politically correct" attitudes about how society and individuals are to be remade, along with (in the best of them) intensive study of test taking to assure entrance into the best colleges. Our institutions of higher education continue this combination of social indoctrination along with the most carefully worked-out schemes of preparation for the highest-paying careers. As I write these words, Harvard University is publicly unwilling to guarantee the small annual deficit—little more than $250,000—of *I Tatti,* Bernard Berenson's extraordinary collection of Italian painting set in the magnificent Tuscan countryside. In every college the great books are indeed taught (or at least talked about)—but taught so as to destroy their entrenched status as classics and reduce them to the level of sociological artifacts, mere examples of past periods of economic, racial, and sexual repression.

And then, miles away from what remains of art and learning, is another kind of human activity to which the word *culture* is applied: the professional sports, the popular music, the films, and the television programs that today take up and, sadly, make up so much of the lives of both children and adults. In all these activities, affecting hundreds of millions the world over, youth and physicality are yoked in the service of money and fame. In a perfect demonstration of our regnant definition of culture, while *I Tatti* struggles for its annual pittance from Harvard, the rock star Prince has just signed a recording contract for $100 million.

The prospect, then, that the institutions of culture will provide Arnold's "best that has been known and thought in the world" is bleak. Arnold, in the 1860s, could see the life ebbing from the Church Establishment, the great universities; he did not trust the energy and forcefulness of the Philistine middle class to find sweetness and light. As Arnold grew older, he felt ever less able to put his trust in these essentially private institutions. The only hope remaining to him lay in the State, initially in its function of provider of universal mass education: for him, and the italics are his, *"The State is of the religion of all its citizens, without the fanaticism of any of them"* [199]. But is the State, any more than our great quasi-private institutions, the answer to our problem of anarchy?

Of course, the English State that Burke, and after him Arnold, idolized was clumsy and rudimentary by our enlightened modern standards. Though Arnold could easily see the looming weaknesses in traditional social institutions, feudalism, in the relations of deference between the classes, still determined much behavior, of elites as well as masses, especially outside of the cities. And such a State as did exist in England was as much, if not more, the creation of social institutions—primarily the church, the landed classes, the public schools and Oxbridge, and perhaps even the press—rather than their creator. England was a people; England was a web of associations; England was a nation; in Arnold's time it was only incompletely a State.

But times were rapidly changing. The triumph of industrialization required central governmental power and regulation. As prosperity brought by industrialization—and the concomitant awareness of poverty too—grew, the English State grew; with the coming of the welfare-state Liberals after 1906, the World War I Coalition Government, the labor unrest and the rise of the Labour party in the 1920s, the Great Depression, rearmament, and World War II, and the problems of postwar economic reconstruction after 1945, the State became the Goliath of today, not the perfecter of our best selves and the bringer of national unity of which Arnold dreamt, but the bureaucratic tyrant that must be endured. And what has been true for the growth of the English State has been true, *mutatis mutandis,* not just in England but in the other free countries of the West as well.

And what of the role of the State in education, the area and the means where Arnold pinned so many of his hopes of self-improvement, self-realization, and self-perfection. Here in America we have a proud and self-confident educational establishment, ever larger, ever more organized, ever more extravagantly funded. On whatever level one considers, whether primary, secondary, undergraduate, or graduate, education is governed either directly by the State or by private institutions in lockstep with legislative requirements and commands. Now we hear talk of national curriculums, national standards, and national testing. Wherever one looks, schools, their faculties and their administrators—whether public or private it hardly seems to matter—arrogate to themselves the most basic decisions, severed from the traditional moral conduct that Arnold called "three-fourths of life," about what children should be taught, how they should be expected to behave, how they should view one another, and how they should live. Could this outcome possibly be what Arnold meant by "sweetness and light" and "the best that has been thought and known?"

Here we have come to the great flaw in Arnold, as he must appear to us today. He understood the anarchy of his day, and he predicted much of ours; he understood the need for high culture in his time, and that need has not changed until today. But he woefully misconstrued the State—not the State he saw in front of his eyes, but what the State was to become under the pressure of modern life. He entirely failed to see that the State bore within itself the seeds of monstrous tyranny; perhaps even more important, he failed to see that the State, by enhancing its own sovereignty through pitting one group against another, actually encourages the anarchy it exists to suppress and, in the process of suppressing what it has encouraged, becomes ever more powerful.

He more than misconstrued the State: he also placed too much weight—or so it seems to this American writer—on the power of religious and educational establishments, no matter how broadly based and no matter how all-inclusive—to build and protect a social consensus. Arnold understood well enough that dissenting establishments of religion, and their educational appanages, could act so as to subvert an established social order; he did not conceive that even so historically grounded an institution as the national church in England, or the nonpublicly established but nevertheless pervasive Roman Catholic church in America, could so act, through its own self-chosen representatives, as to subvert its own claims to universality. Of course it is unfair to tax Arnold not just with minimizing the tyrannical possibilities inherent in the State but also with his inability to anticipate the German radical Rudi Dutschke's remark about winning culture via the long march through the institutions. Above all, Arnold did not understand that the State would tend to replace society, by placing in the punitive force of law the normative functions that had for so long been exercised by an uncodified but nevertheless widely accepted consensus of opinion.

There can be little doubt that Arnold's great value to us today is not as a philosopher of community or of society, let alone of the state; his great value to us is as a lonely spokesman for the individual's search for an inward culture. How ironic it now seems that Arnold the Hellenist, Arnold the achiever of the perfection of the self through the beneficence of the State, is of supreme value to us as the protector of the lonely seeker of the tradition that has made possible the ideal of seeing the object for itself.

Indeed, in this sense, Arnold now seems to us less a Hellenist than an old-fashioned Hebraist, a staunch advocate of just those moral forces that he originally thought overcontrolled by personal decision making. For as we now can clearly see, it is in the individual and the battle for culture that the future of both the individual and culture lies. Curiously, it was Arnold's enemies, rather than his friends, who recognized Arnold's ties to the tradition of English Dissent as well as his obvious origins in the English Establishment and its own ties to culture. Thus, Leonard Woolf, a representative spokesman not just for the Bloomsbury of Virginia Woolf but also for the socialism of the British left-wing intelligentsia, scathingly attacked Arnold in his 1931 book *After the Deluge:*

> He sees himself as a crusader in the cause of culture or "sweetness and light" against Philistinism and English Liberalism. It was the *Zeitgeist,* breathing heavily over Britain, which embodied itself in the Philistine and the Puritan or Nonconformist, so hateful to him, yet he is completely unaware that the priggery of his own mind and the nasal sermonizing of his essays, so hateful to us, are products of the same unholy spirit breathing through him. The Pharisee is full brother to the Philistine, and not even a fig leaf divides the Phariseeism of Matthew Arnold from the Philistinism of his contemporaries.[3]

This is yet another reason that we ought to take Arnold's words about culture seriously. He saw plainly—in distinction to the aesthetes like Walter Pater who followed him—that culture and morality, imagination and conduct, Hellenism and Hebraism, were inextricably linked. I return again to the paragraph in the Preface to *Culture and Anarchy* that Arnold began with the biblical quotation "the days of Israel are innumerable." But now I want to continue with Arnold's own words:

> In its blame of Hebraising too, and in its praise of Hellenising, culture must not fail to keep its flexibility, to give to its judgments that passing and provisional character which we have seen it impose on its preferences and rejections of machinery. Now, and for us, it is a time to Hellenise, and to praise knowing; for we have Hebraised too much, and have over-valued doing. But the habits and discipline received from Hebraism remain for our race an eternal possession; and, as far as humanity is constituted, one must never assign them

---

3. Leonard Woolf, *After the Deluge: A Study of Communal Psychology* (New York: Harcourt, Brace, 1931), 1:281–82.

227
Samuel Lipman

the second rank to-day, without being prepared to restore them to
the first rank to-morrow. To walk staunchly by the best light one
has, to be strict and sincere with oneself, not to be of the number of
those who say and do not, to be in earnest,—this is the discipline by
which alone man is enabled to rescue his life from thraldom to the
passing moment and to his bodily senses, to ennoble it, and to make
it eternal. And this discipline has nowhere been so effectively taught
as in the school of Hebraism.[4] [lviii–lix]

Thus one finally returns both to the importance of Arnold and to the
dislike, verging on contempt, in which he is held today. He understood our
anarchy, he understood our need for culture, and he understood the integral connection between culture and conduct. In so doing, Arnold has
staked a secure place for himself in Western civilization as an apostle of
culture and conduct, of the mental life and the moral life. And that is why
we should read *Culture and Anarchy.*

---

4. This passage about the eternal nature of Hebraism, it must be noted, dates from 1869,
some fifteen years before Arnold's famous remark in his essay "Numbers": "When one
looks at the popular literature of the French at this moment,—their popular novels,
popular stage-plays, popular newspapers,—and at the life of which this literature of
theirs is the index, one is tempted to make a goddess out of a word of their own, and
then, like the town clerk of Ephesus, to ask: 'What man is there that knoweth not how
that the city of the French is a worshipper of the great goddess Lubricity?'" [Super
10:154–55].

Suggestions for
Further Reading

Arnold's prose is to be found in the extraordinary eleven-volume edition, complete with a remarkable scholarly apparatus and extended interpretive remarks, of *The Complete Prose Works of Matthew Arnold,* ed. R. H. Super (Ann Arbor: University of Michigan Press, 1960–1977). His poems may be found in *The Poems of Matthew Arnold,* ed. Kenneth Allott, 2d ed. revised by Miriam Allott (London: Longmans, 1979).

Arnold's letters continue to exist in an unsatisfactory publishing state. The most extensive collection, much vetted by his family, was published as *Letters of Matthew Arnold,* collected and arranged by G. W. E. Russell, 2 vols., 2d ed. (London: Macmillan, 1901). Arnold's important correspondence with his friend the poet Arthur Hugh Clough was published as *The Letters of Matthew Arnold to Arthur Hugh Clough,* ed. Howard Foster Lowry (London: Oxford University Press, 1932). Some interesting, though regrettably few, letters were published by Arnold's grandson, Arnold Whitridge, as *Unpublished Letters of Matthew Arnold* (New Haven: Yale University Press, 1923). A new collection of letters, drawing heavily on Russell and in no way complete, has been published in England as *Selected Letters of Matthew Arnold,* ed. Clinton Machann and Forrest D. Burt (Macmillan, 1992); it is now scheduled to be published in this country (Ann Arbor: University of Michigan Press, 1993). A much-needed complete edition of Arnold's letters, to be edited by Cecil Y. Lang, is said to be in preparation by Harvard University Press, but as far as I am aware no publication date has yet been announced.

Arnold's notebooks, which document his wide reading during his poetic and literary life, have been published as *The Notebooks of Matthew Arnold,* ed. Howard Foster Lowry, Karl Young, and Waldo Hilary Dunn (London: Oxford University Press, 1952).

There are three standard biographical studies of Arnold. The earliest and least satisfactory, again vetted by the family, is G. W. E. Russell, *Matthew Arnold* (New York: Charles Scribner's Sons, 1904); Lionel Trilling's *Matthew Arnold* (New York: Columbia University Press, 1977) is important as an interpretation of Arnold as a writer rather than as a man; Park Honan's *Matthew Arnold: A Life* (New York: McGraw-Hill, 1981) is perhaps as close to a real biography (given Arnold's personal reticence) as we shall ever have.

There is a veritable ocean of writing about Arnold. It is listed and magisterially commented upon, at great and satisfying length, by the Arnold scholar David J. DeLaura in *Victorian Prose: A Guide to Research*, ed. David J. DeLaura (New York: Modern Language Association of America, 1973). More recent Arnold material has been collected in *The Essential Matthew Arnold: An Annotated Bibliography of Major Modern Studies*, by Clinton J. Machann (New York: Hall, 1993). Of this more recent material, three books deserve mention here: Ruth apRoberts's highly suggestive *Arnold and God* (Berkeley and Los Angeles: University of California Press, 1983), James C. Livingston's profound and sympathetic *Matthew Arnold and Christianity: His Religious Prose Writings* (Columbia: University of South Carolina Press, 1986), and Stefan Collini's short study *Arnold* (Oxford: Oxford University Press, 1988).

Acknowledgements

The idea for this new edition of *Culture and Anarchy* first came from Jonathan Brent, senior editor at Yale University Press. In the two years that we have been working on this project, his encouragement and kindness never wavered, and his important suggestions for the overall shape of the book have been valuable and, indeed, necessary. I also want to thank Steven Marcus, Gerald Graff, and Maurice Cowling for their provocative essays. Thanks are also due to Richard Miller for his very intelligent and detailed copyediting. I am grateful to my friends William and Joan Hyland for finding the birth date of Arnold's wife in the church graveyard at Laleham, Surrey. In my work, I have profited immensely from the scholars who have labored so long and so well on Arnold; in particular I want to pay my respects to R. H. Super, the editor of the *Complete Prose Works of Matthew Arnold*, without whose wisdom and erudition this work, and many others on Arnold, would scarcely have been possible; I have also owed much to the notes and commentary in J. Dover Wilson's pioneering edition of 1932 and in Ian Gregor's edition of 1971.

To my colleagues Hilton Kramer, Norman Podhoretz, Joseph Epstein, Neal Kozodoy, Roger Kimball, and Christopher Carduff I also give my thanks for their help, their friendship, and their intellectual companionship. To my wife, Jeaneane, and our son, Edward, I give not just gratitude but devotion. They both stayed with me during a very difficult period; my son also took time from his busy work at Cambridge to help with important checking of references. I should add that the final responsibility for everything in this book save the original Arnold text, and the essays by Messrs. Marcus, Graff, and Cowling, is entirely mine.

Samuel Lipman
New York, September 1993